Ramon Novarro

Ramon Novarro

A Biography of the
Silent Film Idol, 1899–1968;
With a Filmography

by ALLAN R. ELLENBERGER

To Norm,
Thanks for your support.
Best of luck — see you
at Cinecon !!
— Allen R Ellenberger
9/2/18

McFarland & Company, Inc., Publishers
Jefferson, North Carolina, and London

ALSO BY ALLAN R. ELLENBERGER
AND FROM MCFARLAND

Celebrities in the 1930 Census (2008)

The Valentino Mystique (2005)

Margaret O'Brien (2000; paperback 2004)

Celebrities in Los Angeles Cemeteries (2001)

Frontispiece: Novarro in his finest and best-remembered role as Judah Ben-Hur in *Ben-Hur* (1926, MGM); courtesy of the Academy of Motion Picture Arts and Sciences.

The present work is a reprint of the library bound edition of Ramon Novarro: A Biography of the Silent Film Idol, 1899–1968; With a Filmography, *first published in 1999 by McFarland.*

LIBRARY OF CONGRESS CATALOGUING-IN-PUBLICATION DATA

Ellenberger, Allan R., 1956–
     Ramon Novarro : a biography of the silent film idol, 1899–1968 :
with a filmography / by Allan R. Ellenberger.
          p.   cm.
     Filmography: p.
     Includes bibliographical references and index.

     ISBN 978-0-7864-4676-6
     softcover : 50# alkaline paper ∞

     1. Novarro, Ramon, 1899–1968.   2. Actor—United States—
Biography.   I. Title.
PN2287.N6E44 2009
791.43'028'092—dc21
[b]   99-17288

British Library cataloguing data are available

On the cover: Novarro and his lifelong friend Alice Terry in *Lovers?*
(1927, MGM); background ©2009 Shutterstock

Manufactured in the United States of America

McFarland & Company, Inc., Publishers
   Box 611, Jefferson, North Carolina 28640
      www.mcfarlandpub.com

For my mother

Acknowledgments

This biography would not have been possible without the help and cooperation of many people. First, I would like to thank the family of Ramon Novarro. Their cooperation, frankness, and recall of the past were invaluable. My thanks to Ramon Novarro's brother, Jose "Angel" Samaniego; Angel's son, Robert Samaniego; Ramon's brother Eduardo Samaniego; Ramon's sister Carmen de Gavilan; Joseph Samaniego; Theresa Samaniego; and Ramon's personal secretary, Edward Weber.

There were many people who helped and encouraged me over the years that I spent doing research and interviewing people. First, a very special thanks to film historian Kevin Brownlow, who unselfishly shared his research and experience. Also to Jimmy Bangley, a writer and historian who was always there to encourage me. Silent film actress Anita Page was a delight and became a wealth of information about her friendship with Novarro. Also, my experience with Page would never have been possible without the help of MTV film star Randal Malone and photographer Michael Schwibbs; their help was invaluable. Silent child actress and author Diana "Baby Peggy" Serra Carey read an early manuscript of this book and provided invaluable advice and direction.

A special thanks to Novarro costars who graciously gave of their time, including the late William Bakewell, Lois Collier, Kurt Krueger, Marian Marsh, Margaret O'Brien, and the late Myrna Loy. My thanks to celebrities who were friends or acquaintances of Novarro, including the late actress Lina Basquette, actor Patrick Brock, the late author Forman Brown, the late Alan Brock, the late Mae Clarke, Douglas Fairbanks, Jr., the late, great, Lillian

Gish, David Manners, actor Lon McCallister, the late Caesar Romero, and Lupita Tovar.

My thanks to Don Atkins, who graciously and matter of factly told of his relationship with Novarro, and to other friends who shared their memories: the late Samson de Brier, Allan Graener, Jon Keating, John Lanchberry, Joseph J. O'Donahue IV, and Edward Zubbrick, who supplied letters and photographs of his 30-year friendship with the actor.

I also wish to express my appreciation to fellow authors who offered guidance and encouragement: Cari Beauchamp, Eve Golden, Boze Hadleigh, Richard Lamparski, Betty Lasky, Patrick McGilligan, Ken Schlessinger, David Stenn, and Karen Swenson. My thanks also to former employees of Metro-Goldwyn-Mayer Studios: the late J. J. Cohn who shared early remembrances, the late Sydney Guillaroff, and the former makeup girl, who wished to remain anonymous.

I would also like to thank the following for their assistance: Richard Adkins; Army Archerd; Louella M. Benson of the Motion Picture Country Home; Ralph Edwards; Charlton Heston; Mickey Rooney; Marvin Paige; Margarita Lorenz; George Putnam; Roger Mayer and June Caldwell of Turner Entertainment; Kari Johnson; Paramount executive A.C. Lyles; Daniel Swartz and Helga Eike of E! Entertainment; Jose Antonio Ortiz Pedraza, counsel general of Mexico at Los Angeles; architect Eric Lloyd Wright; Robert Taaffe, nephew of Alice Terry; Donald Gallery, son of Barbara La Marr; attorney John Frolich; Cathy Baldrey; Max Pierce; Robert Edwards; Gloria Anne Forney; Ruth Limkemann; John Siglow; Jon Varga; and Marie Yochem.

A special thanks to friends who encouraged me along the way: Mario Comas, Deborah Fullam, Sue and Jere Guldin, Michael Roman, Gina Tronci, Carl Youngblood. Thanks also to Donna Ross, who edited an earlier version of this book. A very special thanks to Freda Novello, who was there from the beginning and provided invaluable research and Novarro memorabilia.

A special thanks to the late author and historian DeWitt Bodeen, whose "Films in Review" article on Ramon Novarro was an invaluable source of information and served as a road map for my research.

My gratitude to the countless people associated with the many libraries and archives: Sam Gill and the staff at the Margaret Herrick Library of the Motion Picture Academy of Arts and Sciences, Beverly Hills; Ned Comstock of the USC Cinema Library, Los Angeles; the late Jim Keppner, founder and curator of the Gay and Lesbian Archives, West Hollywood; Miles Kreuger, curator of the Institute of the American Musical, Los Angeles; David R. Smith, archivist for Walt Disney Studios; Edward E. Stratman, assistant curator of film collections at the George Eastman House, Rochester, New York.

Also, my thanks to the staffs of the following institutions: Los Angeles Central Library; Los Angeles Hall of Records; Doheny Library, USC; UCLA

Research Library; Louis B. Mayer Library of the American Film Institute; Los Angeles City Archives; the Seaver Institute; the Glendale Public Library; the Academy of Television Arts and Sciences Library; the New York Museum of Modern Art; the Beverly Hills Public Library; the Temple of Latter Day Saints; Francis Howard Goldwyn Library–Hollywood.

Contents

Foreword

by Kevin Brownlow

When Valentino left Metro, his mentor, director Rex Ingram, told the front office that he would replace him with a new actor whom he would also raise to stardom. And, against the odds, he did so. Ramon Samaniegos may not have aroused the intense passion incited by Valentino, but as Ramon Novarro he ran him very close.

As Allan Ellenberger points out, he had played an extra role in *The Four Horsemen of the Apocalypse* (1921). Many myths have grown up about their friendship and it is reassuring to have such an authoritative account as this.

When I was researching the silent era in Hollywood in the 1960s, I made several attempts to meet Ramon Novarro—either he was away, or I was double booked. We did exchange a few letters, and a friend, Philip Jenkinson, succeeded in filming an interview with him for the BBC. During my stay in Hollywood, I got to know Alice Terry, Rex Ingram's widow and a close friend of Novarro's. I was impressed by the fact that she regarded him as the best actor of all in the silent era. When you think of the competition, that is a memorable statement. If only more of his work had survived! Novarro had a remarkable career—his experiences on *Ben-Hur* alone would provide a novel—and he deserves this sympathetic and well-researched biography.

The year 1999 is Novarro's centenary. He is being properly celebrated on one side of the Atlantic, at any rate. Ernst Lubitsch's film *The Student*

1

Prince in Old Heidelberg (1927) is being presented with full orchestra at the Royal Festival Hall in London; Britain's National Film Theater is also mounting a retrospective. This book should arouse an even greater fascination in the United States.

Prologue

*But Irving Thalberg wanted me. I was only 25 at the time
and Irving was three months younger than I. It was a case
of youth seeing eye to eye, I suppose.*[1]
— Ramon Novarro

When actor George Walsh was cast to play the title role in the Goldwyn production of *Ben-Hur*, Ramon Novarro was devastated. He wanted to
play the part so much he could taste it. But when the studios of Metro, Goldwyn, and Mayer merged and *Ben-Hur's* director, screenwriter, and Walsh
himself were sent packing, Ramon didn't allow himself the luxury of thinking he had a second chance.

That all changed one Sunday afternoon in June when MGM production chief Irving Thalberg called Novarro at his home. He told the actor he
had something important to discuss with him and asked that he report to the
studio immediately. Novarro drove to Culver City and went to Thalberg's
office, where the "Boy Wonder" got right to the point, asking the 25-year-
old actor if he would like to play Ben-Hur.

Ramon was, of course, both shocked and delighted and replied that he
would. But Thalberg had one request—that Novarro make a screen test.
Putting his entire future on the line, Ramon refused the youthful mogul.
"Why not?" Thalberg demanded.[2]

Ramon reasoned that Thalberg was concerned about his physique and
explained that his body was in good shape. If he had any doubts, all he had

to do was screen his recent film, *Where the Pavement Ends*, throughout which Ramon is half-naked.

Thalberg smiled and agreed, respecting Ramon's bluntness and honesty. He then instructed him to keep his casting secret for now. He would be leaving for New York the next day, and no one must know. Novarro was on top of the world. His dream was at last coming true; the role of a lifetime belonged to him.

The next morning a studio limo picked up Novarro at his home and whisked him to the Pasadena train station. Waiting there were MGM mogul Louis B. Mayer, writers Carey Wilson and Bess Meredyth, attorney J. Robert Rubin and his wife Reba, director Fred Niblo and his wife, actress Enid Bennett, and *Photoplay* correspondent Herbert Howe.

In New York, the group was greeted by Marcus Loew, head of MGM. Loew told Ramon to answer all reporter inquiries with the explanation that he was going on vacation. Just as Loew had predicted, reporters were at the dock, questioning everyone. They were naturally suspicious as to why so many people were traveling to Europe. Fred Niblo fibbed a little, saying he was going to shoot some French exteriors for his recent film with Novarro called *The Red Lily* and then go on to Monte Carlo to begin his next picture with Norma Talmadge.

The night before, director Marshall Neilan and his wife, actress Blanche Sweet, sailed for France on the *Olympic* to make *The Sporting Venus*. The reporters knew the problems that the studio was having in Italy on the set of *Ben-Hur*, and that only fueled more rumors that either Neilan or Niblo was going to take over director's duties from Charles Brabin.

As they were waiting to leave on the steamship the *Leviathan*, frequent Novarro costar Alice Terry arrived to see their departure. Ramon and Alice did an embrace for the cameras which rivaled anything they had done on the screen. At the last minute, Mayer, who was staying behind, gave some words of instruction to Niblo—"Be sure to have a lot of camels in the picture."[3]

After Ramon received farewell telegrams from Thalberg and actress Barbara La Marr, a close friend, the ship pulled up anchor and made its way to Europe. As the ship passed the Statue of Liberty, Novarro leaned over the railing, staring at the beautiful lady in the harbor, pondering his future, and reminiscing about the events which led him to this crossroads of his life.

Chapter One

Childhood and the Revolution (1899–1915)

*My childhood was happy. I remember wonderful summers,
while we were growing up, on the family ranch, where we
lived out of doors, swam, and rode horseback. I'm sorry for
children who grow up in the cities today. They miss so much.*
—Ramon Novarro[1]

Many thoughts may have crossed Novarro's mind as he stood on the deck of the *Leviathan*, gazing at the great expanse of water that lay before him. He may have contemplated the road which had led to this ship bound for Europe, a road that had begun a quarter of a century earlier and had more twists and turns than any desert path he was accustomed to in his native country of Mexico.

Ramon Novarro was born Jose Ramon Gil Samaniego on February 6, 1899, in Durango, Mexico, the second son of a wealthy dentist.[2] Family lore and studio publicity claimed the Samaniego family originated in Greece centuries earlier and migrated to Spain. Eventually, it is said, they sailed to Mexico with Cortez and the conquistadors.

Whether this origin is true or merely invented by some overzealous studio publicity man, the Samaniegos were an influential and well-respected family in Mexico. Many Samaniegos had prominent positions in the affairs of state and were held in high esteem by the president.

Ramon's grandfather, Mariano Samaniego, was a well-known physician in Juarez. Known as a charitable and outgoing man, he was once an interim governor for the state of Chihuahua and was the first Mexican city councilman of El Paso, Texas. It is reported that one uncle was a writer in Spain and another was a successful Parisian painter.

Ramon's father, Dr. Mariano N. Samaniego, was born in Juarez and attended high school in Las Cruces, New Mexico. After receiving his degree in dentistry at the University of Pennsylvania, he moved to Durango, Mexico, and began a flourishing dental practice.

In 1891 he married Leonor Gavilan, the beautiful daughter of a prosperous landowner. The Gavilans were a mixture of Spanish and Aztec blood, and according to local legend, they were descended from Guerrero, a prince of Montezuma, whose name meant "bravery in war." True or not, Ramon believed the legend and would later joke, "I have very little blood of that man. But I may have some of his superstitions."

Mrs. Samaniego was the final court of appeal to all Samaniegos. Remarkable respect was tendered to her by every family member. Before retiring to bed, each child would drop to one knee and receive her blessing. Religion played an important part in Mrs. Samaniego's life, for she was devoted to St. Francis and passed her love of God on to her children.

A favorite parable told of a little Mexican woman kneeling before the image of the Blessed Virgin. Wrapped in her shawl, the little woman knelt on the marble floor of the cathedral; with hands clasped and eyes uplifted, she addressed her love to the Queen of Heaven:

"Oh, dear Mary, my rose, my little dove, my onion, my little cabbage..." A passing priest overheard the old woman's supplication and rebuked her for addressing the Holy Mother in that way. The woman turned mute, questioning eyes and said, "Ah, she will not understand me... My rose, my bird, my little flower..."

Ramon believed that prayer should be simple and unadorned. Unfortunately, religion was never simple for Ramon. He would come to yearn for the peaceful days of his youth and the protection of his parents' home, a very large Durango estate nicknamed the "Garden of Eden." An uncle once said that Adam and Eve would have envied the family that lived there, referring to the abundance and variety of flowers and fruits. Thirteen children were born on the estate.

The Samaniego family began with the birth of a son named Emilio, followed by two daughters, Guadalupe and Rosa. Sadly, young Emilio died of diphtheria shortly before Ramon was born. After Ramon's birth came his sister Leonor, then Mariano, Luz, Antonio and Jose. Unfortunately, the next child was stillborn. The last three children of the Samaniego family were Carmen, Angel, and the youngest, Eduardo.

The Samaniego estate included vine-covered masonry with ironbound

Ramon with his sisters Guadalupe and Rosa (circa 1899).

doors and shuttered windows. There were three inner courts, each with a sunken garden in the center from which a shade tree grew. In the rear was a wide, paved, covered terrace which gave a view of the entire house. From here, Ramon would watch his mother walk through the garden, a rosary in her hand, passing between orange and cherry trees. This would always be for him a vivid memory of his mother in happier times.

Summers were spent at their ranch in the country, where the children would swim and ride horseback. Being wealthy allowed the Samaniegos to lead a comfortable life with all the amenities, including servants and any indulgence they wished to bestow on their children.

One such amenity was the study of the arts, which young Ramon began early. When he was five years old, his mother taught him piano and voice, teaching him first an Italian lullaby. At age six, Ramon made his dramatic debut at his grandmother's birthday party. He and his sister Guadalupe recited a poem by Campamour called "If Only I Could Write." Everyone applauded wildly, which encouraged young Ramon. He had a brief taste of adulation and enjoyed it.

On his eighth birthday, Ramon received a marionette theater as a gift from his mother. Every spare moment was spent producing plays for the neighborhood. Ramon designed the tables and chairs himself, using furniture catalogues from Paris. His sisters did their part by sewing the cushions and embroidering the curtains.

After seeing *The Merry Widow* at a local theater, Ramon rehearsed with his sisters and performed it in their living room. They went about town passing out flyers that read, "Ten centavos for adults and five for children, or a fraction thereof." This policy ensured that people who claimed their children were under six, and therefore entitled to enter free, would have to pay something. Enterprising even at that young age.

To his parents, Ramon's acting and singing were only a hobby, or so they hoped. They had more respectable goals in mind for their son. Dr. Samaniego, of course, wanted his eldest son to follow in his footsteps and become a dentist. His mother, on the other hand, envisioned him as a concert pianist, which might have been a possibility had he not become an actor.

Ramon continued to adapt stories and plays to be used in his marionette theater. On one occasion he performed *Juan Panadero*, a popular Spanish play, for more than one hundred people. "The artistic appreciation of Durango was very high," he joked. His siblings often played a big part in his productions, a practice which continued years later when Ramon had a real theater and entertained not only family members, but movie stars and politicians.

Unfortunately, Ramon's theatrical career was cut short, for in 1913 a revolution loomed on the Mexican horizon. The Huerta government was overthrown, and the country was tossed into turmoil. The rebel Pancho Villa began burning towns and raping the land. The revolution brought the closing of Ramon's school, Our Lady of Guadalupe. Fearing for their lives, Dr. Samaniego moved his family from war-torn Durango to the relative safety of Mexico City.

There they rented a house at 45 Edison Street, and Ramon entered Mascorones College, a military school. He was taught by the Jesuits, who continued Ramon's training in music, encouraging him to sing in the school choir. He resumed his French and English studies, along with a general academic course. He also proved to be very athletic, finding his favorite sport to be la bandera, a Mexican game which showed off his sprinting talent. This sprinting ability helped him win a track championship for the school.

Eventually, the war subsided, and Dr. Samaniego and his wife, along with Ramon and the two youngest children, Angel and Eduardo, returned to Durango. If they found it safe, they intended to return for the remaining children, who were staying with relatives in Mexico City.

Upon arriving in Durango, all appeared to be tranquil. Satisfied that any danger had now passed, Dr. Samaniego sent his wife to Mexico City to return with the children, while he and Ramon stayed in Durango with the two youngest siblings.

While Mrs. Samaniego was in Mexico City, Pancho Villa and his men once again began looting and burning bridges, stranding her and the children. For eleven months the family was separated without any communication or train service between them.

During that time, Ramon became a guardian to Angel and Eduardo. One day the three brothers were returning from their Aunt Carmen's house when they heard the sound of horses clamoring down the street. Ramon grabbed his two brothers and dashed into the nearest house. Fifty or more of Pancho Villa's henchmen were riding into Durango, intent on taking the town. Ramon overheard one of Villa's men say, "Rodriguez, Rodriguez! Do as I tell you! Do as I tell you!"

For more than an hour, the children heard screams and gunfire coming from the streets. When the noise subsided, Ramon and his brothers returned home as fast as their legs could carry them. Later they watched in horror as the captain of the army came down the hill, drew his pistol, and shot a man to death in the street.

Eventually, Mrs. Samaniego and the other children were able to return to Durango, much to everyone's relief. It was then that Ramon's three sisters, Guadalupe, Rosa, and Leonor, declared God's calling in their life. Within two years they took their vows and became nuns. Guadalupe entered the House of the Cross in Durango. Rosa and Leonor, after doing their novitiate in Havana, were assigned to the Canary Islands at the hospitals of St. Lazarus and St. Martin.

Ramon was very proud of his sisters and always spoke of them lovingly. Years later he recalled a story about Rosa, whose duty it was to care for the insane at an institution in the Canary Islands. One day a patient asked Rosa if she had a family that loved her, had money, and was kind to her. Rosa replied that she did have a wonderful family. "And yet you stay here?" the woman asked. "Ah, Sister—it is you who are mad—not I!"

When he heard his sisters' decision, Ramon seriously considered becoming a priest. Being raised in a religious home where letters were sent to the baby Jesus instead of Santa Claus and Judas was burned in effigy on Easter, the thought of dedicating one's life to God was not surprising.

So at the age of fifteen, Ramon decided to study for the priesthood. To prepare for his new calling, he performed servants' duties and awoke at five in the morning to pray and fast. So dedicated was he that the local boys would tease him by singing "Ave Maria" when they saw him on the street. "I wanted to die a martyr and be canonized," he said modestly.

Then one day he noticed a program for the Metropolitan Opera announcing Enrico Caruso and Geraldine Farrar in *Manon*, which reawakened his love for music. "Perhaps it was the devil tempting me," he said. "I'm still not so sure it wasn't."

After much soul searching, he met with the local priest and received his blessing to make music his life's work. Religion was still a major part of his life and that old calling would return several times, but for now, music was his interest and he thought the best place to begin his career was in the United States.

But first he had to convince his parents of his new vocation; it was important to him that they give their blessing. After much discussion, his parents relented, but on the condition that his brother Mariano accompany him. The brothers left by train shortly thereafter for El Paso, Texas, where they had relatives. Two days into their journey, the train mysteriously stopped. Ramon was suspicious, so he and Mariano left and returned by foot to Durango. They later were told that the engineer was one of Villa's men and everyone on board was robbed and some were murdered. Ramon was sure that his mother's prayers were the reason for his caution that may have saved their lives.

Within a few weeks they decided to try the journey once more. With $100 in gold pieces given to them by their father, they again left Durango by train and made their way north through the war-torn countryside. Arriving halfway to the border at a little town called Escalon, they were told the bridges in front of them had been burned. The authorities ordered them to return home. Then word came that the bridges between Escalon and Durango had also been destroyed.

For two days, Ramon and Mariano remained stranded in Escalon. Keeping out of sight of the rebels, they survived on tortillas, beans, and dirty water. Rumors abounded that Pancho Villa was himself in the area cutting off people's ears. "I particularly cared for my ears," Ramon later remarked. "What would a musician be without them?"

Within a week a train from Torreon arrived, repairing bridges as it came. Ramon and Mariano served as escorts to the female passengers, who were also fleeing north through rebel territory. The train kept one step ahead of Villa and his men. Bridges burst into flames almost as fast as the train crossed them.

Meanwhile in Durango, the Samaniego family heard reports of fighting in the northern country. Mrs. Samaniego, terrified about her sons' safety, repeated again and again, "It was not meant to be."

Hours turned into days as the train stopped for passengers and refueling. Villa's men, not far behind, were killing villagers and burning the land. Eventually, however, the train made it to the border and safety. The boys stayed with relatives in El Paso for a few days and then set out for the long trek to Los Angeles. In his wildest dreams, Ramon could never imagine what life had in store for him in the new and wonderful world he was about to enter.

Chapter Two

Remember My Name,
Mr. DeMille (1915–1920)

I found myself in Hollywood going from one studio to another looking for a job. I believe that we usually do the things we want to do. But jobs were scarce and I needn't go into details of those weary days when I interviewed every casting director in town, only to receive the same reply—No!

—Ramon Novarro[1]

With their spirits high, Ramon and Mariano arrived in Los Angeles on Thanksgiving Day, 1915.[2] Only $10 remained of the money their father had given them, so the first order of business was to find a job and a place to stay.

The movie business was still in its infancy in the Los Angeles of 1915. Director Cecil B. DeMille had arrived in Hollywood only two years earlier to film the first full-length Western called *The Squaw Man* (1914). The barn he had rented near Selma and Vine streets had now turned into a whole city block of stages and scenery called Famous Players–Lasky, later to be known as Paramount Pictures.

While filmmakers were operating in and around downtown Los Angeles, it wasn't until 1911 that the first motion picture studio opened just seven miles away in Hollywood. In the boarded-up Blondeau Tavern on the northwest corner of Sunset and Gower, the Nestor Film Company opened its office and filmed Westerns and comedies in the rear. Eventually, other filmmakers made the trek west to take advantage of the California sunshine and to hide from Edison's Motion Picture Patents Company.

The Samaniego brothers rented a room at 842 South Main Street in downtown Los Angeles. Ramon found odd jobs as a grocery clerk, a busboy, and as a cafe singer, singing "Poor Butterfly" to hungry restaurant patrons. For a brief period, he modeled at the J. Francis Smith School of Art and Design with Leatrice Joy, who would later gain fame as an actress and as the wife of screen idol John Gilbert. The money he earned posing nude at the downtown school helped put food on the table.

Ramon found steady employment as an usher at the Clune Auditorium (later renamed the Philharmonic) on Fifth and Olive streets. Simultaneously, he worked as a stage manager and played bit parts at the Majestic Theater Stock Company at 845 South Broadway for the incredible sum of $10 a week. His very first role was as a Japanese bird seller in *The Willow Tree*.

One evening while Ramon was ushering at the Clune Auditorium, Mary Garden, a popular singer with the Chicago Opera Company, arrived for the opening of *Othello*. As she was leaving her box at the conclusion, Ramon approached her. "Miss Garden, I want to sing and play and act and dance for you," he blurted out in a breathless voice. Caught off guard by this young intruder, the opera diva replied, "My! My! What an accomplished young man."[3] She then turned and left the building with her entourage.

Soon Ramon began hitting the local studios, hoping to get roles as an extra. Word was out that Cecil B. DeMille needed extras for his next film, *Joan the Woman* (1917), starring the world-renowned opera singer Geraldine Farrar. Her costar was Wallace Reid, the reigning heartthrob of the day. Ramon was cast as a starving peasant in his first film appearance.

During a break in the filming, Ramon asked Farrar if she would listen to him play the piano. She politely agreed, but during his performance, she nonchalantly turned to chat with Wallace Reid. Ramon suddenly stopped playing and threw her a steely gaze. She became silent, and when he finished she said, "Pretty good."

Ramon was insulted. He considered his talent more than just "pretty good." He later said, "If any phonograph company had offered me a million dollars for my voice at the time, I would have figured I was being cheated."[4]

Ramon's singing was important to him. He was very disciplined and trained his pleasant tenor voice every day. "If only for any hour, I practice singing every day," he said, "not merely for inspirational purposes, but with the consciousness that it is toward my musical career."[5]

Ramon appeared in another DeMille film called *The Little American* (1917). It starred Mary Pickford as an American girl at the beginning of the Great War who sails to France to bring home her aged aunt, but her ship (supposedly the *Lusitania*) is sunk by a U-boat.[6]

Ramon (in turban, holding ice cream cone) appears in one of his numerous extra roles in *The Goat* (1918, Paramount-Artcraft).

DeMille took a liking to the young actor and complimented him on his talent, to which the boy replied, "Remember my name, Mr. DeMille—Ramon Samaniego—it will be known."[7]

A few months later Wallace Reid was working on a film called *The Hostage* (1917) when he learned that director Robert Thornby was looking for someone to play a shepherd in the opening scene. Reid thought of Ramon and recommended him to Thornby, who gave him the part. This led to extra roles in two more films, *The Jaguar's Claw* (1917), starring Sessue Hayakawa, and the Fred Stone film *The Goat* (1918), produced at Paramount.

During the summer of 1917, Ramon entered an amateur contest at the Bijou Theater in Santa Monica. It was hot, and the smell of hot dogs and peanuts wafted through the air. The manager appeared and cleared his voice, announcing, "Ladies and gentlemen, I take pleasure tonight in introducing the flower of Los Angeles and Santa Monica local talent."

The evening began with a saxophone player's rendition of "Poor Butterfly" followed by a juggler who dropped three out of seven balls. An actor reciting Kipling in a green spotlight provided the dramatic entertainment for the evening. There were two ballroom dancers who executed the steps of Vernon and Irene Castle (which had previously won them three loving cups and a shotgun at the Dreamland Dance Hall). Then Ramon appeared, bowed to the audience, and sat down at a piano which was brought out for him. He sat motionless for seconds.

"Looks like he's prayin'," someone whispered. He slowly touched the keys and played Liszt's "Hungarian Rhapsody No. 8," "Pfeiffer's Inquietude," a Chopin etude, and a Beethoven sonata.

As he rose from the bench, everyone burst into cheers. Each performer of the evening was brought out, and the audience was asked to vote by their applause for the winner. Ramon smiled, and the audience acknowledged the young pianist with applause and cheers of "Give him the prize!" The manager lifted Ramon's hand and screamed, "This young gentleman wins the handsome prize of two dollars and a half—in cash!"[8]

In Mexico the revolution continued to devastate the countryside. Dr. Samaniego's dentistry practice had suffered, so he accepted a job teaching English at night school for the Institute of Durango. Other schools had been burned, and most were closed. Mrs. Samaniego was concerned about the children and told her husband, "If the children are going to have any kind of education, we have to leave here."[9]

Dr. Samaniego resisted, but on his wife's insistence he finally agreed to move the family to El Paso, where the children could receive a better education. They rented out the family estate and traveled to El Paso in November 1917 and stayed with relatives. That winter was harsh, and it was the first time the Samaniego children experienced snow. To them, El Paso was a wonderful place.

Because the family had been separated for such a long period, Dr. Samaniego decided to move to California to be with Ramon and Mariano. In August 1918, the Samaniego family arrived in Los Angeles and rented a house at 2323 W. 23d Street, where they lived for two years until a fire forced them out. They relocated to 1340 Constance Street, just south of Pico Boulevard.

One of Ramon's many pursuits was as a busboy at the Alexandria Hotel on Fifth and Spring Street in downtown Los Angeles. It was here that one myth about Novarro was born, and it involved film idol Rudolph Valentino. According to legend, Ramon met the young Valentino at the Alexandria, and they became lovers. The entire relationship between Novarro and Valentino has been cloaked in mystery. No two parties can agree on the circumstances. While it appears the two were acquaintances, nothing more can be proved or disproved.

Some claim that Valentino worked at the Alexandria as a dancer. There is proof that he danced at a roadhouse called Baron Long's Watts Tavern and at the Maryland Hotel in Pasadena, but there is no record of his appearing at the Alexandria. It is true that Valentino frequented the Alexandria, but his purpose was to further his career by attracting the attention of the many stars who visited there.

At any rate, Valentino and Novarro were acquaintances at some point, and according to certain family members, they even partied together. One beloved female relative delighted in regaling interested listeners with stories of Novarro and Valentino at wild parties held at the Roosevelt Hotel.[10] Other family members claim they probably knew each other but were in competition for the same parts, making it unlikely they were friends.[11] Novarro, however, told Betty Lasky in a 1965 interview that he "definitely was not Valentino's rival."[12] Actress Lina Basquette, who was acquainted with both Novarro and Valentino, said, "I doubt whether Ramon was ever too friendly with Valentino."[13]

By the time Novarro began working on the Metro lot, Valentino had already been signed by Paramount. It is speculated that Novarro doubled for Valentino in one film, and he also appeared as an extra in *The Four Horsemen of the Apocalypse*. A rare photo exists from that film showing Valentino and Novarro in the same scene.[14]

In a 1962 interview with talk show host Joe Franklin, Novarro claimed that he hardly knew Valentino. He told another interviewer, "I met Valentino only once, it was through Natacha Rambova when I was ushering at the Philharmonic here."[15] Was he telling the truth or simply trying to hide a dark secret? It is possible the two did have some degree of a relationship whether it was a one-night stand, an on-again, off-again affair, or simply a friendship. Unfortunately, we will never know the truth.

As for the autographed "Art Deco dildo" that Valentino supposedly gave to Novarro for his success with *Scaramouche*, it never existed. It was not mentioned in the police or autopsy reports after Ramon was murdered, nor was it brought up at the subsequent trial. James Ideman, who was deputy district attorney and prosecuted Novarro's murderers, stated in the book *Madam Valentino*, "With reference to the claim that Mr. Novarro was choked to death by means of an Art Deco dildo, I can tell you that that did not happen." Ideman went on to state, "I certainly never made any statement to the effect that such an instrument was used. I did not even know of its existence."[16]

Had an object of that importance and obvious value existed, it would almost certainly have been mentioned in the list of Novarro's possessions or in his last will and testament, but this was not the case. The part it was alleged to have played in his death was the figment of a writer's wild imagination. Regardless, there are many who still wish to believe this legend and the supposed relationship between the two Latin lovers, and no amount of evidence will dispel that.

One night in late summer of 1919, Ramon was appearing in a play at the Majestic Theater. In the audience was Marian Morgan, the famed vaudeville choreographer and lover of director Dorothy Arzner. Morgan was impressed with young Samaniego and approached him after the play, offering him a job in her dance company. "But I've never danced," he confessed. "That doesn't matter," she replied. "You have the physique."[17]

Shortly, Ramon was on his way to New York City for rehearsals in a pantomime called *Atilla and the Huns*. For weeks he went without pay as he practiced his routine. To make ends meet until the play opened, he worked nights as a busboy at an automat on Broadway, between 46th and 47th streets. In fact, he worked so hard at both jobs that he developed sore feet, which slowed up the rehearsals. Morgan angrily accused him of slacking off and fired him. Fortunately, his replacement didn't fare much better, and she asked Ramon to return.

While living in New York, he stayed at an old rooming house next to the Portmanteau Theater on 49th Street. Spanish influenza was raging that winter, and Ramon believed that daily cold baths saved his life (much to his landlady's disdain). He survived on buttermilk and stale bread (which cost him ten cents a day), and every evening he would snatch two apples from the automat. This little indiscretion amounted to $1.75 which he promptly paid back with his first week's salary. After sending money home, he used the remainder to buy a derby, spats, bulldog shoes, and a cigar.

After a stint in New York, *Atilla and the Huns* toured the Orpheum Circuit through towns and cities all over the country. The revue and Ramon were such a success that Marian told the young hopeful, "You have an unusual gift. You'll be a great actor."

"Thank you," said Ramon.

"Don't thank me. Thank God. It's just been born in you."[18]

Soon the troupe arrived at the end of the line in Los Angeles. With all this valuable training under his belt, Ramon besieged the studios for weeks, but to no avail. When this effort failed, he continued his dance training with Ernest Belcher, an Englishman who had started a dancing school several years earlier in Hollywood.

Belcher's stepdaughter was a child actress named Lina Basquette.[19] At thirteen years of age, young Lina became smitten with the more mature Ramon and developed her first crush. Lina and Ramon danced at several Hollywood functions, including a rendition of *Carmen* at the Hollywood Bowl a few years later. During that performance, director Rex Ingram and his fiancée, actress Alice Terry, were in the audience and sent young Lina a basket of flowers, from which Ramon plucked one and placed it behind his ear.

Lina believed Ramon was an artist devoted to art, music, acting, and dancing. "Certainly one of the most handsome of his contemporaries, with charming manners," she said. "Women tried everything to attract him."[20]

While at Belcher's Dance Studio, Ramon met a young man named Louis Samuel, who was training to be a ballet dancer. The two young men became instant friends. He was about the same age as Ramon but entirely opposite in appearance and temperament. Later Samuel would become Ramon's personal manager.

Lina, who did not like Samuel, recalled him as being "insanely jealous of man, woman or child that Ramon felt a friendship or affection for. He had a sullen disposition and seldom did his eyes stray from Ramon."[21]

At the time there were already rumors circulating about Ramon's preference for men. Lina knew nothing of such things and resented her mother calling Ramon a "sissy." Recalling his days at Metro, Lina said, "His studio was already busy trying to build him up as a lady-killer, arranging dates for him with some of the most glamorous gals in the business."[22]

The last time Lina saw Ramon was in 1925 in New York City. He had just arrived from Italy after filming *Ben-Hur*. Later Lina married Sam Warner, a cofounder of Warner Bros.

"I never saw him again after I was married to Sam Warner. Ramon's lifestyle was strictly taboo within that family which had many skeletons in their own closet," Lina recalled. "I shall always remember him as a charming friend and a dance-partner of great talent."[23]

Although his dancing ability would prove useful in several films, it was Ramon's acting and striking good looks that would win him acclaim. After a few more disappointments and false starts, Ramon found that his patience and years of training were about to pay off.

Chapter Three

Stardom (1920–1922)

Here in Hollywood, the people who are struggling are happy; it is only those who have achieved that are discontented. When I was working as an extra and in small parts, I was always happy because I was always living in the future.

—Ramon Novarro[1]

While Ramon worked at the Alexandria Hotel, he made sure he always bused the table of the legendary director D. W. Griffith, who lived at the hotel and also ate lunch there. "He always said he discovered me," Ramon later joked. "Actually, I discovered him."[2]

One day he heard that Griffith was looking for a new leading man for his next film. Ramon was positive he was right for the part, so he bribed a chambermaid for Griffith's room number. He obtained a letter of introduction, compiled a résumé, and went knocking on the great director's door. When Griffith appeared at the open doorway, Ramon offered him his papers and said, "My future is in your hands, Mr. Griffith."[3]

Griffith, who was impressed by the young Latin's good looks, perused the documents and sternly told the young actor to report to the studio the next morning for a test. Ramon anxiously arrived before 8 A.M. the next day. He put on his makeup and waited.

After several hours, Ramon received a treat when his favorite actress, Lillian Gish, arrived on the set to pick up some wardrobe items. "When I

18

discovered that he was waiting for Mr. Griffith," Gish recalled, "I told him that it might be hours before he arrived."

"I'll wait, thank you," Ramon told her politely.[4] Finally Griffith arrived at four in the afternoon and guided Ramon in a brief test that lasted about twenty minutes.

"I thanked Mr. Griffith," Novarro said years later, "but I never heard another word from him. Sometime later I learned he'd signed Joseph Schildkraut as his leading man. I sometimes wonder if he even had film in the camera when he made the test of me."[5]

Ramon returned to extra work in films and bit parts on the stage, including the Hollywood Community Theater, where he was reunited with Marian Morgan. She grew to trust his talent and had him rehearse all the parts for the benefit of the other players. Morgan said, "Ramon is like a slot machine—put in a nickel and any character will come out."[6]

Ramon soon found work in the prologue at the California Theater on Main and Eighth streets. One day Morgan called to ask him to audition for a dance sequence in the Allen Holubar film *Man, Woman, Marriage* (1921), which she was going to choreograph. "I would like to speak to Mr. Samaniego," she told the manager.

"We have no one here by that name," he told her. Unknown to Morgan, Ramon had changed his name to Ramon Zerreco. "I'm sure he's there," she insisted. "He's very young. Never does anything twice alike. He's kind of crazy."

"Oh yes, he's here," he said, and he promptly called him.[7]

Ramon next worked as an extra for the near bankrupt Metro Studios in *The Four Horsemen of the Apocalypse* (1921). The film classic was being directed by Rex Ingram and starred Alice Terry and Rudolph Valentino in roles that would bring them both great acclaim. Ramon and his sister Carmen, who was an accomplished dancer herself, were cast as extras. Originally, Ramon's role was more prominent. Ingram noticed during the rushes, however, that everyone's eyes wandered from Valentino to Ramon, so to keep the emphasis on the star, Ingram trashed the footage and put Ramon in the background, where he would not be noticed.[8] When it was released, *The Four Horsemen of the Apocalypse* was a huge hit and put Metro's finances once again in the black.

Marian Morgan again called Ramon to dance in a film she was choreographing for Mack Sennett that was called *A Small Town Idol* (1921); it was a slapstick comedy starring Ben Turpin and Marie Prevost. In the film, Ramon was scantily dressed in a loincloth and danced a sexually tantalizing number with Derelys Perdue.

Ramon and Derelys were earning extra money dancing at night at the Kinema Theater. Actor Richard Dix, who was dating Perdue, would pick her up after the performance. Dix remembered seeing Ramon in a Mabel

Normand picture and thought he had talent. He felt so strongly that he asked Paramount to give Ramon a test, but they declined.

At the time, Dix was working with Colleen Moore in a Rupert Hughes film called *The Wall Flower* (1922), so he sneaked Ramon into the studio in the back of his roadster and personally directed him in a screen test. Afterward, he tried again to get Paramount interested but was not successful. He even tried to persuade Samuel Goldwyn to use Ramon in *Hungry Hearts*, a role which Dix had just turned down. Even Goldwyn was indifferent.[9]

Ramon finally received a break when he was cast to play the lead in an art film directed by Ferdinand Pinney Earle called *The Rubaiyat of Omar Khayyam*.[10] Ramon's leading lady was Kathleen Key, a fun-loving, boisterous girl who became his good friend and later appeared as his sister in *Ben-Hur*.

Unfortunately, after the film was completed, it was shelved because of a lack of interest and funding. It was finally released in 1925 under the title *A Lover's Oath* (1925) several months prior to the opening of *Ben-Hur*, obviously to take advantage of the hype that film produced, but to no avail. The film still did very little business.

Ramon landed his first screen credit in a small role in *Mr. Barnes of New York* (1922), which was produced by Samuel Goldwyn (who had evidently changed his mind about Ramon) and starred Tom Moore and Anna Lehr. Ramon played Antonio, a Corsican youth who is killed in a duel at the beginning of the film.

After this brief bit of encouragement, Ramon returned to stage work. At the Hollywood Community Theater,[11] he appeared in *The Spanish Fandango*[12] with actor Starke Patterson. In the summer of 1921, the house was full almost every night to see a handsome, sensual Ramon dance a Spanish pantomime. In the audience one evening was director Rex Ingram and his young fiancée, actress Alice Terry. Ingram was a handsome young Irishman who had achieved moderate success in films, first as an actor, then as a director at Universal.

Ingram and Valentino had quarreled during the filming of *The Conquering Power* (1921) when the star voiced dissatisfaction with his role. According to Alice Terry, Valentino's attitude had changed after making *The Four Horsemen*. "I always had the impression that I was playing with a volcano that might erupt at any minute," the actress said.[13]

Valentino stormed off to Paramount followed by his benefactor, screenwriter June Mathis. Legend has it that in rebuff, Ingram declared that he had made a star out of Valentino and could do the same with any extra. After seeing Ramon perform at the Hollywood Community Theater, he remembered

Opposite: **Ramon's first starring role as Ben Ali in *A Lover's Oath* (1925, Astor Pictures). Also pictured is Kathleen Key, who would later play his sister Tizrah in *Ben-Hur*.**

Ramon in *The Prisoner of Zenda* (1922, Metro Pictures Corp). From left, director Rex Ingram, Ramon, Barbara La Marr, and cameraman John Seitz.

his work on *The Four Horsemen* and maintained that he would make him a star. In reality, Ingram did remember Ramon from *The Four Horsemen* and was impressed by his work in the play but thought nothing more of it.

At the time, Ingram was in fact working on the film *Turn to the Right* (1922). Margaret Loomis, who was a friend of Ramon's, had a part in the film. She suggested that he should audition for the role of Rupert of Hentzau in Ingram's next film, *The Prisoner of Zenda* (1922). Ingram was not opposed to using an unknown if he thought he or she was right for the part.

Ramon arrived on the Metro lot on October 12, 1921, Columbus Day, but was turned away by the casting director. As he was leaving, he happened to run into his friend Mary O'Hara, who wrote the scenario for *The Prisoner of Zenda*. She was at Metro helping Ferdinand Pinney Earle edit the soon-to-be shelved *The Rubaiyat of Omar Khayyam*.

Ramon told O'Hara about the problem he was having, so she took him to Earle, who was a close friend of Ingram's. Earle wrote Ramon a letter of introduction on his personal stationery, which read, "Dear Mr. Ingram: Columbus made a great discovery on this day. I believe you will too. Here is an artist."[14]

Upon presenting the letter, Ramon was quickly ushered into Ingram's office. Ingram was polite but told Ramon that he was not the type he wanted for Rupert of Hentzau. "Exactly what type are you looking for?" inquired Ramon.[15]

Ingram explained that he envisioned Rupert to be tall and blond and about 35 years of age, with a beard and mustache. Then Ingram turned over Earle's letter and began sketching what he had in mind. When Ramon saw the sketch, he realized it would take months to grow a beard on his young face, but he pulled out the makeup kit he always carried with him and began applying a false mustache and beard. Ramon was good at makeup, and Ingram watched curiously as Ramon molded his features into the image that he had created on the back of the letter.[16]

Ingram took Ramon to an empty set to make a test. One thing that bothered Ingram was Ramon's youth, but he brought him back three times that week for more tests. Finally he suggested that Ramon wear a monocle. This simple change convinced Ingram, and he signed Ramon Samaniego to play Rupert of Hentzau. After five years of working as an extra in more than a hundred films, Ramon got his first major break.

The Prisoner of Zenda was based on Anthony Hope's 1894 novel and the stage play adapted by Edward Rose. The dependable Lewis Stone played the dual role of the dashing English adventurer and the look-alike mythical Ruritania ruler. Stone once gave Ramon a valuable piece of advice. "When people praise you for your acting ability, and tell you that you are a great actor—don't believe it! You'll know you are a good actor when they say, 'Even I could do that.' In other words, you've made it look so natural that it appears to be simple."[17]

Ingram had Ramon practice tossing his monocle into the air and catching it in his eye until he had the trick perfected. This feat caused Herb Howe of *Photoplay* to remark, "With one flip of a monocle, he won the American public."[18]

The beautiful Barbara La Marr was cast in a supporting role as Antoinette de Mauban. Ingram spent an entire afternoon perfecting a scene in which Barbara slaps Ramon. With each slap, Ramon's face got redder and the sensitive Barbara felt more guilty. Ramon was beginning to think that Ingram had it in for him, but finally the director got what he wanted; Barbara and Ramon then searched for an ice bag.

The Prisoner of Zenda was a box-office success and so was Ramon. *Photoplay* said of him: "There is a new young man on the screen who threatens to become as spectacularly famous as did Rodolf [*sic*] Valentino. He is another Rex Ingram discovery, a Spaniard, Ramon Samanyagos [*sic*]. The director considers him one of the most promising actors he has ever worked with. If Samanyagos doesn't make good in a part like that, he never will."[19]

Photoplay added, "Ramon Samanyagos, who does a fine bit of acting as Rupert of Hentzau, seems a decided find and an entirely new type."[20]

Ingram had another hit, proving that *The Four Horsemen of the Apocalypse* was not a fluke and that he could have a career without the much-laureled Valentino. Years later Ramon commented, "When I was told that I was to have the role of Rupert of Hentzau in *The Prisoner of Zenda*, I really felt that my career had begun. It had too, because Ingram had truly taken an interest in me and gave me every part that he thought I could play."[21]

Ramon's next film for Rex Ingram was titled *Trifling Women* (1922)[22] and again costarred his dear friend Barbara La Marr, as well as Lewis Stone. Ingram later said *Trifling Women* was his best picture, and most critics agreed. The *Moving Picture World* said that, "Mr. Ingram's direction of this production is superb and practically faultless. The story moves at a deliberate tempo which allows the full force of every scene and act to be impressed on the spectator and the film holds your undivided attention throughout. Artistically the production is an achievement."[23]

Variety, however, thought the production value of $250,000 did not live up to the public's expectations and considered the title better than the film. The periodical also noted that Ramon's part "could have been assumed by almost any juvenile of pictures."[24]

Michael Powell, a filmmaker who once worked for Ingram, described *Trifling Women* as "moonlight on tiger skins and blood dripping onto white faces, while sinister apes, poison, and lust kept the plot rolling."[25]

Before *Trifling Women* premiered, Metro executives changed Ramon's name. When the New York office heard the name Samaniego, they wired Ingram, "That's a hell of a name."

"So was Apocalypse," Ingram replied.[26]

Many stories have been told as to how the name Novarro was chosen. Supposedly, studio executives believed that Samaniego sounded too much like "ham and eggs." Another claimed that *Navarro* was the name of a town in Spain where the Samaniegos originated. The most widely used story was that it was his mother's maiden name, which was not true. Even though *Navarro* was a common Spanish name, it was not on either side of Ramon's family.

According to Novarro's brother Angel, the studio simply pulled the name out of the air and altered the spelling to make it more unique, although it would continually be misspelled.[27] *Trifling Women* (which today is a lost film) would be the first to bear Ramon's new name.

Samuel Goldwyn saw an advance screening of *Trifling Women* and was so impressed that he offered Novarro a contract of $2,000 a week. When Ingram heard the offer, he was troubled because he was only paying the actor $125 a week and could never match Goldwyn's price, so he encouraged Novarro to take it. But Ramon thought his loyalty to Ingram was more important and turned down Goldwyn's offer. "Also, I was more than a little annoyed," Novarro recalled, "because Mr. Goldwyn had gone to my family, trying to get them to persuade me to accept."

Besides, the actor reasoned that Goldwyn had had his chance a few years earlier when Richard Dix tried to get him interested in Novarro and he turned him down. "No, Goldwyn can't have you," Ingram proclaimed. "He didn't take you when he could have, so he shouldn't be allowed to have you now at any price!"

Novarro later told an interviewer, "Mr. Ingram had given me my break and the least I could do was stay with him."[28]

For the next two years, Novarro would work exclusively for Rex Ingram, making three films, all of them hits. The tide had turned for the new Latin heartthrob, but soon the film capital was abuzz with the news of a new motion picture epic, and both Ingram and Ramon wanted in on it.

Chapter Four

Rex Ingram (1922–1923)

He acts by thought rather than by gesture. I'm always curi-
ous as to what he's going to do next, so I watch his eyes to
know what he's thinking. And that's fatal!
—Alice Terry[1]

Novarro's popularity continued to grow with each new film, causing his fans to clamor for more information. Without missing a step, the Metro publicity team sent out press releases concerning their budding star. "Michelangelo's David with the face of an El Greco Don," Rex Ingram supposedly said. When Novarro read this, he jokingly told Ingram, "Well, that proves what Mary Pickford once said—that my face and body do not match."

Pickford had recently asked to borrow Novarro to costar in her next picture, *Rosita* (1923). Upon hearing "America's Sweetheart's" statement about his up-and-coming star, Ingram stubbornly declared, "If she thinks your face and body do not match, she can't have you."[2] Ironically, the actor chosen for *Rosita* was George Walsh, whom Novarro would later replace in *Ben-Hur*.

Metro's official biography of Novarro falsely claimed that he was a Spaniard. And even worse, they said that his father had died shortly after his arrival in the United States, which must have been annoying to the very much alive Dr. Samaniego.

Dr. Samaniego suffered from facial neuralgia, which became worse over the years. At times the attacks were unbearable, and several operations failed to totally ease the symptoms. The illness forced him to give up dentistry, so he returned to school and earned a second degree as a chiropractor. His new occupation gained him a fair amount of accomplishment, but he mainly wanted to keep busy and in that he succeeded.[3]

Meanwhile, the Goldwyn Pictures Corporation bought the screen rights to General Lew Wallace's novel, *Ben-Hur*.[4] It was left up to F. J. Godsol, president of Goldwyn, to find the proper players for the epic. It was Godsol who convinced A. R. Erlanger, the play's producer, to allow Goldwyn to produce the new film version. Erlanger insisted on full control over choice of director, stars and scriptwriter. June Mathis was chosen to adapt the screenplay, and Rex Ingram hoped to be selected as director. He was among the many candidates, who included Erich von Stroheim and Marshall Neilan. Rumors and public opinion insisted that Rudolph Valentino should play the title role, but that would mean a special arrangement with Famous Players–Lasky, which was unlikely.

While the Goldwyn committee was making its decision, Rex Ingram took Novarro and Alice Terry to Florida to film his next picture, *Where the Pavement Ends* (1923). This one, Novarro's third picture for Ingram, was based on John Russell's story *The Passion Vine*. Ingram was now paying Novarro $500 a week, influenced by the actor's performance in *Trifling Women* and the generous offer made by producer Samuel Goldwyn.

Where the Pavement Ends was filmed in and around Miami and on the island of Cuba. Novarro played Motauri, a young islander who falls in love with Alice Terry's character, Matilda, a beautiful missionary's daughter.

The script called for a large waterfall, which they had difficulty finding. Finally, film editor Grant Whytock rushed into the hotel where Ingram was playing billiards and told him they had found what he was looking for. "They're the tallest falls you've ever seen," he told Ingram breathlessly, "and there's only an hour of light left." Because of the lack of time, Ingram sent doubles in place of Ramon and Alice. "Hell," Whytock said, "It was only long shots! Who would know."[5]

Motauri knows he can never marry Matilda because of their racial differences, so he gives her his cache of pearls and jumps to his death from the waterfall. Metro felt the ending was too depressing for moviegoers, so it had Ingram film a happier ending in which Motauri discovers he is the sun-tanned lost son of a white trader, which means that he can now marry Matilda. The studio gave exhibitors the choice of which ending to play.

"I favor the tragic ending if it is the logical thing," Ramon said. "People are getting into the frame of mind where they don't care what is happening to the characters of the story, because they know there is always a happy ending. The producers are making a mistake in trying to put out pictures that everyone will see. They put something into each picture that will please every taste and they seldom really satisfy anyone."[6]

Ingram's contract included a clause which stated that if *Ben-Hur* was produced by another studio, Metro would allow him time off to direct the epic. While in Florida, Ingram received a telegram from Godsol telling him that he was out of the running as director. Ingram, who was accustomed to getting what he wanted, suddenly had to contend with the realization that someone was telling him no. The shock was so great that his personality changed overnight. Novarro claimed that it was hard for him to adjust to the disappointment.[7] "His reaction, when he lost it," Novarro said, "was a hundred percent Irish—and you know what I mean."[8]

Director Marshall Neilan was originally offered the picture but turned it down when he learned it was to be filmed in Italy. Eventually, it was announced that English-born director Charles Brabin (the husband of screen vamp Theda Bara) would direct *Ben-Hur*. This shocked most of Hollywood because he was not one of the original choices.

He was June Mathis' choice, however, and she wielded considerable control over the production. She selected Brabin because he had been a student of Bible history for many years, knew Europe well, and was an accomplished linguist. To add salt to Ingram's wound, Mathis stated that she had selected Ingram for *The Four Horsemen of the Apocalypse* only because he had at one time worked under Brabin.

The filming of *Where the Pavement Ends* continued, however, and the picture made Novarro even more popular. In his first interview with the *Los Angeles Times*, Novarro told the reporter: "We went to Miami for this picture. Incidentally, California is the place to make pictures. They have few facilities there [in Miami], and the climate is not so agreeable. We were there three months making scenes that would have taken us seven weeks here."[9]

Variety commented, "Ramon Novarro would be rather too conventionally and spiritually good looking for a regular hero, but in these surroundings he is a picturesque figure."[10]

Reviewers and fans alike noticed Novarro's striking good looks and sometimes ignored his acting ability, which frustrated him. Regardless, Novarro's popularity was increasing. He received 1,300 fan letters a week, and movie magazines clamored for any kind of trivia. "Ramon Novarro has a new hobby—surf board riding," wrote one magazine.[11]

Ramon's contract was coming up for renewal, and Metro president Marcus Loew had plans to make him a star. After several months of negotiations with Loew and Metro's lawyers, Novarro walked away with the best part of the deal. The bargain he drove gave him final say on all his productions for the next five years and earned him $10,000 a week. Nicholas Schenck once said, "There's nothing wrong with this business that a star worth $10,000 a week can't cure."[12] Upon hearing this, Ramon knew he was worth every cent.

The new five-year contract called for him to make two more films for Ingram and to spend the remainder of his time making special productions under other directors. He also received a two-month vacation each year.

Because of the shrewd way he handled himself, Loew commented, "Ramon will make a great Shylock."[13]

His next picture for Ingram, *Scaramouche* (1923), would prove to be his most popular to date. Metro spared no expense for Willis Goldbeck's faithfully adapted screenplay of Rafael Sabatini's romance novel of the French Revolution. Aside from a cast of 30 principals, Ingram built two complete villages, one on the Metro lot and another in the San Fernando Valley. The latter site is today the location of Forest Lawn Cemetery–Hollywood Hills.

Novarro played the title role, Andre-Louis Moreau, a French nobleman who outwits his enemies by joining a troupe of actors and becomes known as Scaramouche. Alice Terry played his love interest, Aline de Kercadsious, and once again Louis Stone played the heavy as the Marquis de la Tour d'Azyr.

Production began on March 17, 1923, St. Patrick's Day, and Ingram, being a good Irishman, celebrated appropriately by getting drunk. He continued celebrating for 12 days, shutting down production before it even began.

Novarro's brother Mariano played an extra in the mob scenes. Mariano was no stranger to films, and besides taking English and French classes, he also studied dramatics in the evening. With Ramon's help, he appeared in a bit part as Mariano Novarro in *The Dangerous Maid* (1923), starring Constance Talmadge. Of course, the Novarro name could not hurt, but unfortunately for Mariano, it didn't help because that was the extent of his film career.

Even though he would allow his youngest brother Eduardo to portray him as a child in *The Red Lily* (1924), Novarro did not approve of his family acting in pictures. In fact, he officially banned his sister Carmen from appearing in films. Carmen was a talented "skirt-dancer" with acting aspirations, and years later accompanied Novarro on his concert tours across the world. He believed that working in films would affect her youth and innocence.[14]

During the filming of one scene, Ingram put Ramon through 12 rehearsals, desperate to get what he wanted. He remarked to *Photoplay* writer Herb Howe: "Isn't that boy a wonder? He's the greatest actor on the screen—I've never seen anyone like him."

"But you drove him through 12 rehearsals," Howe responded.

"Yes, but did you notice I had the camera grinding at all times?" Ingram said. "I'll use his most spontaneous moments."[15]

When *Scaramouche* was in preproduction, a Metro executive wrote, "The picture would be expensive and doubt its popular appeal. The public might be interested in the historical sequences, but would they care about Andres or Scaramouche?"[16]

The picture was expensive, costing more than $1,140,000. The film, which opened at New York's 44th Street Theater, was a major success and sealed stardom for Novarro. *Variety* said, "Ramon Novarro as the young lawyer, actor-duelist-hero of the story is made for the future."[17]

Novarro displaying a drawing of him as *Scaramouche* (1923, Metro Pictures Corp.).

A Los Angeles critic reviewing *Scaramouche* referred to Novarro as the Barrymore of the screen. Shortly after the review appeared, Novarro ran into the actor at a costumer's shop on Hollywood Boulevard. The two had never met, but Barrymore promptly held out his hand. "And so," exclaimed the thespian, "the Barrymore of the screen meets the Novarro of the stage."[18]

After *Scaramouche* completed filming, Marcus Loew had Ingram secretly make a test of Novarro for the role of *Ben-Hur*.[19] Loew had faith in Ramon and thought he was the best actor for the part. As much as Rex Ingram wanted to direct *Ben-Hur*, Ramon wanted to star. By now rumors abounded as to who would play the coveted role. The obvious choice was still Valentino, who surprisingly did not want the part. He told Francis X. Bushman, "What if I do that? Where can I go after Ben-Hur? I have no place to go but down."[20]

Among the others tested for the role were Edmund Lowe, John Bowers, Ben Lyon, and Valentino's pick, Antonio Moreno. By now it had been almost a year since plans for *Ben-Hur* had been announced, and still there were no prospects. The film was fast becoming a joke to the Hollywood press. Herb Howe of *Photoplay* sarcastically wrote: "It looks like *Ben-Hur* might win the *Photoplay* Medal for being best picture of 1940, if there isn't a world war in the meantime. We have a tip on the actor who will finally get it. It's Jackie Coogan. Our sleuths in Hollywood report that Jackie spends several hours every day driving his scooter in training for the big chariot scenes."[21]

In September 1923, after submitting his screen test to the Goldwyn committee, Novarro vacationed in New York City. While there, he learned that George Walsh had been cast in the part that he so desperately wanted. Most critics reasoned that Walsh was chosen because of his role in *Rosita*, which Rex Ingram had turned down for Novarro.

In a press release, F. J. Godsol stated, "George Walsh has been chosen. after exhaustive screen tests had been made of many and the choice was made not only because of his ability as an actor but for his physical attainments as well."[22]

Director Brabin, along with Edward Bowes, vice president of Goldwyn and future radio talent scout, and J. J. Cohn, a studio account executive, sailed for Europe on the *Leviathan*. They began setting up the groundwork and contracting for locations. The original budget for *Ben-Hur* was set for $1.3 to $1.5 million, but the studio thought it was possible to make the film in Italy for only $500,000. Cohn disagreed and thought the same results could be achieved on the back lot, but he was overruled by Mathis and the studio.[23]

Disappointed that he had lost the part of Ben-Hur, Novarro boarded a train back to Los Angeles to begin work on his next film, *Thy Name Is Woman* (1924), which was to be directed by Fred Niblo and was to costar his good friend Barbara La Marr.

Meanwhile, problems were developing at the Goldwyn Studios.[24] Although the studio had many talented stars and directors, its management staff was weak and indecisive. A year earlier the studio had merged with William Randolph Hearst's Cosmopolitan Productions in one of the biggest mergers in history.

Surprisingly, Metro was experiencing the same problems as Goldwyn. The loss of Valentino to Famous Players–Lasky was a blow that nearly crippled the studio. Marcus Loew suggested merging the two studios and combining the talents of both. Details for the merger were handled by attorney J. Robert Rubin and Nicholas Schenck, Loew's second in command. It was agreed that Loew would take over the Goldwyn Studios. A share of Goldwyn stock would be traded for a share of the new company to be called Metro-Goldwyn, and the entire organization would be controlled by Loew's Inc., the parent company.

After the merger was approved by the shareholders and the board of directors of both companies, Rubin and Schenck set about to find someone to oversee the new studio. Rubin approached Loew and suggested a friend, producer Louis B. Mayer,[25] and his assistant Irving Thalberg.[26]

Little did they know at the time that this pairing would make film history. Both future moguls would have an impact on the young Novarro's career. Until then, Ramon had one more picture to make for Rex Ingram, one which would take him to the farthest reaches of the earth.

Chapter Five

Mayer and Thalberg
(1923–1924)

Mr. Ingram's pictures were beautifully designed. He was an artist, and a good one. Every frame was a tasteful and exciting picture in itself. And we actors were rehearsed. We knew exactly what we had to do when it came time to appear before the camera, and we did it.
                                    —Ramon Novarro[1]

Marcus Loew wanted to make sure he had the right man to head his fledgling studio, so while visiting California, he decided to check out Louis B. Mayer for himself. One day he and Rubin stopped by the Mission Road studios, where Mayer gave them a tour of his facilities. They stopped by the set of *Thy Name Is Woman* to watch Fred Niblo direct Novarro and Barbara La Marr. In between shots, Mayer lectured the group about the use of film stock, cameras, costumes, and lighting, stating that the same equipment was used by all the studios. "There's only one way a producer can be different," he told those gathered around him. He tapped his forehead and said, "Brains!"[2]

Thy Name Is Woman was Ramon's first starring picture without Rex Ingram. It was taken from the popular German stage play *The She-Devil* by Karl Schoenherr and translated by Benjamin Glazer. Metro had bought the treatment from Universal a year earlier on the advice of June Mathis. In this film, Ramon played Juan Ricardo, a Spanish officer who makes love to the

Novarro with the "too beautiful" Barbara La Marr in their third film together, *Thy Name Is Woman* **(1924, Metro-Goldwyn).**

beautiful wife of the head of a band of smugglers in hopes that she may betray her elderly husband.

The role of the wife went to Barbara La Marr, known around Hollywood and to her fans as "the girl who was too beautiful."[3] Ramon was very good friends with La Marr and knew about her problems with drugs and alcohol. Many times he tried to help but to no avail. One day after the picture was completed and they were viewing the film, Barbara turned to Ramon and told him that he would have a wonderful career on the screen.

"But," he said, "your career will be as great as mine."

"Oh no," she replied, "In two years I will be forgotten."[4] That statement proved somewhat prophetic. In two years Barbara La Marr would be dead, and her funeral would turn into one of the biggest riots Hollywood ever saw.

Novarro's last picture for Rex Ingram was based on Edgar Selwyn's play *The Arab* (1924), which Cecil B. DeMille originally filmed in 1915. Novarro played the title role opposite his frequent leading lady, Alice Terry. Ingram and photographer John Seitz left for Tunisia, where the movie would be shot. The rest of the cast and crew would arrive later.

In the meantime, Novarro endorsed his first promotional ad for the United Fast Color Eyelet Company. "Off stage," the ad read, "Mr. Novarro is no less fastidious in his selection of the details of his wardrobe. He insists that his footwear invariably be finished with visible eyelets, the mark of excellence in quality and workmanship."[5]

Novarro was the perfect representative for a company stressing apparel for the well-dressed man. He was developing a reputation as one of the best-dressed men in Hollywood and was tagged "Ravishing Ramon" by the press. Years later he told film historian Dewitt Bodeen, "During the first two years of my stardom, I never entered the studio wearing anything but a black suit and tie. Even when conventions were relaxed, it would never have occurred to me to arrive for work wearing Levis or a T-shirt, as some of the male stars do today."[6]

Novarro, Terry, and the rest of the cast left for Tunisia on the S. S. *Majestic*, along with *Photoplay* correspondent Herb Howe.[7] Novarro and Howe began a close friendship on the trip that would continue for many years. At one point there were rumors that he and Novarro were more than just friends, but there was never any tangible proof.

At the time, not many in Hollywood knew that Ramon Novarro was a homosexual. There were rumors whispered about the studio lot, but no one was certain. It was, of course, not known to the public, for that would have meant certain box-office death. He was becoming a big moneymaker to the studio and needed to be very discreet. Hollywood was a liberal town and privately accepted any lifestyle, but if an actor's lifestyle was abhorrent to the public and was revealed, it would end his or her career. It happened with such stars as Wallace Reid, Fatty Arbuckle, and Mabel Normand. Had Novarro's "secret" become known, he never would have worked again.

On the second day of the voyage, Novarro was seasick when Howe visited him. He had interviewed Novarro in New York the previous year and wanted to reacquaint himself with the actor. The ailing Novarro groaned recognition while fingering a huge medal imprinted with the miracle-working image of the Virgin of Guadalupe.

The next day the Holy Mother had apparently performed her miracle and Novarro was completely restored. That evening he joined Howe for dinner. "You are not at all like they say you are," Ramon told him with conviction.

"What do they say I am?" Howe replied.

"Cynical, sophisticated, mercenary," Ramon blurted.

"They are quite right," he said, " so far as they are concerned. You know the verse from Corinthians: 'I am made all things to all men'?"

Ramon laughed, "But you will find I am sold on my own ideas."[8]

When the ship docked in Tunisia, a caravan met the members of the party to escort them to their hotels. After settling in, they went to the Oasis of Gabes, where Ingram had set up filming. Ingram used authentic Arab costumes, weapons, dancers, and extras and made friends with many of the local leaders. The Bey of Tunis presented him with the Order of Niftkan Itchkar and made him a gift of his own court jester, an Arab dwarf with asthma whom Ingram called Shorty. He adopted him as a mascot and used him for several years in his pictures.

One day during shooting, Ramon and Alice were doing a love scene on a crimson rug in a tent situated on a hill. Below them on the sand was a myriad of black tents of nomad encampments. Extras were crouched about small fires preparing the evening meal. In the distance were giant palm trees waving in the breeze, and across the horizon, a Bedouin in a white burnoose raced over the hill. The scene was set. "All right now Ramon, kiss Alice," Ingram screamed into his megaphone. Turning to the crew, he continued, "And when they kiss, start the camels across."[9]

As the camels started, one tripped and fell into a tent, almost landing on the extras inside. Five sheiks who were serving as Ingram's assistants began screaming at the camels, and the players in the Arab orchestra of pipes and drums went running wildly. In the midst of the pandemonium, a little Bedouin girl came bounding across the camera lines with a basket of eggs, thinking she was still on cue. She tripped and nearly scrambled her eggs all over Ramon.

Christmas of 1923 was spent in a Tunisian hotel, but because they were so far away from their loved ones, everyone was downcast. Ramon took it upon himself to brighten their spirits, so he designated himself chief entertainer. He knew that Alice Terry loved to laugh, so he tried some of his best—and worst—jokes. "His jokes are terrible," Alice said, "but he laughs at them so hysterically himself that you can't help joining in."[10]

Ramon impersonated such entertainers as John Barrymore and Charlie Chaplin and "did Ed Wynn better than Ed Wynn."[11] Later he sat down at a beat-up piano and serenaded the group with "Serenata Chusca," a humorous Mexican ballad, and an assortment of arias and popular songs. Promptly at midnight, he departed for mass, despite everyone's protests. Upon returning, he continued by singing "Ave Maria" and "Crucifix" by Faure.

While in Africa, Ingram was informed of the merger between Metro, Goldwyn, and Louis B. Mayer. He told Marcus Loew that he wanted no part of it, claiming it had nothing to do with his dislike of Mayer. He explained to Loew that he was tired of having someone else tell him how to make films. "My sympathies are all with those directors who stand or fall on their own merits," he said. "I have too often seen a good picture, and the career of a promising director, ruined by supervision."[12]

Because Marcus Loew respected Ingram and his past contributions to Metro, he agreed to set the director up with his own studio in Nice, in the south of France, where Ingram could work virtually free of any supervision. The new studio would distribute his pictures and provide him with whatever he needed.

Mayer did not approve of Ingram's arrangements with Loew and claimed he had never been impressed with any of the director's pictures. He knew *The Arab* was being edited without him and demanded to see the uncut version. He hated the film and insisted on having the rushes shipped to him from France, which infuriated Ingram.

When *The Arab* premiered in July 1924, it opened to mix reviews. The so-called "sheik craze" was waning, but *Variety* still thought it was "the finest sheik film of them all."[13] Another reviewer said, "Ramon Novarro is 100 degrees in the shade!"[14] Others thought the film was beautiful to look at but was boring and slow.

Meanwhile, plans for the studio merger in Hollywood were progressing at a rapid pace. Loew offered to buy Mayer's company for $76,500, so Mayer traveled to New York in January 1924 to settle the negotiations. New additions were also announced for the cast of *Ben-Hur*, including Carmel Myers and Francis X. Bushman.

On February 6, 1924, June Mathis sailed for Italy with a script of 1,722 scenes. The next day Mathis wired Abraham Lehr, "Many thanks. Shall do everything in my power to make you proud of me."[15]

Novarro returned from Tunisia in time for the opening of the new studio. A few formalities had to be ironed out, however, before the papers were signed. First, Samuel Goldwyn had to be bought out of his remaining shares of the Goldwyn Studios for $1 million. He also insisted that Goldwyn remain part of the new studio's name.

Mayer also wanted to be prominently named, so it was decided that all films would be released under the trademark Metro-Goldwyn or Metro-Goldwyn-Mayer, according to whatever Mayer thought best. If the shorter version were used, then a subtitle would read, "produced by Louis B. Mayer." Because of the confusion this eventually caused, Metro-Goldwyn-Mayer became the studio's official trademark in the fall of 1925. Through it all, Thalberg stood by his conviction that he did not want his name on anything. "Credit you give yourself isn't worth having," he said.[16] On April 10, 1924, papers were formally signed for the merger of the three studios.

Three days before the opening ceremonies, Novarro appeared in Superior

Court to legally change his name. "Why do you wish it changed?" asked the judge.

"It's too hard to say," he replied. "Everybody calls me salmon eggs and things like that."

"Well, that must be annoying," the judge remarked. "What do you wish it changed to?"

"Ramon Novarro," he answered promptly.

"But isn't that the name of a famous actor," the judge said. "He will not like it."

"No, it will be perfectly all right," Novarro responded. "There will be no hard feelings, I guess, because I *am* Ramon Novarro." From that point on, Jose Ramon Gil Samaniego would forever be Ramon Novarro, though he would retain the name Samaniego for his legal signature (Ramon Novarro Samaniego).[17]

Novarro's next picture was another film for Fred Niblo called *The Red Lily* (1924), which costarred Niblo's wife, Enid Bennett. Screenwriter Bess Meredyth adapted Niblo's original story of *The Red Lily*, in which Novarro played a Frenchman in love with the daughter of the mayor, who objects strongly to their romance.

Niblo was having difficulty casting the part of the boy who was to play Novarro as a teenager and asked the actor for a picture of himself as a youth. Instead, Novarro brought in his younger brother Eduardo, who looked much like Ramon at that age. When Niblo met Eduardo, the director cast him in the part. Movie magazines speculated as to what the future would hold for young Eduardo Novarro. "Will Eduardo succeed his brother in the hearts of film fans?" they queried.[18]

They need not have worried, for this would be the young man's only film appearance. Eduardo had other goals, and Ramon would make sure that his youngest brother achieved them, as he did for all his siblings. He became a guardian to them all, insisting that they were well educated. Eduardo Samaniego grew up to be a talented and respected Los Angeles architect.

It was just as well that young Eduardo gave up acting because there was room for only one romantic star in the Samaniego family and Ramon was it. And that star would soon shine even brighter, for unknown to Novarro, a series of events were unfolding that would propel him to the biggest role of his career.

Chapter Six

Metro-Goldwyn-Mayer
(1924)

*Of all the young cinema celebrities, Ramon Novarro is the
least known and the most worth knowing about.*
—Herbert Howe[1]

In Italy, work on *Ben-Hur* was deteriorating. Labor disputes delayed the
building of the Circus Maximus and the Joppa Gate sets outside the Porta
San Giovanni. Italian labor was inexpensive, but slow. Originally, Mussolini
had offered the Americans all the help they needed, but when he discovered
the differences in salaries between the Hollywood workers and the Italians,
he became indignant.

Mismanagement seemed to hit every aspect of the filming. When Francis X. Bushman arrived in February, director Brabin told him they would not
get to his scenes until August. To fill his time, he went on a 25-country tour
with his sister. Carmel Myers had time to do a picture in Germany, and after
three months without looking at a camera, Gertrude Olmstead complained,
"It looks as though I've signed on for life!"[2] When the actors who were to
play the Three Wise Men arrived, a studio official refused to meet them at
the train station, saying he had met enough wise men from Hollywood.

But George Walsh received the worst treatment of all. Thinking that
his role would make him a star, he had agreed to a salary cut of $400 a week
and second-class accommodations on the boat trip.[3] During his four months

in Rome, however, he was totally ignored and appeared before the cameras only once—to do a test with an Italian actor. It was June Mathis' understanding that she was to supervise the production, but she soon learned differently. Brabin would not allow her any input except to approve or reject changes to the script.

Brabin had hoped for 70 ships for the filming of the sea battle but was only given 30 at a cost of $200,000. When finally completed, they were hauled out into the Mediterranean, but the Port Authority ordered them back to shore after several boats overturned. Weeks later they tried again, but the ships were still not seaworthy, so they had to be anchored.

Nothing seemed to go right. The sets cost a fortune but still looked cheap. The script wasn't completed, and a lot of time and money were being wasted. The morale of the entire company was at an all-time low, and it appeared that Ben-Hur would be the biggest film fiasco that Hollywood had ever seen.

Back in Hollywood, the terms for the studio merger were being finalized. The combined authorized capital stock from each studio was approximately $65 million.[4] Louis B. Mayer was named vice president in charge of production, and the board of directors included F. J. Godsol, president of Goldwyn Pictures, and Edward Bowes, vice president of Goldwyn. In a statement to the press, Marcus Loew commented: "The motion picture business is going through a stabilizing process and is working itself out on sane, economic principles. Through combining our forces in the best interest of all parties to the merger, Metro, Goldwyn, Cosmopolitan and the Louis B. Mayer Company are going a long way in the right direction."[5]

The deal included the distribution contract of William Randolph Hearst's Cosmopolitan Pictures, the services of the directors and stars of both Metro and Goldwyn Studios, and the use of the chain of Goldwyn theaters, including New York's Capitol Theater, the largest in the country. Also included were two theaters in Los Angeles, the California and Miller's, and the facilities of the Goldwyn Studios in Culver City, which were valued at $14 million.[6]

The studio building was impressive from the outside. Its Corinthian columns and fences ran about 800 feet along Washington Boulevard. Inside it looked much like any other studio. The stages were made of metal frame and glass (like a greenhouse), and there were dressing rooms, carpentry shops, and a modest administration building. Mayer arrived on the lot in January 1924 and transferred the cameras and lights from his Mission Road studio. Metro's glass studios were dismantled and shipped across town to be reassembled among the stages already standing.

Mayer decided to keep the logo of the Goldwyn Studios that was designed by Howard Dietz in 1921—a roaring lion's head encircled by the words Ars Gratia Artis (Art for Art's Sake).

The new parent company, Loew's, Inc., officially took over the studio during a formal ceremony on Saturday, April 26, 1924, at 2:30 in the afternoon. Fred Niblo presided as the master of ceremonies. Among the stars present were Novarro, Antonio Moreno, Barbara La Marr, Lon Chaney, and Norma Shearer.

A platform trimmed in the Stars and Stripes was built on the front lawn, and a pastel portrait of Marcus Loew was hung prominently in front. Mayer read telegrams of congratulations from President Coolidge, Will Hays, and the Warner brothers. The army and navy were well represented: more than 300 navy men were assembled and 10 army planes flew over the studio in formation. Will Rogers arrived late, riding in on horseback. "Sorry I'm late folks" he quipped. "I forgot my chewing gum and had to ride home to get it." Abe Lehr, vice president for Goldwyn, handed Mayer a giant key bearing the word *SUCCESS*. "This is a great moment for me," Mayer told the assembled visitors. "I accept this solemn trust, and pledge the best that I have to give."[7]

The following Monday, Mayer and Thalberg began work on building a dream factory that would become one of the most prestigious studios in Hollywood history. One of their first projects was to save *Ben-Hur*. When Marcus Loew suggested that Mayer supervise the film, one of the executives said, "Why not? After all, Mayer knows how to salvage junk!"[8]

In a letter to Marcus Loew, Joseph Schenck said he should consider Rubin's idea of sending Fred Niblo to Rome with an officer of the studio to dismiss June Mathis. Loew was concerned about the reaction from A. R. Erlanger, who had chosen Mathis in the first place. "The worst Erlanger could do," Schenck told Loew, "would be to cancel the contract for producing *Ben-Hur*, which probably would be the very best thing for you."

Schenck reminded Loew that it was Mathis who had written the scenario for *Greed* (1924), which was now 24 reels, and in his opinion could not be edited to a desirable length. Mathis was also responsible for two of Goldwyn's biggest flops that year. "I am not trying to undermine Mathis," Schenck concluded, "but just to point out to your necessity of immediate action."[9]

When Loew addressed Mayer and Thalberg about supervising the production of *Ben-Hur*, they told Loew they would take the job only if June Mathis, Charles Brabin, and George Walsh were removed. They also insisted that the script be rewritten. These demands meant they would have to start from the beginning.

Mayer approached Fred Niblo about replacing Brabin on the film. Less than enthusiastic, Niblo replied: "Personally, I will be more than pleased if you will count me out entirely. It is not too big of a job for me, but if I can't do it right, I don't want to do it at all." Niblo felt the assembled cast was the most uninteresting and colorless he had ever seen in a big picture. "There is not one outstanding personality," he told Mayer. "They were all selected by Miss Mathis with the same judgment that she selected George Walsh."

Having worked with Niblo on several pictures, Mayer was positive he was the man for the job and eventually convinced him to take it. Dubiously, the director accepted the challenge, but he commented: "*Ben-Hur* can be the biggest thing that has ever been done. It can also be the biggest flop."[10]

On Sunday afternoon, June 8, 1924, Novarro was having lunch at his home when he received a call from Irving Thalberg requesting him to come to the studio. The "Boy Wonder" broke the exciting news that Novarro was going to play the part of a lifetime: he was going to take over the role of Ben-Hur from the unsuspecting George Walsh.

The following day an entourage from MGM that included Novarro, Louis B. Mayer, attorney J. Robert Rubin, Fred Niblo, and Herb Howe left from the Pasadena train station for New York. Within a week they were sailing for Europe on the steamship *Leviathan*, which also carried such esteemed passengers as actor, David Warfield, General John "Blackjack" Pershing, and comedian Buster Keaton.

It wasn't long before the news spread that Brabin and Walsh were out and Niblo and Novarro were in. Francis X. Bushman read in the *Telegraph* that Novarro had been signed for the lead and showed the article to George Walsh. "Do you know anything about this?" he asked Walsh.

"You know, Frank," he said, "I felt this was going to happen. But to leave me over here for so long, to let me die in pictures—and then to change me!"

Years later, in a letter to film historian Kevin Brownlow, Walsh stated, "The great injury I incurred, was in their not announcing publicly the full facts. Unfortunately for me, the public figured I had failed to fill the bill."[11]

Indeed, Walsh's career went nowhere after his dismissal from *Ben-Hur*. He returned to America and signed with a poverty-row studio, Chadwick Pictures, making low-budget films. Eventually he did supporting roles in a few films for his brother, director Raoul Walsh, and he made his last picture in 1936.

The mood on the *Leviathan* was somewhat more upbeat, with Marcus Loew hosting dinner parties every evening. Ramon, as usual, charmed everyone on the ship, especially the young ladies. Everyday notes were shoved under his cabin door from mothers who had actress daughters and from women who wanted to recite love sonnets to him. "I'm the girl who smiled at you on deck 'A' this morning," one note read. "I'll be on the boat deck at ten tonight."[12] When attorney J. Robert Rubin found out, he ended the flirting for fear of blackmail. Every possible scenario had to be considered because so much was riding on the success of *Ben-Hur*.

During the voyage, actress Pola Negri was quoted as saying that Ramon Novarro was the greatest actor of the screen and could be compared to Barrymore. Negri further declared her admiration by stating, "When I saw Mr. Novarro as *Scaramouche*, I took my hat off to him." Many thought this was a great compliment, and someone commented, "Anyone who can make the fiery Pola remove her chapeau is just about the greatest conqueror since Alexander."[13]

The night before arriving in Europe, Novarro hosted a benefit concert for the entire ship which was broadcast on radio as far east as Egypt. The proceeds went to the Seaman's Benefit and the Actor's Fund. General Pershing, who was introduced by Fred Niblo with a bugle flourish, shook hands with Novarro but said he would not donate anything to actors. "Movie actors get all the money in the world," he said. "I'm going to give just two-thirds of what I intended, and it will all go to the seamen."[14]

It was raining when the *Leviathan* landed at Cherbourg, France, the next day. From there, the group traveled to Paris, where Ramon was recognized by a young prostitute who offered her services for the evening. Novarro politely refused, much to the delight of the entourage. Nonplussed, the young lady made the same offer to another gentleman.

Having only one evening to explore Paris, Novarro and Howe set out for a night on the town. They had dinner at the Foyot and afterward went to the Casino de Paris, which was similar to the Ziegfeld Follies except that the young ladies entertained in the nude.

On the trip to Rome, the customs inspector entered at five in the morning as the train crossed the border from France to Italy and pounded on Novarro's compartment. Ramon heard the conductor explain that the coach contained movie people, to which the inspector replied, "Rottoni!" which freely translated meant, "The dirty rats!"[15]

Despite the inspector's apparent disapproval, American movies were favorites of the Italian people. *Robin Hood* (1922) ran for two consecutive months in Naples, Mary Pickford was their most popular actress, and Charlie Chaplin's *The Kid* (1921) was shown continuously in Italy and all over Europe.

The company arrived in Rome in the middle of a thunderstorm and checked into the Excelsior Hotel. Metro-Goldwyn had already made the announcement from New York about the film's replacements. In Rome, Marcus Loew began the unpleasant task of breaking the bad news to the company, waiting three days, however, before informing George Walsh. On June 30, Rubin wired Mayer, telling him that everything had been arranged. "Niblo now has everything in hand," he told Mayer. "Believe things will go satisfactorily. Made adjustment with Walsh, took tests of Novarro—looks wonderful."[16]

Upon returning to the States, Brabin filed a lawsuit against Metro-Goldwyn for $583,000 in damages. He alleged that he was not provided the necessary equipment to do a proper job. He eventually dropped the suit, however, and a few years later he again signed with MGM and directed one of Novarro's more popular talkies, *The Call of the Flesh* (1930).

June Mathis decided to stay in Rome for a few months with her soon-to-be husband, Silvano Balboni, who had been a cameraman on the film and had also been replaced. In statements to the press, Mathis blamed all the problems of the film on Charles Brabin. She asserted that all control of the picture had been taken away from her by Brabin and said she could no longer associate herself with the film. In a letter to Kevin Brownlow years later, Novarro said that June Mathis "reacted bravely about the takeover. In fact, she told me of a dream she had in which she had gotten hold of some object that was on fire and then threw it away. But, as we say in Spanish, 'we see faces, but we do not know what goes on in the heart.'"[17]

Even though Novarro was sensitive to the feelings of the ousted cast and crew, he had to remind himself that this was his big break. He knew there was a lot of work ahead of him but sometimes doubted whether he was up for the challenge. If he had only known what lay ahead of him over the next several months, he might have changed his mind and gone back to America with June Mathis.

Chapter Seven

Ben-Hur (1924)

*I wonder sometimes when people congratulate me upon
my performance in* Ben-Hur *how much that performance
would have mattered had I had a fat stomach.*
          —Ramon Novarro[1]

Novarro was immediately put into physical training upon his arrival in
Rome. In a letter to Louis B. Mayer, scenarist Bess Meredyth wrote: "Ramon
looks splendid in his costumes—he is exercising daily and getting into great
physical condition. He is more enthusiastic than ever about the part."[2] According to J. J. Cohn, who was production manager for the studio, Novarro arose
at six in the morning, and after 30 minutes in the gym, he went for road work
with a trainer. On occasion, he would row and swim in the Tiber River.

However, all of Novarro's training could not solve one problem. George
Walsh and Francis X. Bushman were approximately the same height, but
Novarro, at five feet, eight inches was at least three to four inches shorter. As
a solution, they added heels and padding to Novarro's sandals, which gave
the actor an additional inch and a half of height.[3]

Soon more problems arose, and filming was halted for a month and a
half. "Condition serious," Niblo wired Mayer. "Must rush work before November rains. No sets or lights available before August 1. Two hundred reels of
film wasted; bad photography; terrible actors."[4]

By all calculations at the time, *Ben-Hur* would cost close to $3 million.
As a precaution, Mayer sent Alexander Aronson, the head of MGM's new

Paris office, to Rome to make sure Niblo followed orders. Aronson and Niblo disagreed about everything from the start.

Filming finally began under the new team on August 14, 1924. The temperature was running 100 plus in the shade, and everyone wished they had stayed in Hollywood. That morning Niblo wired Mayer in California, "Started shooting today, will bring home the bacon."[5]

Meanwhile, back in Hollywood, *Ben-Hur* jokes were still popular. In one cartoon, two men are watching an old man with a cane and a floor-length white beard walk down the street. One man says to the other, "Rip Van Winkle?" "Nope," the other replies, "Ben-Hur!"[6]

While he was in Rome, Novarro made sure he took advantage of the city's hot spots, and he sometimes dined at the Castello dei Caesari, which commanded a beautiful view of Rome. Many nights he would arrive at the restaurant in a carriage pulled by a horse named General Diaz. The driver, knowing who Novarro was, would always charge a few lire more than what the meter showed. "But that's to be expected with a general leading us," Ramon would always say.[7]

After dinner, Ramon would usually attend the theater or opera. One evening he and his companions arrived late at the Eliseo for a rendition of Verdi's *Requiem Mass* and was told to wait. When he saw that a retinue of uniformed men were being seated before him, Ramon suddenly bolted past them and seated himself, not knowing that one of the entourage was an Italian prince.

When he had a free day, Novarro would often set off to a museum or other historical spot. On one occasion, he and Herb Howe traveled to Pompeii to visit the famed ruins. Hoping not to be recognized, they arrived unshaven and ill-kempt and ate lunch at a little tavern where 20 members of an American touring party were also eating. The duo's disguise was evidently not foolproof because every female suddenly turned her gaze on Novarro. Finally, one of the ladies approached him and said, "I live next door to Tom Mix, so I thought I would introduce myself."

Throughout the afternoon, the star-struck women followed Novarro down the streets of Pompeii until he finally found sanctuary at the Lupanare, a place where women were not allowed. The Lupanare had five stone couches and numerous uncensored pictures of couples in different positions of intercourse. "Here," said the guide, "they held countless orgies. Orgies every night."[8] As a respite, Ramon napped on a stone couch, far from the ogling of his admirers.

By September, Thalberg and Mayer finally had a chance to view the rushes that Charles Brabin had filmed. "Saw Brabin stuff tonight," Mayer wired to Niblo. "Certainly congratulate you on the wisdom of discarding every inch and a great fortune not having Walsh." Thalberg agreed that the Brabin footage was inferior and was amazed that such work could have been done.

"I inwardly breathe a prayer of relief that we have taken the hysterical action that was necessary to make a change. It is beyond my conception," Thalberg continued, "that such stuff could have been passed by people of even moderate intelligence."[9]

For the part of the sheik, Thalberg wanted to cast Wallace Beery, but before the deal was finalized, Beery signed with Famous Players–Lasky. By then, Thalberg was having second doubts about the actor. "He is getting very, very difficult to handle," he wrote to Niblo. "He now announces at what hour he will start work and what hour he will end."[10] With Niblo's current problems, Thalberg was certain that the director did not need one more temperamental actor on the set.

Another cast change took place in October when May McAvoy arrived to replace Gertrude Olmstead in the role of Esther. "*Ben-Hur* was a tremendous undertaking," May recalled, "and shooting on it seemed interminable. I don't know why Esther had to be a blonde doll, but I had to wear a golden wig which I didn't like. The Italian-made wig, which had been fashioned at great expense for Miss Olmstead, was too big for me, and I could never get the new one the way I wanted."[11]

On their days off, Ramon, May and May's mother would often go sightseeing. They sometimes invited Carmel Myers to go with them, but she was always too busy posing for pictures. McAvoy later declared, "I think magazines featured candid shots of Carmel photographed against the ruins of the Roman Empire for the next two years."[12]

Deciding that it was time he inspected the *Ben-Hur* location, Louis B. Mayer arrived in Rome on October 12. The mogul tagged along to watch Niblo shoot the sea battle at the port of Livorno. Charles Brabin's inferior ships had been discarded, and stronger, more seaworthy ones had been built. This was the scene that had become Brabin's downfall, but his problems were minuscule compared to what was about to happen.

That morning Niblo discovered a pile of real swords under a canvas on one of the ships. He was later told that the casting director for the extras had separated the men into fascists and antifascists and planned to instigate an authentic blood-drenched war. After that was resolved, the filming of the two ships colliding commenced, and a high-speed motorboat pulled the pirate ship into the slave boat. The force of the collision panicked the extras, and they fell on their knees in fervent prayer.

Next it was time to film the ship burning, but the flames spread out of control throughout the entire vessel. Panic again seized the extras, and forgetting their safety instructions, many began jumping overboard. Concern for the men's safety prevailed because some were wearing armor, which naturally weighted them down. Still others had lied about being able to swim because they did not want to be replaced. Dinghies were standing by in case of an emergency, but there were not enough to handle all the men. Hearing their cries for help, the cast and crew watched in horror from the shore as the men flailed helplessly in the water. Bushman screamed at Niblo, "My God, Fred, they're drowning I tell you!"

"I can't help it," the director shrieked. "Those ships cost me $40,000 apiece."[13]

Novarro, who was standing next to Niblo, was able to save a couple of men who swam to shore, and later he claimed that he was certain no one had drowned. Other sources differ as to whether any lives were lost that day. One account said that several extras were missing, so Niblo, Enid Bennett, and Claire McDowall stayed up all night checking off names. Three sets of clothing went unclaimed, and reportedly, an assistant director was sent to dump them at sea, along with any bodies he might find along the way. Fortunately, the missing extras turned up three days later, after a fishing boat rescued them farther down the coast. When Mayer returned to America, he had Bess Meredyth smuggle the footage of the burning ship in her suitcase, so that it could be shown in newsreels at home.[14]

The next day, after viewing the rushes, Mayer accused Francis X. Bushman of upstaging the younger, less experienced Novarro. The mogul knew this role was a break for Bushman and believed the actor was doing everything to use it to his advantage. Another story circulated that Mayer paid a visit to Bushman's dressing room but was told by his valet that the star was too busy to see anyone. Infuriated, Mayer allegedly swore he would break the actor. Bushman later tried to explain that his valet simply did not recognize Mayer and that it was not his fault, but Mayer wouldn't listen. In any case, Mayer never again lifted a finger to help Bushman.

Not long afterward, Mayer collapsed with unbearable pain in his jaw. A dentist diagnosed that his gums were abscessed and eventually removed all of his teeth for fear that the infection would kill him. At times Mayer was delirious, and Cary Wilson wired Thalberg in Hollywood, begging him to have Mayer returned to California. "Naturally paralyzed with fear over possibility of Mayer being seriously ill," Thalberg wired to Wilson. "Strongly recommend he leave Rome at once, go to some European resort."[15]

Thalberg wired Alexander Aronson in Paris and ordered him to return to Rome again to oversee the production. Under the title of general director, Aronson's job was to see to it that Niblo worked according to Mayer's wishes until the mogul recuperated.

More problems plagued Niblo when he found that the Coliseum was still not finished after seven months of work. One day Bushman walked on the set and happened to find the workmen sitting on the ground. Furious, he approached the foreman. "You promised to have this arena ready in seven weeks and here it is seven months and you haven't finished yet," he screamed.

"Well, Signor Bushman," the foreman said, "we have no work when this is finished. Why should we work ourselves out of a job?"[16]

Second-unit director William Reaves "Breezy" Eason was chosen to direct the Coliseum's chariot race. Eason had experience with horses and had directed several low-budget Westerns. He let nothing stop him from getting what he wanted, but horses were being killed at an alarming rate. Whenever a horse was injured, it was shot.[17]

Novarro and Bushman went through intensive training for the chariot race. Once during practice the chariots were rounding a curve when a wheel broke. The driver of the chariot flew 30 feet into the air and landed on a pile of lumber; he later died of internal injuries.

Another time Bushman crashed into Novarro's chariot, which had turned the wrong way in front of him. Everyone was sure that Novarro was dead. Miraculously, he crawled away unscathed, but one of his horses died. Bushman claimed that Novarro's driving technique was all wrong. "He held the reigns like he was on a carriage. You've got to wrap that stuff around your wrist, jam your feet up against the front, and lean straight back," he explained.[18]

It was late November when they filmed the scene where Ben-Hur and Arrius (played by Frank Currier) are rescued from a raft. The weather was very cold, and Novarro was dressed in a skimpy loincloth. Currier, who was 75 years old, had to fall from the raft into the icy waters. After several hours, Novarro realized that the cold was severely affecting his older costar, so he suggested that Niblo use extras for the scene. The doubles worked for only 20 minutes before screaming at the top of their lungs. "What do they want?" Novarro asked.

"They want someone to double for them," replied an assistant. "They're cold and are afraid of getting the flu." So Novarro and Currier returned to the raft and doubled for the doubles. As Novarro pulled Currier onto the raft for the fifth time, the elder thespian coughed out water and gasped, "Hereafter, my boy, I play only bankers."[19]

It was soon Thanksgiving, but the cast and crew thought they had very little to be thankful for. To add to their misery, the hotel chef would not make turkey dressing, even though Carmel Myers' mother gave them her recipe. Novarro and Howe decided to have dinner at a little cafe under the trees of a stone-paved piazza. It was while there that Ramon remembered it had been nine years since he and his brother Mariano had arrived in Los Angeles. Thinking back on that Thanksgiving and remembering how he had had only $10 to his name soon cured his depression.

The following week they filmed the galley scene where Ben-Hur has been chained to an oar for three years. It was a very emotional scene for Ramon, and at one point, rowing to the agonizing beat of the horator's gavel sent the actor into a frenzy. Suddenly he screamed, straining from his chains, collapsing limp across the oar. Everyone in the studio was silent. Then a spontaneous cry arose from the 300 Italian extras. "Bravo, Novarro!" they cheered, but the scene ended up on the cutting room floor. Not too disappointed, Ramon said, "But remember all my bad ones that didn't make it."[20]

The next day Novarro and Howe took a short vacation to Venice. After checking into the Hotel Daniel, they strolled on the Piazza di San Marco. Stopping at one of the local shops, they saw signed pictures of Douglas Fairbanks and Mary Pickford adorning the walls. Suddenly the proprietress stopped and gazed into Ramon's eyes. "You look like someone famous," she said, looking at Ramon's beard and long hair. "Yes, let me think! Not a cinema actor. No!" Suddenly the woman stood transfixed. "I know... Jesus Christ!" she said, which prompted Ramon to stop at the nearest barber.[21]

Even though this brief trip to Venice was enjoyable, Ramon remembered that he had to return to Rome and continue work on *Ben-Hur*. He was beginning to feel the anguish and frustration that had plagued the original company and soon began to question his participation in the film and whether he should stick with it or just quit.

Chapter Eight

Rebellion in Italy (1924–1925)

I do not mean to deprecate Mr. Niblo, who was always a meticulous craftsman, but I do think that Rex Ingram would have brought more artistry and sophistication to Ben-Hur.

— Ramon Novarro[1]

The pressure placed on director Fred Niblo was beginning to take its toll. The fact that the Italian actors did not speak English and the studio's continual interference eventually caused Niblo to lose control. At one point, he began throwing things at the extras, which infuriated Francis X. Bushman, who walked off the set. "I was through, I wouldn't have him doing that," Bushman declared.[2]

Fortunately, Enid Bennett became the stabilizing force on the set and was able to persuade her husband to apologize, but the problems continued. Because he wanted complete control of the film, Niblo refused to give scenes to his assistant directors, Christy Cabanne and Al Raboch. Add to that the constant rain each day, and you had a cast and crew who were irritable and edgy and hated Niblo more every minute. Alexander Aronson urged Thalberg to fire the director and send producer Harry Rapf to take control.

"Have definitely decided picture will never be made under present management," Aronson complained. "Nothing he [Niblo] can do will change my opinion. I will remove him from picture indefinitely and without reservation. Will go ahead without him until you send me a new director, preferably Vidor or someone similar, willing and anxious to work."[3]

Both Mayer and Thalberg refused to fire Niblo and instead encouraged the members of the team to sit down and work out their differences. In order to establish harmony, Niblo and Aronson met for an all-night conference and came to an agreement that both could live with. But by Christmas things had slowed down so much that even Mayer insisted that Niblo hurry things along. The mogul was concerned about the morale of the cast and urged Niblo to utilize his assistant directors. "Remember," he told Niblo, "we promised them quick work with three directors so they can get home early."[4]

On Christmas Eve, everyone gathered for a party at the Excelsior Hotel. At one point, a depressed Kathleen Key (who had just received a Christmas cable from her mother) rose and gave an emotional speech. Looking out at the several hundred people gathered, she said, "I'm all alone here in Rome," which brought a much needed roar of laughter from her peers.[5]

On January 2, 1925, Novarro left word for Aronson that he was sick and suddenly left Rome. He had been severely battered while training for the chariot scene and was fed up with the way things were being handled. He no longer had faith in Niblo and decided it was better to be fired and sent home than to continue with the director's sarcastic abuse.[6] He and Herb Howe traveled by train to the French Riviera, but they left in such a hurry that he forgot to bring his passport. To make matters worse, Howe discovered his French visa had expired.

Arriving in San Remo, they tried to get past the border guard by coyly flashing a copy of Mrs. Myers' turkey dressing recipe; it was on engraved stationary and looked official. The guards refused to accept the bogus credentials or the 100-lira notes that Novarro fingered temptingly.

As a final resort, Ramon wired Alexander Aronson to either send their passports or ask the American consul to help them get across the border to Monte Carlo. The American consul was silent, and Aronson insisted that they return to Rome at once. Stubbornly, they rented a car and drove to Ventimiglia, the first Italian border town, and decided to plead with the French consul. In desperation, Howe told the consul that he was *Photoplay*'s special representative and the gentleman with him was a powerful cinema star of great influence. Not impressed, the consul refused their appeals and said, "Not a chance!"

Their only recourse was to check into a hotel near the border and sneak across, but the hotel clerk informed them that the guards were on 24-hour watch. He did suggest that they could take a rowboat across the bay but added, "Of course, they might shoot at you."

There was one other way. The clerk told them how many people had crossed the border by descending over a rock precipice to a narrow beach by the sea. So the next morning they left their luggage behind, made their way along the ledge to the beach, and hurried down the narrow strip of sand to the French border. Just as they were about to cross, they were stopped by two guards, who asked to see their passports. Novarro lied and said they were guests of the little French hotel above them and were out for a morning stroll. Observing that they were without baggage, the guards allowed them to pass.

Thirty minutes later they arrived at the Hotel de Paris at Monte Carlo, but because of their unkempt appearance, the maitre d' refused to admit them. For four nights they played in the casino and lost all their available cash, but by then, the studio had tracked them down and ordered them to return to Rome at once. Novarro's reply was, "Thank you. Don't count on me till next Wednesday."[7]

Novarro was obstinate and traveled to Nice to visit Rex Ingram and Alice Terry. Somehow Aronson found out where the duo had gone and wired Novarro at Nice with threats of discipline. Reluctantly, and at Ingram's insistence, Novarro and Howe returned to Rome.

Aronson was so infuriated that he informed Marcus Loew of Novarro's behavior, knowing the influence the older man had with him. Loew gently scolded Novarro by telegram, asking him to be more cooperative with Aronson.[8]

When Novarro returned to Rome, an article appeared in the *Paris Tribune*, telling of the young actor's recent adventures in France. "Among the distinguished visitors at the Hotel de Paris the past week was Mr. Ramon Novarro, the famous American cinema star who has created a sensation recently in France with his *Scaramouche*," the article stated. "Mr. Novarro came so quietly, with practically no baggage, that he was not recognized before his departure."[9]

Aronson took Novarro aside, and after expressing dismay over his actions of the past week, he informed him that the entire company was returning to California. "When do you think I will be able to leave?" Novarro anxiously asked. Aronson estimated that the scheduled filming would be finished within two weeks. Novarro then requested that he and Herb Howe be permitted to leave before the rest of the company. Although Novarro gave no reason for the request, Aronson agreed and arranged for their passage on the *La France*, which was to sail on January 24. In return, Novarro promised Aronson his full cooperation in order to wrap things up.[10]

The next day the *Ben-Hur* company was invited to meet members of the Italian royal family. On January 8, everyone was collected in the Circus Maximus set and told that no one was to speak to the royal entourage except Niblo. Disappointed and cold, the cast finally saw three automobiles arrive with the royal family. Fred Niblo approached and bowed low to the smiling, fur-draped queen but made no move to introduce her to the cast. The royal family was led to the platform, where they viewed the actors through a camera. "They didn't even say hello," muttered Kathleen Key.

After several minutes, the royal family descended the platform and again passed the little group of artists standing patiently in the chilly breeze. As the procession left the Circus Maximus, Fred Niblo was heard saying to the king, "We are scouring the libraries of the world for stories."

"He's encouraging him to write scenarios," observed Novarro, who threatened to put in for pay as an extra for standing around for an hour. But when the royal car passed, Princess Giovanna recognized the actor and smiled. "She saved you five dollars," he told the business manager.[11]

A few days later the princesses returned to the set incognito to observe the filming. This time they spoke with Novarro and several cast members and expressed their interest in art studies. "All the royal family are greatly beloved of the people," Novarro later told the *Los Angeles Times*. "They are much interested in pictures. They have a projection room in the palace and everything. They are very interested in the technical and artistic end."[12]

The following week Novarro again rebelled, refusing to do several close-ups on the Circus Maximus set that Niblo wanted in case they didn't return in the spring. Aronson was again called in to negotiate and said, "At least I would have those close-ups for future use, irrespective of their quality, which no one could know in advance."

After a long session with Aronson, Novarro agreed to do the last four shots in the galley sequence and the close-ups that were needed. He told Aronson he would work that evening and all the next morning if he could leave for Nice in the afternoon. Aronson agreed and took lights and heaters away from Christy Cabanne, who was filming with Carmel Myers. That evening the production manager called Aronson at the Excelsior Hotel and told him that Novarro was too tired and could not make it for the galley sequence that night. Ramon promised that he would be in makeup by 9:30 the next morning and would give them two and a half hours to get the shots they needed. "Although I rebelled at taking dictation from an actor," Aronson said, "realizing the importance of getting this stuff, I swallowed my indignation, knowing that in two and a half hours we could get what we wanted, and hence the quarrel was not needed."

The next morning Novarro did not arrive until 10:45 and had completed only two long shots by noon. He then told Aronson he was finished and refused to do the remaining close-ups. In order to arrive in Nice on time, he had to leave immediately. "Whether he has a girl in Nice, or whether he wanted to see Rex Ingram and spend a few days with him, I do not know," Aronson said. In any event, Aronson sent a letter off to MGM attorney J. Robert Rubin, describing Novarro's behavior the past few weeks.

"I have no quarrel with Novarro," he told Rubin, "nor do I purpose making this an issue, because I realize that the two close-ups could be done just as well at home. I am just citing this to you showing his utter lack of responsibility and lack of cooperation.

"He has not been the only one of our problems," Aronson continued. "It seems to me that many of our actors feel that with the tremendous investment of money that we have in this picture, they can run us! If this picture had cost one-tenth of what it actually has, I would have put Novarro on the carpet."

Why was Novarro, who usually was very cooperative, suddenly being so mutinous? In his meetings with Aronson, Novarro told him that as far as he was concerned, pictures had been a disappointment to him. "None of my dreams have come true," he told Aronson. "I am through with pictures. I care neither for fame or for money!"[13]

Fifteen minutes after Novarro completed the galley sequence, he and Herb Howe were on a train bound for Nice. While packing, Ramon discovered his watch had been stolen by his Italian valet, who at one time had worked for the king. "Probably the king missed his crown one day, and that's why the valet wasn't working for him anymore," quipped Ramon.[14]

Several days after the company left Rome, a fire swept through the property warehouse. This was the final straw for Thalberg, who thought the entire project was madness. He was happy the company was returning to California under his watchful eye. Mayer had hoped the film's problems would work themselves out after his trip to Rome, but he finally agreed with Thalberg. After a storm knocked down part of the Joppa Gate, all the sets were destroyed except the Circus Maximus, which was left standing in hopes of returning in the spring. Later Thalberg decided to rebuild the arena in California.

Novarro and Herb Howe sailed on January 24, 1925, on the steamship *La France* to New York. The remainder of the company left several days later on the *Berengaria*. Ramon stayed in his cabin during most of the trip, playing his guitar and allowing his beard to grow. As they were packing their trunks on the eve of their landing in New York, Ramon showed Herb a notebook that contained a line which he had written before sailing for Rome. It read, "If my *Ben-Hur* is remembered, I have not lived in vain."[15] They both began to laugh.

Novarro's popularity increased dramatically as a result of his participation in *Ben-Hur*, but not everyone thought he was the best choice for the role. "It will be a crime against filmdom and the memory of general Lew Wallace if Ramon Novarro is allowed to play *Ben-Hur*," wrote one fan to *Photoplay*. He stated that producer A. L. Erlanger would not like the picture. "Believe me," the writer continued, "I cannot visualize Novarro struggling to fit his small feet into the huge sandals of Ben-Hur."[16]

Feedback from the letter was swift, and another reader disagreed, saying, "I, for one, will not be disappointed at the outcome of that picture, I can hardly wait its completion."[17]

Novarro on location with the cast and crew of *The Midshipman* (MGM, 1925). Visiting the set is actor John Gilbert.

That sentiment was shared strongly by Mayer, Thalberg, and the entire cast and crew. Thalberg was not thrilled about the project in the beginning, but now he found it a challenge and took over the responsibilities, which was fine with Mayer.

Thalberg assigned MGM's art director Cedric Gibbons and A. Arnold Gillespie the task of designing a new arena. After several delays, a site was found at the intersection of Venice Boulevard and Brice Road (now La

Cienega Boulevard). Eight hundred men worked night and day to complete the construction.

Meanwhile, filming on interior scenes and close-ups resumed at MGM studios on February 18, 1925. Filming was finally wrapped up, except for the chariot race, which would have to wait for the completion of the Circus Maximus set.

Before shooting began on Novarro's next film, *The Midshipman* (1925), Thalberg gave him a well-deserved vacation. Ramon bought himself a new Lincoln Coupe, whose special feature was an extra gas tank that Novarro considered a "source of comfort."[18] He also purchased an old-fashioned, roomy house at 2265 West 22d Street in the exclusive West Adams district for $12,000. He spent $100,000 on the renovation, which took several months. Novarro added his own private wing with a suite of dressing rooms, servants' quarters, and something that had been a dream for him—his own theater.

Ben-Hur assistant director Christy Cabanne was assigned to direct *The Midshipman*.[19] Carey Wilson's story of life in the U.S. Naval Academy was produced with the complete cooperation of the Navy Department. MGM sent a production unit numbering 250 people to the Naval Academy at Annapolis, Maryland. Novarro was chosen by the officers at Annapolis from a list of 11 popular leading men, and the choice was later endorsed by Washington.

For one scene, Cabanne tried to get a Navy goat (nicknamed "Nothin' Else Butt" by the crew) to eat a few tin cans. "Why don't you put honey on the cans?" Ramon suggested, and it worked.[20] That was a simple problem compared to the controversy that arose for the planned graduation scene. Studio executives eagerly suggested that President Coolidge should hand out the diplomas himself, but that idea was quickly scratched by Washington. As a compromise, MGM was granted permission to have Novarro join the graduating class so that he could march up and receive an unsigned sheepskin.[21]

With another picture now under his belt, Novarro had to contend with the filming of the chariot race for *Ben-Hur*, arguably one of the most exciting sequences ever filmed for a silent picture. An incident was about to occur, however, which could have spelled the end of his career and closed the gates of Metro-Goldwyn-Mayer studios forever.

Chapter Nine

The Chariot Race (1925)

Mr. Mayer was an uncouth little man with very little learning or background except how to make money.
—Ramon Novarro[1]

One of Novarro's new acquaintances was actor William Haines, who was known to his close friends as Willie. It was rumored that the two had a brief affair, but unlike Ramon, Haines was not shy about his homosexuality. He would often bring his lover, Jimmy Shields, onto the lot, much to Mayer's loathing. Haines knew all the hot spots in town and on occasion would take Ramon with him.

Haines often spoke his mind and once declared to a friend that actor Lew Cody was a vain stuffed shirt. Upon hearing the remark, Cody replied, "What do I care what that old queer thinks." To retaliate, Cody allegedly told Mayer about Haines' latest rendezvous at a male brothel on Wilshire Boulevard. According to writer Anita Loos, "Willie got called in on the carpet for that one."[2]

What Mayer didn't know at the time was that Haines had taken Novarro with him that night. When he found out, Mayer hit the roof. How dare Haines risk the future of MGM by exposing the star of *Ben-Hur* to a scandal that would have ruined the picture before it was even released? Mayer reasoned that no one would watch a religious picture with a homosexual hero.[3]

Mayer used his influence with the Los Angeles Police Department and had the bordello closed. He was about to fire Haines[4] when William Randolph Hearst interceded and told Mayer, "Marion [Davies] is fond of Willie."[5]

Before this, Mayer was in the dark about Novarro's homosexuality. He liked Ramon and admired the way he treated his family, but being a homosexual was something Mayer could not tolerate. He knew *Ben-Hur* was going to make Novarro an even bigger star and a moneymaker for the studio. He warned Novarro, who was shaken by the entire incident, that if it ever happened again, he would be out on the street and would never make another film. He advised the actor to find a nice girl and settle down.[6]

Reluctantly, it was the last time that Novarro socialized with William Haines. From that point, he would try to make any rendezvous as private as possible, a practice he would follow until his death. He was not always successful, however, and would have other scrapes with Mayer and the law.

Ben-Hur had its own problems, and in April 1925, Fred Niblo argued with Mayer over his choice of Betty Bronson to play the Virgin Mary. Niblo felt Bronson was incapable of expressing the compassion and tenderness that was needed to play the Mother of Christ, but Mayer disagreed. When the picture premiered, *Variety* said of Betty Bronson's brief appearance, "It is without a doubt the most tremendous individual score that any actress has ever made with but a single scene with a couple of close-ups."[7] Once again it seemed that Louis B. Mayer was right.

Novarro suddenly discovered that his services were in big demand. UFA Studios in Neubabelsberg, Germany, was preparing to produce the Goethe poem *Faust* (1926). They originally wanted Lillian Gish to play Marguerite, but she was not available at the time. When Gish signed with MGM, she was still interested in playing Marguerite, so the studio tried to work out a deal.[8]

UFA also wanted Novarro to play the title role, but the actor was not eager to play the part. If the entire Goethe poem were produced, it would be a long picture, and he was not willing to go into another lengthy production so soon after *Ben-Hur*. He worried about being forgotten by the public, needlessly as it turned out because the deal fell through and the film was made without Novarro or Gish.[9]

The remodeling of Novarro's house on West 22d Street continued, along with the construction of his theater. He had a brilliant neon sign installed over the entrance which read "Novarro's Teatro Intimo." Inside, the auditorium was slightly larger than a drawing room. The walls were a cream-tinted plaster, and the floor was laid in thick taupe carpets. There were seats for about 60 people, and the stage was large enough to accommodate a company of 30. An orchestra pit big enough for 12 musicians was concealed by a parapet.

A huge, intricate switchboard offstage controlled the best theatrical lighting system of that time. Instead of scenery, a complex pattern of lights was used to paint images against a background of plain hangings. A box office issued tickets, and programs were distributed by ushers. There was no projector or screen in the theater.

Novarro's theater served as a training ground to try out new numbers for his future concert tours and to put on plays for the benefit of his family and friends. Over the next few years, many stars and politicians would visit Novarro's Teatro Intimo.[10]

The family residence was a huge, rambling, old-fashioned house with 17 rooms, including 6 bedrooms and quarters for the servants. Ramon's wing was located in the back of the house next to the theater, with a secret passageway from a private side entrance. His red and purple bedroom was influenced by *Ben-Hur* and had a large bed in the center.

A tall brick wall surrounded the house, which had glass-enclosed porches stretched across the front on both floors. Throughout the yard were scattered numerous odd and assorted gnomelike statues, which were rather Viennese in character. When asked about the unusual statues, Ramon replied, "We like them."[11]

Ramon's studio, where he practiced his music, was located above the auditorium of the theater. Stairs led from the back of the stage to a rooftop garden with an aviary. In the studio, velvet-covered spired windows of pale amber cast a copper color on the carved wood ceilings during sunset. A fireplace was located in an arched recess on an Italian grate, with bookshelves on either side. A Venetian chest sat in one corner, and between the fireplace and window rested one of Ramon's pianos. Deep-cushioned chairs provided places of rest in front of a large processional crucifix that hung reverently on the wall.[12]

The West Adams district was home to the famous and wealthy, such as lawyers and bankers. Actor Lon McCallister, who appeared in such films as *Stella Dallas* and *Stage Door Canteen*, was raised nearby. McCallister was a child when Ramon moved in. He had never seen a Novarro film but knew the name well. "It [Novarro's estate] was kind of a compound within the city," McCallister recalled. "I can remember once, climbing up on the wall of his estate. Someone had told me that was where Ramon Novarro lived."

He climbed up and looked over the wall but never saw Novarro. In the early 1960s, Lon McCallister met Ramon Novarro at a beach party in Malibu and related this story to him. "Oh, I'm so sorry you didn't climb over the wall and come in," Novarro told him. "Those were wonderful days in my life and I would have loved to have met you, but I am glad to have the opportunity now."[13]

To take advantage of Novarro's growing popularity, Ferdinand Pinney Earle released the actor's first starring vehicle, *The Rubaiyat of Omar Khayyam*, under the title *A Lover's Oath* (1925). The picture was a novelty, and the bizarre, imaginative sets were considered the one bright spot of the film. Critics also noted that Novarro was very Apolloesque but had little to do but murmur sappy love words such as, "O moon of my delight! I will build for thee the alabaster palaces of my dreams."[14] The picture disappeared long before *Ben-Hur* was finished filming.

On Saturday, October 3, 1925, filming of the chariot race began on the massive Circus Maximus set at Venice and La Cienega. The grandstand was 3,000 feet long, and Horace Jackson and set designer A. Arnold Gilespie devised an optical illusion with the help of a hanging miniature that was a closely guarded secret for several decades. "The hanging miniature was quite close to the camera itself, probably 12, 14 or 15 feet away," Gilespie revealed years later. "The lower portion of the hanging miniature tied in structurally to the full size set some several hundred feet beyond."[15]

Nearly every MGM stock player and an additional 3,000 extras arrived at 6:30 A.M. in order to be costumed, bearded, and bewigged. The man in charge of this monumental task was Adolph Seidel, chief costumer for MGM. Seidel, who had dressed the companies of the Berlin and Vienna grand operas, had worked through the previous night and began sending extras into the stands as early as 7 A.M.[16]

Fred Niblo supervised 42 cameras from a 100-foot tower with his chief assistant and head cameraman, Percy Hilburn. This was the largest number of cameras ever used for one scene, and they were set up in every possible location. Some were hidden behind a soldier's shield or inside huge statues, and some were buried in the ground to create the effect of horses and chariots driving out from the screen and over the heads of the audience.

Niblo rehearsed 62 assistant directors recruited from every studio and dressed them in costumes in keeping with the groups they had to direct. Breezy Eason and his assistant, Silas Clegg, supervised the race from ground level. One of the assistants recruited from Universal was future director William Wyler.[17] "I was given a toga and a set of signals," Wyler recalled. "The signals were a sort of semaphore, and I got my section of the crowd to stand up and cheer and to sit down again, or whatever was called for. There must have been 30 other assistants doing the same job. People have said that I was the assistant director on the entire sequence, but that's all I had to do."[18]

A special platform was built for the many stars who arrived that day to watch the filming, including Douglas Fairbanks, Mary Pickford, Lillian Gish, Marion Davies, and John Gilbert. Harold Lloyd left his company waiting in the studio while he stood beside Niblo on the tower for more than eight hours. At the end of the day, Lloyd and Fairbanks staged a mock duel to the delight of the crowd. Soon the arena began to fill with the cast and extras. At 8 o'clock, Irving Thalberg asked production manager J. J. Cohn how many people were assembled. Even though there were about 3,900 extras, Thalberg told Cohn to find more. "Where am I going to find anyone now?" Cohn asked.

"I don't care, Joe," Thalberg replied. "Pull them in off the street if you have to, but we need more people!" So Cohn and his assistants scoured the neighboring diners, bus stops, restaurants, and markets until they found and dressed an additional 400 people. But filming was halted once again when a morning fog rolled in from the ocean. Not until 11:30 was it bright enough to begin, but by then it was time for lunch.

Cohn insisted on filming a couple of scenes, but Niblo disagreed, thinking the crowds would riot if they weren't fed. The problem was that there were only 3,000 lunches for more than 4,300 extras, and some of the policemen had already eaten two lunches. Cohn ignored Niblo and had assistant director Charlie Stallings bring the horses into the arena. "Joe, you can't do that," Niblo insisted, "the crowd will riot if they don't get their lunch."

"Good," Cohn shot back. "That'll add realism to the scene. Now get the horses."[19]

It was nearly noon when the 54 Roman imperial guards rode in on horseback.[20] Carmel Myers, Nigel de Brulier, and May McAvoy were in their boxes, while all about them thousands of costumed Romans, Jews, Egyptians, and Assyrians gesticulated and chattered in anticipation of the great race. During filming, the caterers arrived with extra lunches and served them to the hungry crowd. Fortunately, they were so far away from the camera, they were never noticed.

Finally, it was time to begin the race. According to one story, to heighten the excitement, Breezy Eason offered prizes for the winning chariots: a $150 first prize, a $100 second prize, and a $50 third prize. Future director Henry Hathaway, who was an assistant on the film, later gave the credit for the prize money idea to studio comptroller Eddie Mannix, who allegedly offered $5,000 to the winner.[21] Whichever story is true, the idea worked because the drivers raced around the arena with astounding speed.

Staying true to the original story, Novarro's chariot was pushed into ninth position at the beginning of the race, while Bushman's was in fourth. The chariots drove lap after lap, which at first seemed very boring. Then during one lap, a horseshoe went flying into the crowd, barely missing some of the spectators. Things were now beginning to liven up.

The second race went smoothly until two chariots became tangled as they rounded a corner. The other chariots behind them could not see what had happened and came speeding around and collided into the wrecked chariots. Set designer Gillespie was sitting on the hanging miniature and had a bird's eye view of the entire crash. "Some extra came out and tried to stop the oncoming chariots because he could see what happened, and of course that spoiled that particular part of the film."[22]

Opposite: **Novarro practices driving his chariot (in dress shirt and tie) with a trainer on the Circus Maximus set of *Ben-Hur* (1926, MGM) located at La Cienega and Venice boulevards.**

Actually, the scene was used, as is, in the film. If you look closely, the extra can be seen running out onto the raceway; that extra was Henry Hathaway. "I was out there trying to wave them down," Hathaway explained, "but they weren't going to stop, 'cause they wanted to win."[23] Novarro's chariot, which was directly behind the others, rode over the top of the wreckage but miraculously continued on and won the race.

By the end of the day, the race had been so thrilling that it was thought filming was completed. Actually, Eason spent several more weeks filming close-ups in the empty arena, including Messala's wreck and death. The script called for his wheel to be torn off by Ben-Hur's chariot, and as the chariot crashes, the ones behind them collide and crush Messala's body. The wreck went off as planned, and even though there were some cuts and bruises, no one was seriously injured.

Francis X. Bushman claimed there were five horses killed in that wreck. "MGM had convinced everyone that not a horse had been killed," Bushman said.[24] J. J. Cohn insisted that no horses were killed, but Bushman disagreed. No one came forward, however, to back him up.

Both actors had done a fantastic job. Even Bushman was pleased at how Novarro had mastered driving his chariot. Many sources claimed that doubles were used for the leading players, but Cohn insisted they were used only for the more dangerous scenes that were filmed at a distance.[25]

On the last day of filming, everyone shook hands and some had tears in their eyes. Even though at times it had been hell, this group had been through a lot and had become very close. Special effects men set off smoke bombs and fired pistols in celebration. After more than three years, *Ben-Hur* had finished filming.

Chapter Ten

Novarro's Teatro Intimo (1925)

In my Hollywood home, I have a teatro intimo accommo-
dating 60 guests. When people first see it, they invariably
exclaim: "Oh, a projection room in your home." "No," I
emphatically reply, "pictures never enter this theatre."
                                             —Ramon Novarro[1]

Ramon chose the 34th wedding anniversary of his parents to celebrate the opening of Novarro's Teatro Intimo. The invitations were inscribed in Spanish on parchment scrolls and lettered in crimson and gold. Translated to English, the invitation read:

> I am honored in inviting you to the inauguration of my little theater with the first edition of the Novarro revue, which is given to celebrate the thirty-fourth wedding anniversary of the beloved authors of my days, Senor Doctor don Mariano N. Samaniego and Senora dona Leonor Gavilan de Samaniego; presented on the twenty-fourth of the current October at eight-thirty (prompt).[2]

Many of the guests were Mexican and Spanish, but Herb Howe and *Los Angeles Times* columnist Harry Carr were also included. Priests, artists, musicians, and government officials attended, including representatives of

President Calles of Mexico, who extended an invitation for Ramon to attend the opening of *Ben-Hur* in Mexico City.

Ramon was taking singing lessons from the acclaimed opera singer Louis Graveure, who was the guest singer that evening. "I have never given up studying here with Louis Graveure, the great Metropolitan tenor," Ramon said.[3] The opera singer raved about Ramon's vocal talent, saying, "In addition to possessing a tenore robusto voice of exceptional quality, Mr. Novarro is a thorough musician and an accomplished pianist. He is the coming great tenor."[4]

The revue consisted of one-act plays, songs, and dances performed entirely in Spanish by younger members of Los Angeles' Latin community. The audience burst into applause as one talented young man declared, "All credit must be given to Ramon who directed us."[5] The theater's opening was a success, and Ramon's theater would witness many concerts over the next 10 years.

While Ramon was celebrating his success with Novarro's Teatro Intimo, the editing of *Ben-Hur* was in its final stages. The publicity department was gearing up for the lavish premiere, scheduled for December 31, 1925. Carey Wilson and Bess Meredyth each squabbled over screen credits, demanding separate title cards, while June Mathis' lawyer insisted on proper acknowledgment for his client.

Problems continued, and changes were made until the very end. There were many who speculated that the stress Thalberg was shouldering through it all was the cause of his heart attack near the end of November. His doctors were uncertain whether he would recover, but within a few weeks he was editing the chariot race (projected on the ceiling above his bed) in time for the preview at the Criterion Theater in Pasadena on December 2, 1925.[6]

On December 18, Novarro, along with Fred Niblo, Enid Bennett, May McAvoy, and Francis X. Bushman, left by train for New York City. During the trip, Novarro caught a severe cold and was ordered by the studio doctor to stay in his hotel room for the duration of the visit. But even without Novarro's presence, opening night was a huge success; *Ben-Hur* was met with thunderous applause. Members of the audience stood on their seats and cheered during the chariot race. At intermission, a friend approached Francis X. Bushman and asked, "Well Francis, how do you like yourself?"[7] Bushman was so overcome by the spectacle that even he was speechless.

Friends and admirers gathered around Fred Niblo to offer congratulations and praise. Director John Stahl telephoned both Mayer and Thalberg to report how wonderfully the picture had been received. The following day Nicholas Schenck enthusiastically wired Thalberg in Hollywood: "Well kid," he wrote, "you were repaid last night for all the hard work. It was the most magnificent opening I ever witnessed."[8]

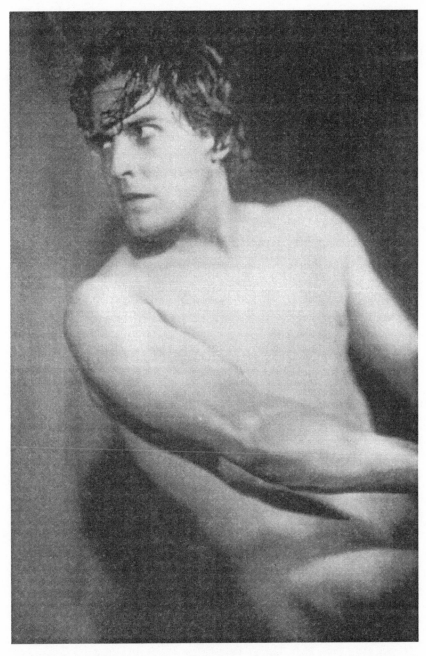

Novarro in a publicity photo for *Ben-Hur* (1926, MGM). The original caption read, "This picture proves rather conclusively that he has no intention of entering a monastery or taking up the profession of concert pianist."

The reviews were unanimous in their praise. *Variety* said, "As the industry today stands, so does *Ben-Hur* stand: the greatest achievement that has been accomplished on the screen for not only the screen itself, but for all motion picturedom."

Of Novarro's performance, *Variety* said, "He may never have appealed before in former productions, but anyone who sees him in this picture will have to admit that he is without doubt a man's man and 100 percent of that. Novarro is made for all time by his performance here."[9]

The studio publicized the film with a photo of a half-naked Novarro, just barely showing his pubic hairs. The caption read, "This picture proves rather conclusively that he has no intention of entering a monastery or taking up the profession of concert pianist."[10]

A. R. Erlanger, who owned the rights to *Ben-Hur* and produced the original play on Broadway, said: "The picture is mightier than the play. I have employed a dozen or more Ben-Hur's, including some very distinguished names in theater history. But to my mind, Ramon Novarro is the greatest of them all."[11]

Upon seeing the film, Novarro's mentor and friend, Rex Ingram, sent Novarro a telegram which simply read, "You give a great performance, Ramon. I am very proud of you."[12]

Around the world, people agreed that *Ben-Hur* was a masterpiece. One exception was in Italy, where much of the epic was filmed. Dictator Benito Mussolini thought the hero of the film would be the Roman, Messala, so when he saw Bushman's character defeated, he had the film banned from Italy. "*Ben-Hur* was a great joke on Mussolini," Bushman recalled. "He thought we were about to recreate the grandeur that was Rome. When he saw the film, he almost had a stroke. The hero was a young Jewish follower of Christ, and a Roman was the villain of the picture."[13]

Ben-Hur became the most expensive silent film ever made.[14] The picture cost just under $4 million and made more than $9 million at the box office. After everything was tallied up, MGM lost more than $1 million, but it had a motion picture classic which was the beginning of its fledgling film studio.[15]

After the success of the premiere, Novarro returned to California and discovered that his dear friend Barbara La Marr was critically ill with nephritis, or inflammation of the kidneys. The public was not told that the kidney infection was the result of chronic drug and alcohol abuse. When Novarro visited Barbara, he found her in good spirits and was told that she would recover with the proper rest and care. Being encouraged by this good news, Ramon continued with plans for a trip to Europe and sent Barbara a letter and a basket of flowers before he left.

Two days later, Barbara suffered a relapse and sank into a deep coma. Gradually, she grew weaker, and she died on January 30, 1926. A photograph of Ramon Novarro was next to her bed. When Novarro heard the news, he canceled his travel plans and returned to California.[16]

La Marr's family delayed the funeral until the following Friday so that Novarro could attend. Several thousand fans were waiting outside the mortuary when Novarro arrived at 2:15 P.M. During the service, mass hysteria broke out as throngs of onlookers fought to catch a glimpse of the star's casket and the celebrities who gathered to mourn. As La Marr's remains were placed in the hearse, the crowd broke through the police line and rushed the funeral procession. Five women fainted and were rescued by police from being trampled to death. It took 15 minutes to push the throng back enough to allow the remaining cars to continue to Hollywood Cemetery.[17]

After the funeral, Ramon decided against going to Europe and instead asked Herb Howe if he would accompany him to Quebec. Howe agreed, and a few nights later they arrived by train in the Canadian city, greeted by the twinkling lights of the little shops along the streets. While they were registering at the Chateau Frontenac, the clerk informed them the rooms would be $10 a day. After he read Novarro's name on the register, however, the clerk smiled and extended his hand. "We are glad to have you, Mr. Novarro," he said. "The rooms will be $8 a day."

"So the name of Novarro must be worth $2," laughed Ramon.

Word leaked out that Novarro was in town, but the gracious people of Quebec did not impose upon him. Several theater managers called to welcome him but did not ask for personal appearances. He was besieged for autographs by young girls, and even though he changed his room three times, determined females would bribe the chambermaid for his room number, just to get a look at their idol.

The editor of *Le Soleil*, the local French newspaper, offered to give Novarro and Howe personal guided tours of the city, and each day the newspaper published bulletins on their activities. When the citizens learned that Ramon collected old song sheets for his library, he received several calls from people offering him music. "What gracious people these Quebec-ers are!" he remarked.

As a gesture of hospitality, the premier of Canada extended an invitation to Novarro to visit the parliament buildings. As they were leaving, the premier told Ramon, "We regard you as an aristocrat of pictures. Ben-Hur is a true nobleman."[18]

The next day the two travelers left Quebec happy and well rested. This was a pleasant vacation for Ramon, and to show his appreciation, he wrote telegrams of thanks to everyone in Quebec who had made his trip enjoyable.

As evidenced in Quebec, Ramon's popularity skyrocketed after the release of *Ben-Hur*. The MGM publicity department reported that he received more than 2,500 fan letters a day, some addressed simply to "Mr. Ben-Hur, Hollywood, California."[19]

Fans devoured every bit of information about their movie idol. Magazines reported about Ramon's love of music and his secret desire to become a priest. Astrologers plotted his horoscope, mystics foretold his future, and graphologists tried to decipher his handwriting. No matter what the magazines spewed out, the fans ate it up and begged for more.

Writers made fantastic observations, especially about his good looks. Even the respected journalist Adela Rogers St. Johns was quoted as saying, "Lyric charm, poetical charm, plus the beauty of a Greek boy. Think of him when you read of Keats, when you read of Byron, when you read Romeo and Juliet."[20]

Theater owners were polled and asked, "Who else do the exhibitors look upon besides Gloria Swanson and Harold Lloyd as a meal ticket?" One exhibitor said, "Well, among men, we are looking forward to the future work of Ramon Novarro as being the biggest puller that has ever been known to the box office. This young Novarro is a clean-minded, upright, idealistic young boy. Women like that, but, strange to say, men like it still better."[21]

Writers tried to romanticize Ramon to his fans. *Los Angeles Times* columnist Harry Carr once wrote: "I have a theory of my own about Novarro. At first it seemed so strange and outlandish, I have hesitated to tell it to anyone. I am firmly convinced that this boy is the window through which the light and the learning of a people long since vanished from the earth shines again."[22] Privately, all this attention and obvious studio hype bothered Novarro.

Novarro's ancestry was popular fodder among gossip columnists. Depending on whom you read, he was either descended from Cortez or Montezuma or both. In reality, this was an attempt to romanticize Ramon's Mexican ancestry, which was never denied but was also not openly publicized. At the time, Mexicans, especially those with dark skin, were depicted in films as villains. In 1922 the Mexican government made a smart move and banned all movies featuring Mexicans in a negative light. Producers complied, but the stereotypes continued. The offending characters were no longer called Mexican, or "greasers," but no one was fooled.

Other Mexican stars of the silent era such as Gilbert Roland, Lupe Velez, and Dolores Del Rio all experienced the same racial stereotypes with the studios. Very seldom did they play their own race. Even Novarro played every nationality, including French, English, Polynesian, and even American, but never Mexican. Not until he made *The Big Steal* in 1949 did he finally play someone from his homeland.

Dolores Del Rio once said, "I tried to interest my producers in stories about Mexico. I wanted to play a Mexican. But they preferred me to play a French woman or Polynesian."[23] Del Rio, who was a second cousin to Novarro, first met him after his success with *Ben-Hur*.[24] A bond developed between them that lasted until Novarro's death. Dolores would prove to be someone he could confide in about everything, including his homosexuality.

There would be, of course, others with whom he could share that secret. Most were attractive women who wanted to spend an evening with a charming man and not feel threatened. Not all were outwardly attractive, however; and many were women older than he who found Ramon fascinating. One such woman made a reputation for herself during World War I and on the Broadway stage. She would prove to be a true and loyal friend.

Chapter Eleven

The Student Prince
(1926–1927)

*Ramon was apparently everything I had been told, but
my informants, sleuths and guides who led me to the stage
where he was working, had neglected to tabulate his greatest attribute, his sense of humor.*

—Elsie Janis[1]

On the stage from the age of eight, Elsie Janis was a talented comedi-
enne who had the uncanny ability to mimic anyone she saw or met. Known
as the "AEF Sweetheart" during World War I, Elsie was the only woman
allowed behind enemy lines to entertain the troops.[2]

After the war, Elsie returned to Broadway, but she realized the theater
was not the same, so she wrote and produced her own show called *Elsie and
Her Gang.* Using a cast of ex-servicemen, the show toured the Orpheum Circuit and became a huge success.

One evening in 1923 Elsie and her troupe played the Los Angeles
Orpheum Theater to an audience that included both Rudolph Valentino and
Ramon Novarro. Members of the cast gazed at the duo through a peephole
trying to decide which one was more handsome. Elsie said they were all crazy
because no one could hold a candle to her Rudy. During the performance,
her eyes were glued to the Italian and never once strayed to Ramon, although
she could hear his applause and laughter. After the show, Elsie was delighted
when Valentino came backstage to pay his respects.

Novarro visits a friend, Broadway star Elsie Janis, on the set of her film *Madame Satan*. Novarro is in costume for his film *Call of the Flesh* (1930, MGM).

Ramon was a great admirer of Elsie Janis' work and invited the star and her company to visit him at MGM. Elsie, however, refused, and went to Famous Players–Lasky to watch Valentino. That evening her troupe told her how courteous and gentle Novarro was, but Elsie was basking in the glow of her visit with the original Latin lover.

Fast forward several years and Elsie and her gang are once again passing through Los Angeles and Ramon is again in the first row. This time, however, Elsie was the one who was doing the peeping at him. She had just seen *Ben-Hur* and was very impressed with the actor. She began asking friends if they knew Ramon Novarro. "No one knows him," they answered. "He never goes to parties. They say he is going to become a priest."

"The robes will be very becoming," she replied.[3] She arranged a visit to MGM the following day and was introduced to Novarro. The two hit it off immediately and began a friendship that lasted until Elsie's death 30 years later.

The studio was now churning out Novarro pictures to keep up with the demand. His next effort, *A Certain Young Man* (1928) with Marceline Day, had problems, however, from the start. Remarkably, Novarro was cast as a gray-haired gentleman devoted to a life of sensual pleasure. Producer Bernie Hyman hated the rushes, so with Thalberg's permission, he scrapped everything and started over. Two months later Hyman presented the finished picture to Thalberg and Mayer, who were so aghast by what they saw that they shelved the film.[4]

On a more positive note, *Ben-Hur* had its Los Angeles premiere at the Biltmore Theater on August 2, 1926.[5] The premiere was a complete success and was attended by the entire cast and such Hollywood notables as Eleanor Boardman, Norma Shearer, Mr. and Mrs. Antonio Moreno, Coleen Moore, and practically every star in town.

In her review of the film, Louella Parsons declared, "Not to see *Ben-Hur* would be like not seeing the Passion Play if it came to Los Angeles." Of Novarro's performance, she said, "I can think of no actor who could have played the adventurous Ben-Hur, his vicissitudes, his victories, and his final restoration, with the finished air that characterizes young Novarro. A less experienced actor would have been swayed by his emotions, but Mr. Novarro exercises an admirable restraint."[6]

Respected stage actor David Warfield wired Novarro after the opening and said, "Accept, please, my congratulations upon what I consider a great performance."[7]

Later that month Rudolph Valentino died in New York, reportedly of peritonitis after being operated on for an acute gastric ulcer and a ruptured appendix. The riot that occurred at Campbell's Funeral Parlor eclipsed the uproar seven months earlier at Barbara La Marr's services in Hollywood. When Valentino's body was returned to Los Angeles and laid to rest at Hollywood Memorial Park, Novarro escorted "the Sheik's" former costar Alice Terry to the ceremonies. Novarro was quoted as saying that Valentino's death had "robbed art of a true son. His work and his personality were inspirations to all who knew him."[8]

Shortly after the funeral, Novarro began his next film, *Lovers?* (1927),

Novarro and his lifelong friend Alice Terry in *Lovers?* **(1927, MGM), their last film together.**

in which he was reunited with his dear friend Alice Terry, whom he persuaded to take the part. During filming, rumors began to spread about town that MGM might produce Shakespeare's classic, *Romeo and Juliet.*[9] It was no secret that the studio had wanted to do a production of the bard's play for some time. German director Ernst Lubitsch was offered *Romeo and Juliet*, but he was more interested in another picture MGM was preparing called *Old Heidelberg*. John Robertson was already assigned, however, to direct that project with Novarro in the starring role.

It was thought that Lubitsch might want Novarro as Romeo, and, if so, production on *Old Heidelberg* would be postponed. The coveted part of Juliet would then go to Norma Shearer, whom Irving Thalberg was personally grooming for stardom.[10]

As things sometimes go in Hollywood, Novarro was not meant to be Romeo. Plans for the film were scrapped for the time being, and Ernst Lubitsch replaced John Robertson on *Old Heidelberg* (retitled *The Student Prince of Old Heidelberg*), with Novarro and Shearer in the starring roles. "The

Eastern office had to be consulted," Novarro later said, "and they consulted their salesmen, who consulted the exhibitors, who consulted I don't know who. Anyway, *Romeo and Juliet* is not being produced. You begin to feel, after a few adventures in this maze, that you are up against a monster without a head."[11]

At the same time, Cecil B. DeMille, who left Famous Players–Lasky to establish his own studio down the street from MGM, asked to borrow Novarro for the lead in his next film, *The King of Kings* (1927).[12] Mayer was not in the habit of loaning out one of his top stars, and politely turned down the director, much to Novarro's disappointment. He liked the idea of working for DeMille again and also thought playing the role of the Nazarene would be a beneficial use of his acting ability. Mayer convinced him that he had to finish *Lovers?* and then begin work on *The Student Prince*, so he would not have time for DeMille's picture.

Filming on *Lovers?* continued, and one day during a scene with Alice Terry, Novarro suddenly collapsed and was rushed to the studio hospital, where doctors diagnosed him with influenza. Cautiously, the studio kept his illness secret for three days, until his temperature reached 105 degrees. Fearing public criticism in light of Valentino's recent death, Mayer finally released word of his condition to the press.

Several days later Ramon's temperature broke, but he was ordered to stay in bed for two weeks. Some time later it was revealed that he had ptomaine poisoning and not influenza, as was originally reported. Mayer happily told reporters that Novarro was improved and would be back to work soon.[13] *Lovers?* made a modest profit and proved to be the last pairing of Novarro and Alice Terry. She went on to make two more films before retiring from the screen.

Now that Novarro had pulled through this latest illness, the Samaniego family was again faced with another crisis. Ramon's younger brother, Jose, was playing on the Berkeley University football team when he suffered a severe back injury. Because of improper treatment, it developed into a cancerous tumor. Ramon hired the best doctors, but not much could be done.

At the end of 1926, MGM's publicity brochure named its top box-office attractions as Marion Davies, Ramon Novarro, John Gilbert, and Norma Shearer. At the time, Irving Thalberg was beginning to show a special interest in the career of Norma Shearer. From this concern grew an eventual love affair. In order to see her talent showcased in the best possible light, Thalberg took advantage of Novarro's popularity and paired the two in *The Student Prince in Old Heidelberg* (1927).[14]

Novarro was cast as Prince Karl, who grows from a lonely child in the palace of his father, the king, to a young adult attending school in Heidelberg. There he meets and falls in love with a bar maid, Kathi, played by Shearer. The two carry on a love affair until Karl is called back to the palace and sadly promises the dying king that he will marry a princess he has chosen for him.

The mood on the set was at times very strained. When filming began in December 1926, it became clear that the relationship between the director and his stars was anything but loving. Neither Shearer nor Novarro was comfortable with the Lubitsch "touch."

Both stars were accustomed to rehearsing a scene completely before filming it, but Lubitsch preferred to have his actors do less rehearsing and be more spontaneous. They also disliked his practice of performing the scene and having them imitate it for the camera. Later Norma told a friend, "Ernst keeps trying to get subtleties into my expressions and behavior that my own instincts tell me are inappropriate."[15] Lubitsch was also a perfectionist and once shot a scene 102 times. "Take it easy," he would say. "If I don't get it, I'll do it again—and again."[16]

As usual, celebrities would visit the set to watch the filming. On one occasion, Marion Davies, Mary Pickford, and Ramon's friend Herb Howe dropped by, and Lubitsch asked Howe if Novarro was happy with the picture.

"In seventh heaven," Howe replied, even though he was aware of Ramon's feelings.

"Ya? I am glad," the director replied. "I tell you the truth, that boy is giving a marvelous performance. If this picture is big with popularity, he should be the outstanding man on the screen. This is not masquerade romance. That is acting. This is heart. He is just a simple boy who is a prince. I think that is like as Novarro, not?"[17]

Lubitsch's praise sounded spurious, even to Howe who nodded his head in agreement.

During one grueling day, Lubitsch thought Norma was playing her part too haughtily. After several unsuccessful attempts to get the right attitude from her, he suddenly exploded and told Norma that he could get a waitress from the commissary to do a better acting job.

The actress, by now in tears, insisted that Thalberg be called. Lubitsch quietly sat in his chair pulling on an unlit cigar until the producer arrived. The tension grew until Thalberg arrived and quietly listened as Norma tearfully explained her dilemma. He kissed her forehead and said, "Everyone has a lot to learn from Mr. Lubitsch."[18] End of discussion.

Ramon had far different problems with the director. Lubitsch, through studio gossip, was aware of Novarro's sexual preference. He thought America's Victorian view of homosexuality was humorous because in Germany, it was commonplace. To his amusement, Lubitsch added homosexual innuendo to many of Ramon's scenes.

In Lawrence Quirk's biography of Norma Shearer, he describes a scene in which Lubitsch singled out an apparently homosexual extra for Novarro to hug, and laugh, and sing with. Take after take was demanded with obvious

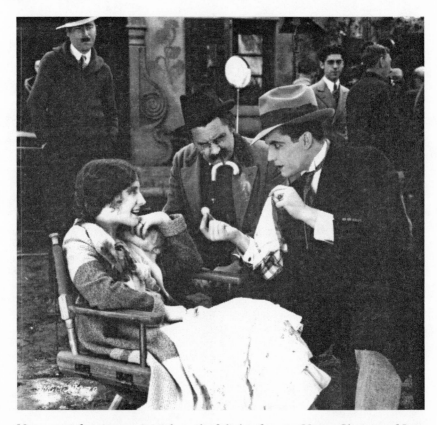

Novarro performing magic tricks to the delight of costars Norma Shearer and Jean Hersholt on the set of *The Student Prince in Old Heidelberg* (1927, MGM).

pleasure by the director, until Norma, who sensed Novarro's discomfort, feigned a fainting spell. According to King Vidor, who relayed the story to Quirk, it was "a better performance than she was giving in the picture."[19] The scene was eventually cut by Thalberg.

Norma knew of Ramon's sexual preference. She had worked with several homosexual and lesbian actors and sympathized with the emotional pressures that accompanied their lifestyle. Like Alice Terry and Rex Ingram, both she and Thalberg were accepting of Novarro.

When asked about *The Student Prince*, Novarro told Quirk, "It was not one of my favorite films, and Lubitsch certainly wasn't my kind of director. I know he did well with others, but he was wrong for me. We just didn't have simpatico, and I was glad when it was over with."[20]

When the film premiered in September 1927 at New York's Astor Theater, critics tore it apart. There were only two showings a day at an increased price of $2 a ticket. *Variety* termed it a nice little picture but not worth the $2 asking price. The film cost $1,205,000 and lost $307,000 at the box office.[21]

Years later *The Student Prince* would be made into a musical, an art form which unfortunately eluded the silent film makers. However, a storm was brewing on the horizon which would soon change that, catching all of Hollywood off guard and sending producers scrambling to adjust to the new sensation—sound.

Chapter Twelve

Talking Pictures
(1927–1928)

I am very proud of the industry to which I belong. There has been so much advancement, and even greater development to come. The people who are willing to learn, to work and prepare themselves for talking pictures will last, the others will disappear. I'm very glad now that I studied voice.

—Ramon Novarro[1]

Construction of Hollywood real estate accelerated during the late 1920s, with buildings being erected on Hollywood Boulevard from La Brea to Gower Street. Many buildings which stand today were built at this time, including the Hollywood Roosevelt Hotel, the former Warner's Theater, and Grauman's Chinese Theater. In all, Hollywood commercial construction totaled more than $9 million in 1927 alone.

The Hollywood aristocracy bought real estate as an investment. Sid Grauman owned two theaters on Hollywood Boulevard and also invested in the Roosevelt Hotel with Mary Pickford and Douglas Fairbanks. Norma Talmadge and her husband, producer Joseph Schenck, owned the Talmadge Apartments at Wilshire and Berendo Street and later sold them for $1,850,000.

Louis B. Mayer invested in a structure at the southwest corner of

Hollywood and Western that housed, among other things, the Central Casting Bureau and the Motion Pictures Producers Association. The basement contained large billiard parlors and a bowling alley.[2]

Novarro built several apartment buildings, including one near Sunset and Fairfax boulevards that he called "The Ramon," with a statue of him erected in the courtyard. He also invested in land in the San Fernando Valley, which was then spotted with ranches and orange groves. After World War II, when the value of Valley property soared, he sold most of it for an enormous profit.[3]

Even though he was 28 years old, Ramon still lived with his family, not feeling a need for a home of his own. Whenever privacy was a priority, he would use two popular Hollywood establishments to entertain. Practically every male star in Hollywood was a member of the Hollywood Athletic Club, located at 6525 Sunset Boulevard. When needed, Novarro and other stars would rent the five-room penthouse under assumed names.[4]

Novarro's other haunt was the Garden of Allah, a group of 25 Spanish bungalows that were built around the main house of silent screen actress Alla Nazimova at the corner of Sunset and Crescent Heights boulevards.[5] Legend has it that actor Cary Grant was once a guest at Novarro's bungalow. The story goes that when Novarro began to charm the young man, Grant refused his advances.[6] If true, Grant was one of the few who rejected Ramon Novarro; his good looks and charming personality were a magnet to both sexes. Ramon would later become good friends with Grant, even costarring in one of the actor's films.

Whenever politicians or foreign dignitaries passed through Hollywood, it was almost certain they would be given the grand tour of the studios. Even American presidents were not impervious to the industry's allure. In the summer of 1927, President Calvin Coolidge visited Southern California and was given a tour of the major studios by Mary Pickford. On their arrival at MGM, the president was brought on the set of Novarro's current film, *The Road to Romance* (1927), costarring Marceline Day. The president and his entourage were introduced to Novarro and the cast, including a trained bear named Bruno.

As filming began, the bear escaped from the trainer and went on a rampage. Everyone ran for cover except Coolidge, who frustrated his Secret Service agents by refusing to get out of the bear's path. Suddenly, the president began laughing and continued to laugh until the bear was brought under control. He later told the press that his visit to Metro-Goldwyn-Mayer Studios was the bright spot of his trip to California.

It had been three years since June Mathis was replaced as scenarist on *Ben-Hur*. After leaving Italy in August 1924, Mathis returned to the States with her fiancé, Sylvano Balboni, and she married him in December. Mathis continued to work and was eventually put under contract by Colleen Moore and Joseph Schenck. The screenwriter had been fighting a weight problem most of her life and had had a heart condition since she was nine years old. Doctors continually warned her to watch her diet.

On July 26, 1927, Mathis was in New York with her grandmother and was attending a performance of *The Squall* at the 48th Street Theater when she suddenly screamed and collapsed. She was taken outside to the alley, where she was attended by physicians from the audience. Within minutes she was dead. A week later she was laid to rest at Hollywood Cemetery, next to her discovery and friend, Rudolph Valentino.

The following month another death occurred that deeply affected Ramon and the entire Hollywood community. MGM president Marcus Loew died at his Long Island home after a long illness. Louis B. Mayer was devastated and attempted to fly east, but bad weather prevented it. He closed the studio for one day and held a memorial service led by Rabbi Edgar J. Magnin. Nicholas Schenck was appointed president of Loew's, Inc., which troubled Mayer because he disliked Schenck immensely.

Unfortunately, Loew did not live long enough to witness the new technology which would permanently affect the motion picture industry. On October 6, Warner Brothers premiered *The Jazz Singer* (1927), with music and a few lines of dialogue. The public's response to the film was so enthusiastic that theater owners clamored for more talking pictures. Until then, the only studios experimenting with sound were Warners and Fox. The others, including MGM, thought it was just a novelty that would never replace the silent film.

Thalberg told *Photoplay Magazine*, "The talking motion picture has its place, as has colored photography—but I do not believe the talking motion picture will ever replace the silent drama any more than I believe colored photography will ever replace entirely the present black and white."[7] So much for the Boy Wonder.

MGM waited until the following summer before releasing its first sound film, *White Shadows in the South Seas* (1928), which was originally a silent film.[8] By this time, Warner's had released *Lights of New York* (1928), the first all-talking picture. MGM production was falling behind while everyone rushed to see the new talkies being produced by other studios. Realizing talking pictures were not just a fad, Mayer had two primitive soundstages erected, and they were used around the clock until fully equipped ones could be built.

The changeover to sound drove up production costs immensely, forcing smaller studios out of business. It also affected the foreign market because English-speaking films could not be shown all over the world. In time, dubbing and subtitles would be a way around the problem, but at first, studios produced foreign language versions of their important films.

The stars themselves were also affected. Actors with heavy accents or speech impediments soon found they were out of a job. The coming of sound was a two-edged sword to Novarro. He had been recently honored for his singing at the Hollywood Bowl and was thrilled at the opportunity to sing in pictures. "Only in talking pictures can opera be made possible to the masses," Novarro reasoned, "and this one thing alone will be of incalculable good."[9]

He was concerned, however, about his accent and wondered if his fans would accept him. He had a very pleasant tenor voice that was well received once MGM gave him the opportunity. At a special meeting to determine which actors had suitable voices for talkies, MGM executives decided that Lewis Stone, Lionel Barrymore, and Conrad Nagel could begin work on sound productions immediately.

At one point, when Ramon Novarro's name was mentioned, an executive said, "He can sing and play the guitar, but what about his accent?" They were about to question whether they could depend on Novarro, when another executive reminded them: "You know, the public is always going to remember Ramon as Ben-Hur. He was a Prince of Judah. We can always cast him in a film where the guy speaks in a foreign accent."[10]

And with that, Ramon was spared the ax, at least for the time being. He seriously considered leaving the screen and devoting his life to music. He always considered motion pictures as a sideline, saying, "I like them very much—do not misunderstand me. Yet since I can first remember, I have wanted to be a singer. That has been my real life."[11]

In mid–November, Ramon took his family to New York for a three-week vacation of sightseeing and attending Broadway plays. From there, Novarro sent his father, mother, and an uncle to Europe to be reunited with his two sisters who were nuns in the Canary Islands. When a reporter asked how his sisters liked his films, Ramon sadly replied, "But no, they are not allowed to see motion pictures."[12]

Ramon returned to Los Angeles with his siblings but would meet his parents later in Madrid after filming was completed on his next film, *Across to Singapore* (1928). Many actresses were tested to find a suitable leading lady for this film set on the high seas. Finally, after a long search, a former Charleston dance contest winner was chosen who now went by her new name, Joan Crawford. Friends continued to call her "Billie."

During filming, Crawford was involved in a torrid romance with Douglas Fairbanks, Jr. Because they would be at sea during Christmas, Fairbanks gave Ramon a pair of jade earrings to give to Joan on Christmas morning. "Billie, Doug feels terrible about not spending this holy day with you," Ramon began. "But he hopes that this little token of his affection will be of some consolation."[13] He handed the small box to Joan, who cried with delight upon seeing the delicate trinkets. When the ship redocked at Long Beach on New Years Eve, Fairbanks was there to meet Crawford. As the new year began, he proposed marriage.

Novarro and Crawford continued their friendship for several years. As for Fairbanks, even though they were never close, he remembered Ramon as a "handsome, pleasant and talented man with charming manners."[14] Ramon, who felt an affection for Fairbanks' mother, Beth, would often visit her for tea and would escort her to social functions.

Across to Singapore was a box-office success. Even though the critics were not kind, the public swarmed to see the picture, which was filled with violence and thrilling special effects. Of his costar, Ramon told an interviewer, "Joan Crawford gives an excellent portrayal in this; you see, it will make her a star."[15]

In February the studio decided to dust off *A Certain Young Man* (1928), which had been shelved two years earlier. Novarro and Marceline Day were called back to do additional scenes and retakes directed by George O'Hara.[16]

Novarro with costar Joan Crawford in *Across to Singapore* (1928, MGM).

For the effort that was placed on the picture, it had many careless moments. *Variety* said, "The result is not bad, although plenty of details give a hint of what a palooka it probably was when first turned out."[17]

Even though the film was a dismal failure, it did not deter Ramon's fans, who were as enthusiastic as ever about their idol. Women still besieged the studio for photographs of their favorite star. Soon Novarro would be able to provide his admirers with some of the most stunning and classic photographs ever taken of him. Those photos would launch the career of a then unknown photographer who would continue to capture the image of Hollywood's most glamorous stars for the next 60 years.

Chapter Thirteen

Hurrell (1928)

*Ramon Novarro was a real Latin heartbreaker. Every-
where he went the women trailed him like a bunch of dogs
chasing a bitch in heat. Funny how much of an animal we
really are and we try so damned hard to always deny and
hide that relationship.*

—Florence "Pancho" Barnes[1]

In 1928, Ramon became friends with Florence "Pancho" Barnes, a woman
flier who became famous for breaking speed records in her plane, *Mystery
Ship*. Years later she founded the Happy Bottom Ranch in the Antelope Valley, which became an oasis in the desert for aviators depicted in the film *The
Right Stuff* (1983).

She was born Florence Leontine Lowe in San Marino. Legend declared
that Florence received the nickname "Pancho" while gun-running weapons
to Mexico on a banana boat as a young girl. Pancho later married the Rev.
C. Rankin Barnes, pastor of the Pasadena Episcopal Church. It was a love-
less marriage that produced one son and ended in divorce.

Pancho was introduced to Ramon at a party, and the two became
an unusual couple cavorting around Hollywood in Ramon's sports cars.
Pancho was not the glamorous type and was known for her profanity, which
she used liberally. Chuck Yeagar, who was a friend of Pancho's in the
late 1940s, said in his autobiography, "She would never use a five or six
letter word when a four-letter word would do. She had the filthiest mouth

that any of us fighter jocks had ever heard. Now that's saying a lot, but it's true."[2]

Regardless, she and Ramon became friends, much to everyone's amazement. "He did everything for me," she later said, "bought clothes, flowers, jewelry and all the romantic stuff." One outfit was a light blue suede flying suit he had made for her in Brazil. To add to the ensemble, he added a pale, powder-blue silk scarf and a pair of leather boots. One day she was at the Glendale airport with several of her cronies, including Roscoe Turner, who had a pet lion named Gilmore.

"While we were all talking," Pancho remembered, "Gilmore pissed on those beautiful boots Ramon had given me and I was infuriated."[3] She grabbed Turner's riding crop and began chasing after the lion. Turner, unaware of what happened, started yelling and chasing both of them. A newsreel company happened to be at the airport and filmed the entire event. However, when the footage was shown in theaters, it was not explained what had started the incident in the first place.

Pancho was a staunch supporter of a struggling photographer named George Hurrell, who had taken many photos of her. Ramon had told Pancho that he was planning to make his concert debut in Vienna and needed some new portraits. She suggested Hurrell, and Ramon asked her to set up an appointment. Pancho excitedly told Hurrell about Novarro's request, to which he replied, "I'm flattered, but why doesn't he use MGM's photographer?"

She explained that Novarro was planning an upcoming concert tour and added, "He doesn't want MGM to know about it right now. If he asked Ruth Harriet Louise to do it, the prints would be all over the studio."[4]

That evening Hurrell prepared his tiny studio at 672 Lafayette Park Place to greet the *Ben-Hur* of the screen. Soon Novarro's sports roadster arrived, and he and Pancho made their way to Hurrell's studio, where the two were introduced. Pancho, who was breathless and giddy, excused herself, explaining she had to meet some new pilots down at Mines Field. Hurrell sensed there was a budding romance between her and Ramon, which was precisely what Pancho wanted people to think.

After Pancho left, Hurrell set up his equipment while Novarro changed. Within minutes, he turned around and saw the actor standing quietly on the landing dressed as a Spanish grandee in a huge sombrero, with silver ornaments and a mustache glued to his upper lip.

Hurrell found that Novarro, whom he nicknamed Pete, had photographically perfect features and was very relaxed. The photographer played classical music, which made Novarro even more responsive. "He could face my camera with a blank expression," Hurrell recalled. "Not at all like some of the men-about-town whom I had been photographing. I had to trick them into losing their solemn expression in order to get an interesting shot, but Ramon was relaxed."[5]

Two days later when the Latin saw the proofs, he told Hurrell, "You have

caught my moods exactly. You have revealed what I am inside." Hurrell photographed Novarro many times over the next few months. When Pancho saw
a photo taken on her estate in San Marino of a tunic-clad Novarro standing
under a tree next to a white horse, the aviatrix noted, "My God, George, even
the horse looks glamorous!"[6]

One day while visiting the set of *The Hollywood Revue of 1929*, Norma
Shearer invited Novarro into her dressing room for a visit. She complained
that she was very unhappy about the recent film roles she was receiving. During the conversation, Ramon spread out a stack of portraits he had just received
from Hurrell. Norma looked from one to the other with obvious interest.
"Why Ramon, no one has ever photographed you like this before," she said.

Ramon told her about Hurrell and his tiny studio in Lafayette Park. Smiling, she said, "He may come in handy. I have an idea."[7] She explained that
the studio was preparing a script she wanted called *The Divorcee* (1930). Her
husband and mentor, Irving Thalberg, did not think she was beguiling enough
for the part. She hoped that if Hurrell could photograph her like a "sex pot,"
Irving would give her the role. So Ramon set up a meeting between the actress
and Hurrell. The photographs were stunning and convinced Thalberg to give
his wife the part. As a result, she won the Academy Award for best actress,
and Hurrell was given a contract as a portrait photographer at MGM.

As a favor to his friend Renee Adoree, Novarro agreed to take a smaller
role in her next film, *Forbidden Hours* (1928). Even so, Novarro received top
billing, which was in his contract. "What he [Novarro] has to do, he does in
real nice fashion," the *New York Telegraph* stated, "but the picture is all
Renee's." *Variety* said of Novarro: "Tough break for the star that he had to
waste such corking frivolous moments on such a yarn."[8]

To create interest in the film, the MGM publicity department devised
a few gimmicks to tease the public's curiosity. Publicists suggested exhibitors
place a placard in front of the theater reading, "Warning! You are forbidden
to park, neck or loiter around or in front of this theater during the showing
of *Forbidden Hours*."[9] Even with a bad film and worse publicity, *Forbidden
Hours* made a profit. People wanted to see a Novarro film regardless.

In April 1928, Novarro left for New York and made an appearance at a
benefit dance. As soon as he began dancing with one partner, another would
cut in, until an argument broke out among the ladies and they began ripping
at his clothes. Three men pushed their way through the melee, took hold of
Novarro, and led him to a back entrance and into a taxicab. He was so grateful that he treated his three rescuers to dinner at a nearby restaurant. The
next day Ramon boarded a ship for Europe and a reunion with his family.

To make sure his time in Europe would be free of incidents similar to
that in New York, Novarro traveled incognito, using the family name of
Samaniego. Wearing a mustache and goggles in Heidelberg, he met three students who mistook him for an eccentric, wealthy tourist. When he was just

Novarro's first formal portrait by photographer George Hurrell, 1928.

another traveler, and not film star Ramon Novarro, he could move about freely. Later the press publicly criticized Ramon for wearing the disguise, claiming it was a publicity stunt. "It's all a pose, all a gag to stress his own importance," they said.[10]

In Paris, Ramon was thrilled to be there at the same time as his old friend Elsie Janis, who was on tour. She had recently become very ill and had to be rushed to the American Hospital; Ramon arrived shortly before she was pronounced out of danger. When Elsie came out of sedation, she was told that Ramon was going to visit her. Soon the hospital was buzzing about the impending arrival of *Ben-Hur* himself. That afternoon Elsie was sunning herself in the solarium when Ramon entered the hospital in disguise. He went to Elsie's room and saw the bathroom door closed; assuming that she was bathing, he discreetly waited in the hallway.

An hour later Elsie returned from the sun porch and found Ramon in the hallway, napping on a chair, wearing dark glasses and a fake mustache and beard. She wouldn't have recognized him at all had he not been wearing his old worn fedora. Elsie grabbed him and took him into her room before anyone guessed his identity. "Ramon, why are you disguised?" she asked.

"Oh Elsie, it's wonderful," he replied "I am seeing everything and everybody and no one recognized me." He paused, looked a bit sheepish, and added, "Besides, I'm afraid to take it off now, for I don't want to know that no one recognizes me anyway!"

That evening he dined with Elsie's mother at her apartment at the Hotel Crillon. Ramon telephoned Elsie and serenaded her for more than 20 minutes. One by one, she allowed the nurses to listen. "What a lovely voice," someone sighed, "I wish we could see him." Recalling his ridiculous disguise that afternoon, Elsie laughed and said. "I wish you could too."[11]

Whenever Ramon took his trips abroad, the only mementos he bought for himself were sheet music. "I don't collect souvenirs," he said. "We forget everything in time. Nothing lasts. We strive to attain things and yet never quite attain them, although we may think we do."[12]

When asked by a journalist if he had visited the popular tourist attractions while in Europe, Novarro replied, "Why should I go to those places? One only meets Americans, South Americans and the English. On this trip I wanted to meet the real people of the countries I visited. I talked to the artists, the writers and musicians."[13]

When Novarro returned to Hollywood, his next film, *The Flying Fleet* (1929), was ready to begin production. They had to contend, however, with scores of workmen on the lot constructing new sound stages to handle the recent demand for talkies. To take advantage of this new sound craze, most films were now being released with synchronized sound and a musical score, but limited or no dialogue. *The Flying Fleet,* Novarro's first picture to take advantage of the new technology, was the story of six young men who are about to graduate from the U.S. Naval Academy at Annapolis and train for the Navy Air Corps.

The director, George W. Hill, was chosen because he had a reputation for creating realistic depictions in his films, often collaborating with his wife, screenwriter Frances Marion.[14] *The Flying Fleet* would be Hill's first attempt at sound, using only music and sound effects. To capture the roar of the airplane's motor, Hill had Novarro hold a microphone in the cockpit during aerial scenes.

Thalberg wanted the picture to be accurate and asked permission to film aerial formations and maneuvers on the aircraft carrier *Lexington*, which was stationed at San Diego. The navy gave permission, except for the filming of planes landing or taking off from the ship. "This is a Naval secret, and never allowed to be photographed," the navy told Thalberg.[15]

Thalberg wired Admiral Pratt at San Diego and asked him to view two navy films titled *Wings of the Fleet* and *Sailors of the Air*. He told the admiral that recent newsreels revealed "more detail than we consider necessary" and would he please reconsider his decision.[16] It wasn't long before the producer received permission to film whatever he wanted on the *Saratoga* and the *Lexington*, which proves how much influence Irving Thalberg had.

Novarro's leading lady was chosen by the actor himself. Before going to Europe, he chanced by the set of *Telling the World* (1928) and was introduced to Anita Page, who was acting in her first MGM film. Novarro was impressed by Page and asked her if she would like to be in his next film. Another pretty blond actress, Josephine Dunn, was also being considered for the role. Producer Bernie Hyman's only objection to Page was her height. He said she was too tall, but Novarro thought that was nonsense. "I can wear lifts in my shoes," he said. "Besides, I played with Miss Crawford and she's as tall as Miss Page."[17]

As Ramon was leaving the meeting, Page was waiting outside and said to him, "Thank you very much, Mr. Novarro. I hope I get the part."

"I think you will," he replied. And she did.

Filming began on August 2, 1928, and moved to location shooting in San Diego the following week. Scenes were shot at the luxurious Hotel Del Coronado, where the cast—including Page and her mother—were staying. Page's father came along and rented a small house so he could be near his wife and daughter.

Ramon and Anita became very close during that month-long stay and often dated while in San Diego and upon their return to Culver City. He always greeted her by kissing her forehead. She sat on his lap between takes, and he would tell her, "Oh Anita, you're such a flirt." At other times he told the crew, "Do you want to see the most beautiful girl in the world?" During one kissing scene, they continued long after George Hill yelled "Cut."

On September 11, filming resumed on the lot in Culver City. Anita and Ramon were becoming closer, and many of the cast and crew teased Ramon, saying, "Why don't you marry the girl?" One day the wife of costar Ralph Graves arrived on the set and noticed the chemistry between Ramon and Anita. She took Anita aside and told her, "I think Ramon likes you."

Ramon was still feeling pressure from Louis B. Mayer about marriage, and the fiasco with William Haines was still fresh in his mind. Ramon was very taken with Anita and loved her vibrancy and joy of life. If anyone could change his lifestyle, he felt she could. He introduced her to his family, and she became good friends with his sister Carmen.

Novarro with costar Anita Page in *The Flying Fleet* (1929, MGM).

On September 29, the last day of shooting, Ramon and Anita were filming a scene when he turned to her and said, "I want you to answer me as though you really mean it." Anita was bewildered as Ramon took her in his arms and said, "I love you. Will you marry me?"

Anita was shocked. At first she thought he was joking and replied, "I might on an off Thursday." Ramon wasn't laughing, and Anita could see the disappointment on his face. One of her regrets was that she never apologized for hurting his feelings. She liked Ramon very much, but her career was just starting and she wasn't ready for marriage.

Anita continued to see Ramon over the next year. Soon she noticed a gradual change in him that affected not only their relationship, but his career and personal life. It was during this year that a series of events occurred that would mark the beginning of Novarro's dependency on alcohol, a habit that would be an albatross around his neck for the remainder of his life.

Chapter Fourteen

Pagan Love Song
(1928–1929)

I worked with many attractive men at MGM, including
Clark Gable, but Ramon was my favorite. He was so good
to me that I hope he knew that I appreciated it.
                                                      —Anita Page

Things were soon smoothed over between Ramon and Anita, and they continued seeing each other. Their last date was at a party at Marion Davies' beach house in Santa Monica. Ramon had been drinking heavily and asked Anita to dance. Clumsily they staggered across the dance floor, almost falling at one point. "Ramon, what are you doing?" she cried, putting an end to the dancing.

Months later, when *The Flying Fleet* premiered at San Diego, the local theater manager asked Ramon and Anita to appear. Other than the opening of *Ben-Hur*, Novarro never made personal appearances or attended premieres. He did not believe in it. "We are an illusion," he told Anita. "The audience does not look at us as real. We are just an image on a giant screen that can never live up to their expectations in person."

He thought his fans would be disappointed to see him in person, but Anita asked him to do it as a favor to her, so he relented and attended the premiere. When they arrived in San Diego, the Naval Air Station crowded 130 planes into the air, flying in review for the occasion.

After a day of posing for photographers, Ramon and Anita walked into the Pantages Theater, arm in arm before a crowd of screaming fans. As the picture began, Ramon's name appeared on the screen and the audience applauded wildly. Anita also applauded, and Ramon turned to her with a shocked look on his face. "What are you doing?" he demanded. "Stop it!"

Anita was astounded at his reaction, but being the independent girl she was, she continued to applaud. They had entered the theater arm in arm, but walked out five feet apart. Anita was so incensed at Ramon's attitude that she didn't talk to him for three days. She never understood his reaction. "Maybe he thought I was being nice to him because he was a movie star," she wondered years later.[1] Of course that wasn't true, for she had great respect for him. It was something that would forever remain a mystery to her.

The last time she saw Ramon was in 1931 on the MGM lot. The studio was looking for a leading lady for Novarro's next picture, and a friend encouraged her to ask Ramon to consider her. She saw him the next day, and they talked for several minutes. Of course, the role did come up in the conversation, but Ramon told her that she was not the right type for the part. Shortly after, she left MGM to do other things, including a Billy Rose stage musical. In 1937 Anita Page married and retired from the screen.[2]

Ramon's next picture would prove to be his most popular and the biggest moneymaker to date. *The Pagan* (1929) also had synchronized sound and music and was directed by W. S. Van Dyke. Novarro's costars were Donald Crisp, Renee Adoree, and newcomer Dorothy Janis. Dorothy and Ramon became good friends, and he nicknamed her "Little Thing."[3] When the cast and crew left for Tahiti in October 1928, Van Dyke promised to have filming completed by Christmas so Ramon could be home in time to begin his European concert tour in January.

Many thought that Van Dyke had underestimated his schedule when he directed *White Shadows of the South Seas* (1928), also filmed in Tahiti. He had spent four months in the islands then but now assumed that because he had been through it once, those same problems would not recur. Van Dyke had figured out the shooting schedule so he could be finished in two weeks and have the remainder of the time to tour the islands. Unfortunately, the weather would not cooperate, and tropical storms ate up more than 30 days of shooting time.

The highlight of *The Pagan* was Novarro serenading his costar Dorothy Janis. *Los Angeles Times* correspondent Harry Carr once said, "If MGM ever starts Novarro singing in his photoplays, he will win laurels that will make his own fine screen record seem tame and cheap."[4] The studio evidently took the writer's advice and had Arthur Freed and Nacio Herb Brown write "The Pagan Love Song" for him to croon. Ramon recorded the song before leaving and would later lip sync the words during filming.

When the company returned from Tahiti, rumors circulated on the lot

Novarro and cast arriving in Tahiti to film *The Pagan* (1929, MGM). Beginning second from left: Donald Crisp, Dorothy Janis, and Renee Adoree in the arms of Novarro.

that the song was terrible. Thalberg planned to replace it until he realized that new lyrics would not match Ramon's lip movements that had already been filmed, so he was forced to keep it. To their surprise and delight, "The Pagan Love Song" became a huge hit that would become Novarro's signature song.

Novarro returned to California on December 23, 1928, just in time to celebrate Christmas with his family, but it was not a happy one. Ramon's brother Jose, who had been diagnosed with a malignant tumor of the spine two years earlier, took a turn for the worse. Shortly after New Year's Day 1929, a doctor was hired to attend to him full time. At 8:25 P.M. on February 22, Jose Vincente Samaniego died at home surrounded by his family. Twenty-three-year-old Jose was very outgoing and was said by many to be better looking than Ramon. Three days later he was buried in the new family plot at Calvary Cemetery.[5]

The shock of his brother's death affected Ramon deeply. He later said that his idea of the importance of success changed at that point. "I was absorbed by my work," he said. "I thought success was everything. And then I came to the realization that it was about the least important thing in my life."[6] He delayed his trip to New York and was about to cancel his concert tour when Elsie Janis intervened and convinced him that Jose would have wanted him to continue on with his life. In spite of Elsie's help, Ramon fell into a deep depression and began drinking more heavily.

In April 1929, Novarro's MGM contract was about to expire. Novarro was trapped in the middle of a power struggle between Mayer and Thalberg. Both wanted the Latin in their corner, even though Novarro knew that Thalberg's first concern was his wife's career. "I was dying to have my career managed by Irving Thalberg," Novarro recalled, "but I soon realized that his only star interest was his wife. If Norma needed something, I could be left sitting in his waiting room for a week until I got it."[7]

Mayer wanted Novarro to sign an exclusive contract that would have been so restrictive that the actor believed the studio would have controlled him "body and soul." At one point during negotiations, Novarro handed the contract back to Mayer and politely said, "Excuse me, Mr. Mayer, you have not told me when I am allowed to go to the bathroom."[8]

From then on, his attorney hammered out the new contract with MGM's lawyers while Ramon stayed home and studied music. He was getting restless making films and wanted to do concerts. Rumors were circulating around Hollywood that Ramon was quitting films to go on a concert tour. "Compared to music," he told friends, "the screen is so dissatisfying!"[9]

Unfortunately, Novarro's attitude towards his movie career was typical. His entire life he yearned for things which appeared out of reach and ignored the talents and the breaks he had received. He was extremely vain and ambitious about his singing, and as a consequence, he brushed off his movie career as being of no real importance. Had he put the time and energy into his acting that he did into his singing perhaps he would have gone even farther.

His planned European tour was to open at Berlin's Philharmonic Hall in March of 1929. Mayer didn't want to lose one of his top stars, so he finally gave in to Novarro's demands and signed him to one of the most remarkable contracts Hollywood had seen at that time. Mayer sarcastically told Novarro, "Ramon, if you ever decide to give up acting, I'll make you head of my legal department."[10]

The new contract called for him to work at MGM six months of the year, making two pictures. During the remaining six months, he would be free to accept concert tours, make records, or do anything he liked, except make films for other studios. Only Al Jolson had a contract with similar latitude. With talking pictures becoming so popular, Ramon would also have the chance to do musicals.[11] "I got things my way on paper," he later said, "so I groaned, signed the contract, and in my opinion, because I had been forced to kiss Louis B. Mayer's ass, I never made a worthwhile picture again at MGM."[12]

To help smooth things over with the studio after the turbulent negotiations, Novarro told the press: "I would rather stay with MGM than go to another studio. Ever since I came to the screen I have been here, first with Rex Ingram at old Metro, and then with MGM."[13]

With his affairs finally in order, Novarro left for New York and then continued on to Berlin, where he was to make his debut in the opera *Tosca*. "It is preferable that I make my debut abroad, rather than in America," he said. "Over there I will be judged as a singer only; here I would first be regarded as 'a movie actor,' and then a singer."[14]

A few days before opening night, Novarro collapsed in his Berlin hotel room. Doctors diagnosed him on the verge of a nervous breakdown and insisted he cancel his scheduled debut. After being released from the hospital, he spent days wandering the streets of Berlin in a trancelike state. To ease his mind, he naturally sought solace in music. "But I couldn't study my music," he said, "or find interest in anything."

One afternoon he was out walking and passed a small concert hall. Hearing the strains of a violin echoing inside, he wandered into the half-filled house and sat in a back-row seat. "A boy in his early 20s was the artist of the recital," Ramon said. "An unknown boy fighting his way to success. He played light, lilting melodies. There was so much youth, hope and eagerness in him and his music, that suddenly I felt a new wave of peace coming over me."

As Ramon listened to the soothing music, he began to awaken from his grief. "I wanted to meet him and thank him," he said, "but I didn't because I was afraid he might think I was a sentimental fool. I don't even know his name, but I shall always remember that hour."[15]

Afterward Ramon recuperated by touring Paris and Monte Carlo. The studio had pegged him to star in *The Bridge of San Luis Rey* (1929) with Lily Damita and wanted him to make some atmospheric shots in Spain. But because of his depression, the studio replaced him with Duncan Renaldo.

MGM was aware of Novarro's hesitation to return to films. To sweeten the pot, Mayer wired Ramon in Berlin and offered to star him in a musical if he returned home immediately. On June 21, 1929, Novarro arrived back in California and told reporters, "It's worth going to Europe just for the thrill of getting home again!"[16]

Once, when asked if he planned to quit acting, he replied, "I am grateful to motion pictures, because they have made it possible for me to study singing, which is about to open up a new career for me."[17]

Novarro's first talking picture was *Devil-May-Care* (1930), directed by Sidney Franklin, one of Irving Thalberg's favorite directors, who guided Greta Garbo in *Wild Orchids* (1929). Novarro reported to the studio for rehearsals on August 1 with costars Dorothy Jordan and the popular opera singer Marion Harris, who only sang one song, much to the dismay of the critics.

In the story, Novarro, a follower of Napoleon, is condemned to death by King Louis for conspiracy against the throne. Cheating death at the last minute, Novarro escapes and takes refuge in Dorothy Jordan's bedroom. She attempts to turn him over to the soldiers, but he escapes and retreats to a friend's chateau, disguised as a servant. Later Jordan arrives at the same house, and, of course, romance follows.

Filming on *Devil-May-Care* ended on September 27 and, probably because of the problems which the new medium of sound incurred, was 16 days over schedule, which did not please Mayer.[18] Even though Sidney Franklin said that the film was "sort of a bootlegged musical," the critics were kind to a point.[19] *Variety* said, "[It's a] Novarro picture all of the way, for a front rank juvenile and actor, whose singing voice is not unlike Maurice Chevalier. Perhaps it's the accent."[20]

When filming was completed, Novarro went to El Retiro, a Jesuit retreat at Los Gatos, California. He spent the week in meditation, receiving counseling from the spiritual advisers. "Oh, that place up there" Ramon commented, "I love it very much. There is always trouble during the making of a picture. There are always things happening unexpectedly which are upsetting. When I come home from there, everything seems so much more beautiful."[21]

Louis Samuel, Novarro's business manager, had been friend, companion, and chauffeur to the actor for 10 years, since their days at Ernest Belcher's dance studio. Samuel had won his trust, so Ramon gave him power of attorney. Unknown to Ramon, Samuel's brother was in the stock market and was

Novarro's Lloyd Wright–designed hillside home in Los Feliz in 1929, shortly after its construction. Later called the Samuel-Novarro House, it was declared a historic-cultural monument by the Los Angeles Cultural Heritage Board in 1974.

unwisely investing the actor's money. When the stock market suddenly collapsed on October 29, 1929, Ramon almost lost everything.

Ramon was devastated, not only because of the loss of money, but because of the betrayal by a close and trusted friend. After an investigation, it was discovered that Samuel had also embezzled funds from Novarro's account. The money could be replaced because he still had a steady paycheck coming in, but the loss of trust was something which would, sadly, never be restored. Because of the friendship they once had, Ramon agreed not to prosecute if Samuel attempted to right his wrong. The only asset the one-time manager had left after the crash was a house in Los Feliz, which he turned over to Novarro.[22] The house had been designed two years earlier by Lloyd Wright, the son of famed architect Frank Lloyd Wright.[23]

On November 14, 1929, Novarro began work on his next picture, *In Gay Madrid* (1930), which was produced by Paul Bern and once again costarred Dorothy Jordan. The filming was plagued from the beginning. Novarro was late to work 10 days during shooting, and the entire production was 13 days behind schedule when it wrapped on December 21. *Variety* said, "Certainly looks like MGM was hard-up for a story for Novarro to go so far afield."[24]

As the new year approached, Novarro was glad to say good-bye to 1929. His beloved brother Jose had been taken from him by cancer. He had gone through the roughest contract negotiations with Louis B. Mayer he had ever experienced. His closest friends, Rex Ingram and Alice Terry, were far away in Europe. The stress of whether his fans would accept him in sound pictures had placed him on the edge, and his European concert debut had failed to take place. One of his closest friends had embezzled his money and had lost almost everything Ramon owned in the stock market crash. With each new heartache, Novarro became more dependent on alcohol.

To make matters worse, he was becoming increasingly bored with acting and needed something that even his singing could not fulfill at the time. So he decided to try something that was almost unheard of for actors in those days. He wanted to direct.

Chapter Fifteen

The Director's Chair (1930)

Directing is very hard work. You toil all day, and at night you must stay and watch the rushes. In my Spanish and French versions, I acted and directed, and believe me, I was laboring night and day.

—Ramon Novarro[1]

The new decade began with the filming of one of Novarro's most popular talking pictures. *The Call of the Flesh* (1930) was chosen for Novarro a year earlier, and almost didn't make it to the screen thanks to many name and story changes. As required, the studio submitted the story to the Association of Motion Picture Producers (AMPP), or the Hays Office as it was sometimes known. The AMPP had some misgivings about the way certain groups of people were portrayed in the screenplay.

In a letter to producer Hunt Stromberg, AMPP executive vice president Fred W. Beetson wrote, "The story will meet objection from the angle of royalty. It is unwise to depict the king and the prince in this manner, and it is possible that offense may be caused by using the church in the manner which is suggested. There is a lot of good material in this story, but I should rewrite it entirely before attempting to produce it."[2] The studio did exactly that and assigned Dorothy Farnum to rewrite the script but keep the Spanish flavor.[3] Charles Brabin had mended his relationship with the studio since the *Ben-Hur* fiasco and was signed to direct the picture.

The supporting cast included Dorothy Jordan, in her third consecutive film appearance with Novarro. Ernest Torrence was cast as Novarro's mentor, and Renee Adoree as the old flame who is still in love with the precocious opera singer. This would prove to be Adoree's last film; the actress had been suffering from tuberculosis for some time but only Novarro knew of her illness.

One day while filming a scene Renee collapsed on the set and began hemorrhaging. A doctor was called and Novarro contacted producer Hunt Stromberg. "Hunt, I am worried about Renee, " Novarro said. "If you replace her with another actress, I will redo all my scenes and you won't have to pay me." Stromberg was impressed but thought it would still be too expensive to replace the actress at that late date.

"I'm sorry, Ramon" he replied. "But I will see to it that she finishes the picture tonight."[4]

A still from the unreleased film *March of Time* (1930, MGM), in which Novarro is singing, "Long Ago in Alcala."

Adoree returned to the set that evening against her doctor's orders, who made it clear to Stromberg that he would not be responsible for anything that happened. As the final scene was being completed, Adoree hemorrhaged again and lost consciousness. She later went to a sanatorium in La Crescenta just outside Los Angeles, where she stayed for five months.

In the hopes of repeating the success of the *Hollywood Revue of 1929*, MGM began production on what was to have been its most extravagant musical, *The March of Time*, to be directed by Chuck Riesner. Novarro, who had been left out of *Hollywood Revue*, along with Garbo, sang "Long Ago in Alcala," written by Andre Messaizer. He performed the song on a wharf background in a French sailor's suit. Other stars in the film included Buster Keaton, Faye Templeton, Karl Dane, and the Dodge Sisters, who danced in front of a five-story prison facade.

Twenty-four segments were filmed before Thalberg pulled the plug.[5] Lavish musicals were losing their appeal, and he decided to quit while the studio was still ahead. The segment with Novarro has never been seen.

In April, Ramon leased a house in Santa Monica at 130 Adelaide Drive that faced the Pacific Ocean.[6] Ramon was concerned about the recent polio epidemic and hoped the sea air would keep his siblings healthy. But just in case, his doctor dispensed nose drops which he hoped would ward off the disease. Novarro didn't want them succumbing to the same fate as the two sons of Ferdinand Pinney Earle, who contracted polio. One son died, but the other, Ivan, a close friend of Novarro's brother Eduardo, survived and later became a talented painter. Whatever the reason, the Samaniego children remained healthy and didn't contract the crippling disease, much to Ramon's relief.[7]

During the filming of *Call of the Flesh*, a feud arose among Novarro's fans in *Picture-Play* magazine. A man named Gene Charteris complained that Novarro was "a slightly portly actor, very conceited and self-sufficient." The critic had recently seen *The Pagan* and thought Ramon had an "unbecoming roll of fat about his face and neck." Soon, women *and* men from all over the world began defending their screen idol.

"Anyone who saw *The Pagan* and thought Ramon 'fat and foolish' must have had a stomachache or a hangover when he wrote the letter!" one fan proclaimed. Another reader attacked Charteris himself, saying, "Perhaps you have a big nose, a mouth the size of the Grand Canyon, and a disposition like a lemon, and every time your girlfriend sees Ramon she tells you of your faults, thus giving you a Novarro complex."[8]

It was evident that Novarro's popularity was at an all-time high. Actress Marlene Dietrich once told a reporter, "I am convinced that Novarro is one of the most valuable, finest and most interesting men in Hollywood."[9] Women adored him and flocked to his pictures, even when they were panned by the critics. But soon his popularity would wane, especially when the Latin lover craze began to decline. Things might have been different had Mayer and

Thalberg known what to do with him once sound came and he could no longer play any role or nationality. With his accent, he was limited to foreign characters. Since MGM had not yet developed its reputation for lavish musicals, Novarro's singing talent almost went untapped. For whatever reason, the studio continued to put him in one bad film after another. Occasionally, the old popularity would flare up with films such as *Mata Hari* and *The Barbarian*, but Ramon would never again see the same quality of work that he enjoyed in his silent days.

As soon as filming was completed on the *Call of the Flesh*, work began on the Spanish language version. Part of Novarro's contract called for him to direct, so the studio gave him his first opportunity. "You see, when you act," he explained, "the audience is an instrument which you play upon. When you direct, it is like conducting a symphony. You draw from your cast the different emotions which you want. It is a much more stimulating thing to me than acting."[10]

Studios were not yet dubbing their movies for the foreign market, so for many of their large budget films they would assemble a foreign cast and shoot the film on the same sets. Many stars appeared in their foreign versions but had to learn the scripts phonetically. Fortunately, Novarro did not have to do this because he was fluent not only in Spanish and English, but also in French and Italian.

Novarro took his director's duties seriously and proceeded as if he were putting on a revue in his private theater. For weeks he interviewed Spanish actors who were well known only in their own countries. One actor from Spain agreed to do a supporting role in the film if Novarro would do the same for him in his country. Novarro tactfully explained that his contract with MGM precluded any such arrangement, so the young actor went on his way. "The Spanish are conceited like children," Ramon told Herb Howe.

"You mean like you," Herb replied.[11] Ramon laughed.

Ramon cast Conchita Montenegro in the part of Maria. She was a former dancer who had played in a handful of Hollywood films. "It has been an enjoyable experience directing little Conchita Montenegro," Novarro said. "She is a spontaneous, lively, impulsive creature." Novarro was sometimes very demanding with the young actress, especially when she would not follow his directions.

"I am very stern," Novarro noted. "And Conchita is so sweet about it. " Conchita would go to Novarro and say: "I will do that scene much better next time. I will try very hard to get it the way you wish."[12]

La Sevillana, as the film was called in Spanish, was a family affair for Novarro. His uncle Ramon Guerrero, an accomplished linguist, adapted the screenplay into Spanish, and his mother, Leonor, played the mother superior.

Unfortunately, during filming for *La Sevillana*, Ramon and his family received some bad news. The family awoke on Monday morning, August 4,

Still from *La Sevillana* (1931, MGM), the Spanish version of *Call of the Flesh*. Shown with Novarro are Jose Soriano Viosca and Conchita Montenegro.

1930, to learn that their 19-year-old cousin, Jacques Samaniego, and his friend William Mossberg had been arrested for murder.[13] Both juveniles were drug addicts who paid for their habit by committing armed robberies.

The young men were accused of murdering 26-year-old Ralph Trump as he sat in a car with his girlfriend, Marjorie Ulman. Evidently, a gun discharged as the duo were attempting to rob the unsuspecting couple. For almost two years the case had remained unsolved, but the two young men were finally picked up by police for a recent pharmacy holdup.

Detectives searched through police records and noticed the two fit the description of Ralph Trump's killers. They questioned each one separately for hours until both confessed to the murder. They were also chosen from a lineup by Marjorie Ulmen.

"I did it, but I didn't mean to," cried Mossberg. "We were both hopped up. We had been taking dope and still take it. When I pointed the gun at the fellow, I didn't know the safety catch was off. It must have been released when I pulled the gun from my pocket. I squeezed the trigger accidentally as I tried to scare the man in the car."[14]

The two were former Manual Arts High School students and told police they had obtained the drugs at a party of high school students on the night of the murder. They also confessed to five recent drugstore holdups and were booked on first degree murder and six counts of robbery. At a preliminary trial a few weeks later, the boys' attorney entered a plea of not guilty by reason of insanity. Both were later declared sane and capable to stand trial.

At first, the information about Novarro's relationship to the young men was kept from the press. Mayer, worried about any hint of scandal, used his influence with the major newspapers, requesting the star's name not be mentioned.

To give the appearance that nothing was wrong, Ramon began work directing *Le Chanteur de Seville* (1931), the French variation of *Call of the Flesh*. The released English version was greeted well by the critics, especially a Spanish dance number Ramon performed with Renee Adoree that critics compared to Valentino's sexy tango scene in *The Four Horsemen of the Apocalypse*.

In the French version, Novarro once again played Juan and was supported by Suzy Vernon and Pierrette Gaillot. At the completion of filming, the cast and crew presented Ramon with a statue of Pagliacci to commemorate his musical numbers and to express their enjoyment of working with him as a director.

The film premiered at the Madeleine Theater in Paris on February 21, 1931, to an invitation-only audience. *Variety* wrote, "Due to Ramon Novarro's draw, film is likely to play to large but disappointed audiences. Patrons expect to see another *Ben-Hur*, and find him in a role which, though he does exceedingly well, is not what they expect."[15]

Novarro was prepared to direct and act in a German version when Irving Thalberg canceled it, saying, "It's too much work for what we can get out of it."[16] Instead, a synchronized version of the film was released in Germany and in Italy.

In mid–August 1931, Elsie Janis' mother died. Elsie had been extremely close to her mother and fell into a deep depression, declaring that she would retire from the stage. Two years earlier, Elsie had attempted to cheer up Ramon when his brother Jose died; now it was Ramon's turn to repay the favor. He told her jokes and sang and danced—anything to see her smile again.

One evening Ramon convinced Elsie to attend a party at the home of opera singer Lawrence Tibbett. As usual, Ramon entertained guests with songs and an occasional Mexican dance. After some coaxing, Elsie joined him at the piano for a musical exchange. Ramon began ribbing the vaudevillian, who replied, "Aw, go on home," and gave him a little shove.

"Of course," Elsie recalled, "then he gave me a little push. I pushed him back, and the first thing you know we were at it hot and heavy." One push too many and the duo fell off the piano bench, much to the delight of the other guests. She pinned Ramon down and sat on his stomach, appearing victorious. However, Ramon "played dead," and when Elsie was distracted, he undulated his stomach, causing her to fall on her right shoulder. "Even then it wouldn't have been so bad," she insisted, "but I wouldn't say I was hurt and so he kept on pummeling me until my shoulder was completely dislocated."

Elsie made some excuse and left the party with Ramon. Not wanting to make Ramon feel bad, she didn't tell him about her injury that night. "I hated to tell on Ramon because he wouldn't hurt anybody for anything. Ramon isn't a big bruiser. He just didn't know I was hurt, and I was too stubborn to tell him."

When Ramon found out, he of course apologized profusely. Elsie laughed and told a friend: "I promise you that the next time it will be different when I take on Mr. Novarro in a wrestling match. He'd better watch out. That's all I've got to say!"[17]

All their frivolity could not change the fact that the trial of Jacques Samaniego was a source of embarrassment for the actor. Mayer had managed to keep the star's name out of the newspapers and away from the proceedings up to this point, but even his influence had its limits. It was expected that Novarro would soon have to go public for the black sheep of the family.

Chapter Sixteen

Secret Life (1931)

[Novarro was] happy, charming, carefree, extremely optimistic, obliging, and eager to please. He was full of laughter, continually leaping from one idea to the next, and for his director, pretty difficult to pin down."
— Jacques Feyder[1]

In May, Novarro participated in a benefit at the Philharmonic Auditorium to aid the survivors of a recent earthquake in Mexico. This was his first appearance at the Philharmonic since his days as an usher. Among those appearing with him were Dolores Del Rio, Raquel Torres, Antonio Moreno, and other famous Mexican players from the stage and screen.

Meanwhile, work began on Novarro's next picture, *Daybreak* (1931), based on Arthur Schnitzler's novel of the same name.[2] French director Jacques Feyder directed the film in which Novarro played an Austrian officer who sacrifices his army career for the love of a girl with whom he has had an affair.

Supporting roles went to Helen Chandler, Jean Hersholt, and William Bakewell. Bakewell had been acting since the age of 17 and had received good reviews the year before in the Academy Award–winning *All Quiet on the Western Front* (1930). Bakewell liked Novarro and thought he was "gracious, charming and easy to work with." Years later Bakewell saw Novarro at a party given by actor John Carroll at his Lookout Mountain home. Novarro approached him from behind and spoke dialogue from *Daybreak*. Without missing a beat, Bakewell returned his lines, and the two completed the scene, much to the delight of the guests.

On February 6, 1931, Novarro's 32d birthday, the studio delivered a giant cake to the set of *Daybreak*, and the cast and crew sang "Happy Birthday." Feyder often found it hard to get Novarro to concentrate on his work because he loved interacting with people. Novarro was adored by the crew and would entertain them with juggling and guitar playing. On the other hand, Helen Chandler, who had just appeared as the female lead in *Dracula* (1931), was a bit more difficult because of her addiction to alcohol and sleeping pills.

In the early 1930s, Novarro frequented the Rector Hotel, which was located on the northeast corner of Hollywood Boulevard and Western Avenue. A former makeup girl at MGM recalled that at the end of a day's filming, Novarro would sometimes invite people to join him. Usually, three or four very good-looking young men would follow him off the set, to the snickering of several ladies. After witnessing this several times and confessing to being naive, she asked someone why they were laughing; she was taken aside and explained the facts of life.

The Rector Hotel supposedly catered to a lower-class clientele. Why Novarro would go there, one can only guess. William Bakewell remembered the rumors about Novarro's sexuality, but it was not something people openly discussed. "Ramon was a member of the MGM family," Bakewell recalled, "and no matter what, he was to be protected. Mayer saw to it that his 'children' were taken care of, and he would not tolerate any derogatory remarks from anyone."[3]

One of Novarro's close friends was director F. W. Murnau, who also was a homosexual.[4] Knowing each other's taste in men, they supposedly procured lovers for each other. Although Novarro never worked with Murnau, the director privately coached him on his dramatics. "It was fortunate, I suppose, that Murnau did not long survive the birth of the talking pictures," Novarro said. "He frequently complained of talkies to the very studio heads who were hiring him and told them, 'You have destroyed the art of acting.'"

"In a way, I feel Murnau was right," Novarro continued. "We of the silent screen had created a pantomimic art that had no language barriers. We were universal—any nationality would understand the story we were telling."[5]

Upon completion of *Daybreak*, Novarro immediately began work on another Feydor picture, *Son of India* (1931), which would be the director's last American picture before returning to Europe. Madge Evans played Novarro's love interest, and Conrad Nagel was cast as Evans' brother. During the preview, Novarro helped collect the comment cards and noticed that one patron had complained about Nagel being in the picture. "Everywhere you go, you see Conrad Nagel," the slip read.

"That was correct," Novarro laughed. "Conrad Nagel makes about 52 pictures a year, it seems."[6]

Publicly, Novarro put on a front for his fans, but privately, his involvement with his cousin's murder trial continued to be a constant source of annoyance to him. The pair claimed they were under the influence of drugs and did not recall committing the murder and were not responsible for what they told police. A ballistics check showed the bullet that killed Trump closely resembled one fired from Mossberg's gun.[7] This, however, was not enough to convince the jury and a mistrial was declared.

During the second trial, defense attorneys decided that Jacques' only chance for acquittal was to have Novarro appear as a character witness. On May 14, 1931, a processor unsuccessfully attempted to serve a subpoena on Novarro at his home on West 22d Street and at MGM. Finally, on May 27, Novarro was served at his home and ordered to appear in court two days later, but he never showed up.[8] No excuse was given, and it appeared to the defense that any hope of acquittal had vanished. The jury deliberated for only four hours, and on June 5, William Mossberg and Jacques Samaniego were found guilty of first degree murder. They were sentenced to life imprisonment, plus ten years.[9]

After the trial, life once again returned to normal on West 22d Street. Novarro's MGM contract was up for renewal, and he wanted to continue his contract as originally written. He would consider signing a six months contract with the agreement that he would sign again after another six months. He was feeling restless and wanted the time to pursue his singing or do some traveling.

Mayer wanted to have the actor at his disposal for at least a year or longer, so Ramon refused to sign. Until their lawyers could iron out the details, Novarro agreed to sign for one picture as the featured lead in Greta Garbo's next film, *Mata Hari* (1931). Ten days later Novarro signed his new contract with MGM obtaining the terms he wanted.

In August, Novarro made formal plans to take over the Louis Samuel house in Los Feliz. Novarro contacted the original architect, Lloyd Wright, and commissioned him to redecorate the house from top to bottom. Wright's plans included not only a refurbishing of the house, but a total relandscaping of the grounds and the purchase of some adjoining land.[10]

Even though it appeared on the surface that Novarro's life was under control, many were aware that alcohol was slowly becoming a problem. His growing penchant for men, in contrast to the teachings of his church, produced feelings of guilt that were more than he could handle. Liquor was his way to ease the guilt, and it gave him the courage to approach men.

Novarro at one time had avoided parties, but now he attended every one he was invited to. "For four years I went nowhere," he said years later. "I dressed entirely in black. After a friend invited me to parties for sixteen consecutive times I concluded I might be missing something. I went, and for two years I was quite a mixer."[11]

It was at one such party that he had his first recorded scrape with the law. On September 13, 1931, Novarro and his secretary, Frank Hanson, attended a party where he met two very attractive young men. Hanson had caught the eye of a young lady, and Novarro decided that the five of them should go to the Garden of Allah, where he had a bungalow. Hanson drove Novarro's car with the young lady beside him while Novarro and his companions sat in the rumble seat. As they drove down Wilshire Boulevard, they were suddenly struck by another vehicle at the intersection of Rimpau Street. No one in Novarro's party was hurt, and the passenger of the other car, Harold E. Wisdom, seemed only dazed.

After police were called, Novarro contacted Mayer and Thalberg, who tried to cover up the incident, but it was too late. They managed to pay off the two men and the woman, who were never heard from again. Fortunately, the incident didn't appear to be that serious, but Mayer took the opportunity to warn Novarro, thinking the embarrassment would be enough to ensure it didn't happen again. That seemed to be the end of the matter.

Several days later, however, as Novarro was leaving MGM, a process server met him at the gate and claimed that Mr. Wisdom had been hurt worse than previously thought and was suing him for damages in the amount of $50,500.

Novarro and his lawyers met with Pete Smith and Howard Strickling of MGM's publicity department, who were experts at covering up scandals. It was agreed that they should find out how serious Wisdom's injuries were. Since witnesses proved too unreliable and sometimes gave conflicting testimony, another method had to be found. "Why can't we take moving pictures of this man who claims he has been so injured?" Ramon suggested. "If it is true, as he says, that his back has been injured, then he certainly cannot object to moving picture testimony of the injury in court."[12]

Smith and Strickling agreed that it was a good idea and instructed a private detective on how to use a camera. For several days the detective followed Harold Wisdom and photographed his every move without his knowledge. Slowly, Ramon was building his case.

Filming of *Mata Hari* began on October 1, and since the stars were Ramon Novarro and Greta Garbo, the worst was predicted. "It was expected that they would clash not only in stellar temperament over close-up footage and 'scene-stealing,' but because their nationalities would bar them from friendliness," wrote one fan magazine.[13]

At the time, Novarro's popularity was waning, and the studio hoped that a pairing with Garbo would be the trick to reignite his fans' passion. The story of *Mata Hari* was based on the life of the beautiful Dutch spy of the same name. Six years earlier Rex Ingram filmed a loosely based silent version called *Mare Nostrom* (1926) that starred his wife, Alice Terry. Marlene Dietrich had appeared in *Dishonored* (1931), which was also about Mata Hari, at

Novarro and the legendary Greta Garbo in the classic film *Mata Hari* (1931, MGM).

Paramount; several movie magazines deplored this film because the studio hadn't been historically accurate.

MGM did not want to make the same mistake. A studio executive claimed to have had several talks with a one-time friend of Mata Hari named Fern Andra, a former UFA star. Claiming to be a princess herself, she allegedly had moved in the same circles as Mata Hari and was able to add much color to the story.

MGM originally picked Robert Montgomery to star opposite Garbo, but he was finishing up another film and was unavailable. Ivor Novello, a friend of Garbo's and one-time actor and composer of some of England's most celebrated musicals, prepared a treatment of the script, but the studio decided to go with a version by Benjamin Glazer and Leo Birinski.[14] It was rumored that Garbo introduced Ramon to Novello, who was also a homosexual, and that they had a brief affair.

George Fitzmaurice provided the direction, and "Garbo's cameraman," William Daniels, handled the photography. Lewis Stone and Lionel Barrymore costarred, and that teaming, along with Garbo and Novarro, prompted the press to declare the cast as the "Metro Tragedy Four."[15]

On the first day of filming, Novarro left pink roses (Garbo's favorite flower) on her dressing room table. A note that accompanied the bouquet read, "I hope the world will be as thrilled to see *Mata Hari* as I am to work with her—Ramon Novarro."

Novarro and Garbo were acquainted with each other from working on the MGM lot for the past six years, but they were not friends. They had heard the stories about each other's temperament, which created some obvious tension the first day. "I felt very strange," Novarro recalled, "and I imagine Miss Garbo also felt some restraint at the time. She was so very charming, however, that I felt instantly comfortable."

The first scene shot was in Mata Hari's apartment. When it was finished, the still photographer set up his camera to take the first photographs. As they posed in the doorway of the bedroom chamber, suddenly both actors appeared self-conscious. "In a way, it was a test," Novarro said. "Perhaps she felt I was watching to see if she would 'upstage' me. Or possibly she was waiting to see if I would try it on her." Whatever it was that caused the tension vanished as soon as the camera shutter clicked. Garbo looked up at Novarro and laughed.

It was common knowledge that Garbo did not like to rehearse. Novarro, on the other hand, needed rehearsals to understand how a scene should be played. "I like to rehearse with the lights, camera, microphones," Novarro explained, "just as it will be when it is actually filmed. When Miss Garbo realized my method of working differed from her own, she graciously offered to rehearse."[16]

Even though Ramon enjoyed working with the seductive Swede, he was concerned about his lawsuit. He had narrowly escaped having to appear in court for his cousin's murder trial, but it seemed impossible to dodge a court appearance this time. In order to avoid the embarrassment of that night, he had to prove that Wisdom was lying. To him there was only one way, and for once he was glad to be involved in the motion picture industry.

Chapter Seventeen

Garbo (1931–1932)

*I liked Garbo very much. It seems to me she was imper-
sonal. I don't think she was ever in love with anyone.
Someone must have frightened her at the beginning. They
say Stiller hit her.*

—Ramon Novarro[1]

Garbo and Novarro became good friends. Director Clarence Brown told
Novarro that no one got on so well, so fast with Garbo as he did. According
to those who worked on the set, there was no friction at all between them,
which was quite an accomplishment for two stars who always had their way.

While scenes were set up, they would sit and talk in Garbo's dressing
room or stroll down the streets of the back lot, going over dialogue. During
one of these sessions, they conceived a love scene which Fitzmaurice used in
the film. "The scene was filmed in the utmost darkness," Ramon recalled, "only
our cigarettes were lit. Nevertheless, it was more erotic than any of these bla-
tant scenes of movies today."[2] The scene was later cut from the film when
New York censors objected to it, saying it was too suggestive.[3]

Filming began each day at 9 A.M. and ended promptly at 5 P.M. Novarro
always questioned how Garbo knew when it was 5 o'clock, until one day he
noticed her maid, Alma, raise up the mirror of her makeup box as a signal.
When Garbo saw it, she began to take the pins out of her hair without bat-
ting an eye.

"She smiled graciously, said good night, and said she would see us at nine o'clock in the morning," Novarro recalled. "No word of complaint or apology. That's all there was to it. No 'I go home!' as I heard so much about. Just an independence and courage to do what she believes is the right thing."[4]

One day Fitzmaurice came to Novarro and requested his help for a scene which needed to be filmed late in the day. The director was nervous about asking Garbo to stay an hour later, so he pleaded to Ramon, "Would you mind asking her? You're such good friends."[5]

Novarro agreed and invited Garbo to his dressing room, explaining the problem over a gin fizz. The actress agreed to stay the extra hour, but having the last word, she arrived two hours late the next morning.

At one point, the question arose as to who would receive top billing. Novarro's contract stated, "Artist to be featured or co-featured, but no one featured or co-featured with him without his consent; and the name of no other person to be in larger type than that of artist."[6] Garbo had a similar clause in her contract, so each willingly agreed to be co-featured with the other. It was the only time in his MGM career that Novarro shared top billing.

Mata Hari became one of the top 15 grossing films of 1932, earning more than $2.25 million at the box office. It was Novarro's highest grossing picture of his career. However, the ever present censor boards would rather have seen the film shelved. The Atlanta Better Film Committee gave it a "not recommended" rating, and the committee's spokesperson commented: "I wish this picture could be destroyed. It is not fit to be shown anywhere."[7]

To spice up Ramon's lagging publicity, the studio trumped up a supposed romance between him and Garbo. One day while having lunch with Ramon at the studio commissary, William Haines asked with a wink, "What's this I hear about your romance with Garbo, Ramon?"

"That's what I'm trying to find out," Ramon replied.[8]

Novarro continued his friendship with Garbo after filming was completed. On one occasion, she expressed a desire to meet Natacha Rambova and asked Ramon to arrange it. Novarro agreed and planned for them to meet at his Los Feliz home, but he made the error of inviting other guests. When Garbo arrived and saw the small gathering, she turned around and left without a word.

Many years later, in a magazine interview, Novarro related his last meeting with Garbo. It was the early 1960s in New York City, and Novarro was walking down Fifth Avenue when he happened to see a newspaper photograph that reminded him of the Swede. Suddenly, he turned and there she was at his side, hidden behind a wide-brimmed hat and dark sunglasses. She looked at him seductively and said, "Hello baby"; then she disappeared into the crowd.[9]

The day following the completion of *Mata Hari*, Novarro was in superior court, defending himself against the personal injury lawsuit. Harold Wisdom took the stand and testified that Novarro's car was traveling at 45 to 50 miles an hour when it crashed into his car. Wisdom, who was a collector for the Southern Pacific, claimed that his back had been injured and it wearied him to make long car trips, which was necessary for his job. Finally, Novarro took the stand in his own defense. "Were you drinking that evening?" asked the plaintiff's lawyer.

"I had one little drink with my friends," Ramon responded, "but my secretary had none. He never drinks."[10] When asked, Novarro claimed he could not remember the names of the two men who sat in the rumble seat with him, nor could he remember Hanson's lady friend.

The following Monday, Ramon's lawyer introduced into evidence a film that recorded the physical activities of the plaintiff since the accident. A flurry of gasps and whispers rushed through the courtroom as the jury saw Harold Wisdom horseback riding, playing baseball, and even rowing a boat. Novarro's lawyer stated that these were all things Wisdom claimed he could not do without pain and discomfort, but as the film clearly displayed he was "doing them with a smile."[11]

Wisdom again took the stand and explained that he engaged in exercise as strenuous as he could stand on the advice of his physician. The judge interrupted him and warned that further testimony might be used against him. Wisdom declined to explain any further.

"It is apparent the plaintiff has made an effort to mislead the court and jury as to the extent of his injuries," the judge declared.[12] He awarded Wisdom only $700 to cover the damages to his car. For once, Novarro's profession helped him out of a scrape.

In December, Novarro traveled to New York to attend the premiere of *Mata Hari* and to make recordings, appear on radio, and begin planning a world concert tour. Soon after arriving at the Savoy Plaza Hotel, a messenger arrived with a box of flowers with a note that read, "With sincere appreciation and best wishes"[13] and was signed "M. H." Knowing they were from Garbo, he ordered three dozen of her favorite yellow roses and sent them to her at the Ritz-Carlton, initialing his note, "A .R." (Alexis Rosanoff).

The next day he attended a revival of *Ben-Hur* at the Rialto. Novarro was embarrassed by his performance in the film classic (which had been equipped with sychronized sound) and wondered why the audience wasn't laughing at him strutting and puffing across the screen. In a review of the modified *Ben-Hur*, the *New York Times* reported, "Notwithstanding its age and a good deal of amateurish acting, it is still an unusually interesting production and one that benefits by the added periodical audibility."[14]

In Novarro's next picture, *Huddle* (1932), he played Tony, the son of an Italian immigrant who works his way through Yale on a football scholarship. Sam Wood directed this unbelievable tale in which a 33-year-old Novarro plays an 18 year old. He was discouraged about the pictures the studio was choosing for him and was becoming weary of the stereotyped young Galahads he had to play. He honestly could not see himself as a college football hero, but for some reason he could not convince the studio.

The critics yawned at *Huddle*, declaring it to be too long, but otherwise felt Novarro executed his role well. Of the star they wrote, "Novarro makes his Tony believable and they've opened up a sequence for him to strum his guitar and toss an Italian ballad to the girl."[15]

Meanwhile, remodeling of the Los Feliz house continued, and once restored, it was a stunning masterpiece. Novarro gave MGM art director Cedric Gibbons his own ideas for the interior decoration. The main entrance led to a landing that was covered by an iron grill in modernistic zigzag patterns. A pair of steps led down to the lower floor, and another pair led up to the guest bedroom, which was painted in two tones of blue and enclosed by glass on three sides.

On the main floor below, the beige library also served as an informal drawing room and had a panoramic view of Hollywood. On a slightly lower level, behind folding metal doors was the dining room, with a black carpet and a matte pearl-gray ceiling. On the walls were chromium-plated chains on top of a black background. The dining room table was made of black and white aluminum, covered in dull black satin with an onyx and glass table top. A breakfast terrace overlooked a garden filled with shrubs and trees, including Monterey Cypress, cherry, and plum. Grape vines grew in one corner opposite the walled-in swimming pool.[16]

After 33 years of living with his family, Ramon at last had his privacy and a private place to entertain. He no longer needed such haunts at the Garden of Allah to indulge himself. The parties Novarro held there over the next few years were legendary, and guests were awed at the design of the house. It was said that whenever you attended one of Novarro's parties, you had to dress in black and silver to match the interior.

"I had to get away from home, to live alone in a house of my own," Ramon said. "I had to cater to whims and notions of my own that would be impossible for others to live with. For instance, I am frequently seized with a sudden desire to play my piano when I am somewhere en route between my bath and my bedroom, clad as God made me. Now, living alone, I can gratify this desire."[17]

Now that he was finally on his own, Hollywood and Louis B. Mayer hoped he would tie the knot. Mayer, who had played matchmaker for other couples, even offered to fix him up with a nice girl on the MGM lot, but Novarro refused. The Hollywood fan magazines and the fans themselves began speculating on Novarro's love life. "The Man No Woman Can Vamp," declared one story. Another read, "I'll Never Fall in Love, Predicts Ramon Novarro."

"There have been stories," he told one interviewer, "to the effect that

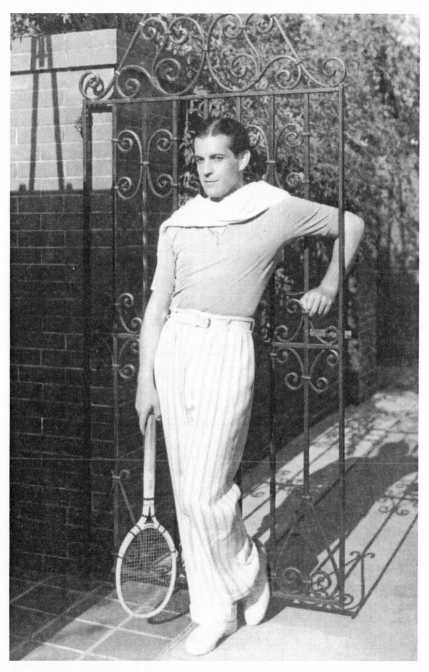

Novarro posing at the front gate of his family home at 2265 W. 22d Street in the West Adams section of Los Angeles.

when I meet the *only girl*, I shall marry. But there will never be an *only girl* for me. I shall never marry."

He claimed his reason for not taking the plunge was that he was supporting of his family. He intended to put his younger siblings through college, and that kept him busy. His brother Angel had just graduated from Berkeley and wanted to get his master's. Eduardo, who was studying to be an architect, would finish the following year. "If God had intended me to marry and have children of my own, He would not have given me these ready-made children," Ramon reasoned. "He would not have placed me in a position of so much responsibility."[18]

Ramon had no regrets about the obvious self-sacrifice he made for his family. Even though everything he said was true, the only interest he had in women was as friends. "Friendships mean a great deal to me," he once said. "There are some whom I love, and when I want to play, I seek them out. Ruth Chatterton is one of my very dear friends. We talk music together, listen to music, and argue for hours over aesthetic questions."[19]

Besides Ruth Chatterton, his many women friends included Alice Terry, Renee Adoree, and Elsie Janis. They all adored Ramon and accepted his attraction to men, which surprisingly did not include movie stars or influential producers. He was more interested in the blue-collar worker, such as stagehands or other crew members, which bothered Louis B. Mayer immensely. Although Mayer hated what Ramon was, he liked him as a person, unlike William Haines, whom he detested.

Ramon would content himself with one-night stands and the occasional short-term lover, which increased his loneliness and his desire to drink. This isolation would shadow him the rest of his life, and in the end would be a contributing factor in his death.

In Novarro's next film, *The Son-Daughter* (1932), his leading lady was Helen Hayes, who had performed in only one other film at MGM but was well known on the New York stage. Louis B. Mayer admired Hayes' acting ability but was distressed by her looks. "What shall we do with you?" Mayer told the actress. "Too bad you don't have a face like Garbo to go along with that great acting talent." He once suggested that she wear one of Norma Shearer's elegant dresses, to which she replied, "But Mr. Mayer, I'll still look like Helen Hayes."[20] So the studio cast her in *The Son-Daughter*, where her appearance as a Chinese bride would be totally unrecognizable.

Although Hayes and Novarro were cordial during filming, no great friendship developed. "I first saw Ramon in *The Prisoner of Zenda*," Hayes recalled. "I thought he was an exceptionally adept actor. Acting technique on the silent screen differed so greatly, I was interested in the things he was able to do with a move of the head or a gesture."

Novarro, who actually shaved his head and endured hours of makeup to achieve the desired transformation into a Chinese immigrant, also admired

Hayes' great acting talent. "When I saw Helen on the stage in *Clarence*," he said, "I wondered if I could ever manage to speak a line with the consummate art and naturalness she did."[21]

Regardless of the mutual admiration the two actors had for each other, the picture was a dismal failure. The critics called it slow-moving and laborious and complained that Helen Hayes was playing Helen Hayes and Novarro's Latin dialect clashed with the "stilted" English dialogue.

The studio decided that Novarro's image needed bolstering to enhance his slipping box office. Edith Farrell, who was in charge of the fan mail at MGM, noticed an elderly lady that constantly sent letters and gifts to Novarro. She suggested that Ramon meet Grandma Baker—as she signed her letters—with all the fan magazines as witnesses.

Grandma Baker, a Belgian-born Catholic who lived in Oak Park, Illinois, spent her afternoons watching Novarro's films and writing him letters. Her daughters warned her, "Your wasting you're time writing to a movie actor. You'll never hear from him."

Undaunted, Grandma Baker was rewarded when she received a telegraph from Ramon that read, "Will be passing through Chicago Wednesday. Would love to see you, Grandma. Ramon Novarro." That day his train was two hours late, but Grandma Baker was still waiting when Ramon put his arms around her and said, "I'm so glad to see you, Grandma."

Ramon was so taken with his new grandmother that he brought her to Los Angeles for a six-week visit during the Christmas holidays. She constantly waited on Ramon, not allowing his valet to do anything. "She knows more about my pictures than I do," Ramon said. "And the way she reads my publicity—well, when I tell you she has more clippings about me than I have, you'll understand."[22]

When the time came for Grandma Baker to leave, she gave Ramon a chain that she had worn as a little girl in Belgium; it became his treasured keepsake. Grandma Baker died not long after her visit to Los Angeles and would always be remembered by Ramon.

During her visit, Grandma Baker was most certainly serenaded by Ramon. Even though Novarro's fame and fortune was made in motion pictures, he could never suppress his ambitions to be a concert singer. So he made plans for another tour of Europe, which he hoped would not end up a fiasco like the first one.

Chapter Eighteen

European Concert Tour
(1932–1933)

Unfortunately, in 1933, fashions in screen lovers were changing. Ramon was still a big star, Metro's reigning exotic lover, but things were beginning not to work so well for him. His career was shaky, and he knew it. He'd invested his earnings wisely, so that wasn't a problem, but it's still a very sad thing, that irrevocable slide from stardom.
                                                                            —Myrna Loy[1]

Plans for Novarro's new concert tour of Europe were unfolding on schedule. Robert Ritchie, Jeanette MacDonald's fiancé at the time, was now managing Ramon. Ritchie planned to have Novarro open at the Empire Theater in London after he finished his next film, *The Barbarian* (1933). In line with his contract, the studio gave him a six-month leave of absence that was to start after he finished the picture. However, *The Barbarian* was being delayed, and Ramon warned the studio that if filming did not start soon, he wouldn't do it at all.

To fill his time, Novarro was inspired to write a play about the life of a movie star called *It's Another Story.* "I was having a party at my home on New Year's Eve," Ramon said, "but left my guests at the stroke of 12 in order to usher in the new year right by setting down the first words of my play."[2]

A few months later Novarro was at another party at the Hollywood Hills home of actress Una Merkel, his costar in *Huddle.* The gathering was attended by such stars as Jean Harlow, William Bakewell, Ginger Rogers, and her date, Howard Hughes. After several drinks, Novarro disappeared from the gathering. Suddenly, a scream was heard from upstairs, and shocked guests found an inebriated Novarro, stark naked, with only a bandanna around his head. Jumping up and down on the bed, he screamed, "I'm Queen Victoria on her deathbed! I'm Queen Victoria on her deathbed."[3]

Several guests, including William Bakewell and Howard Hughes, calmed Novarro down and dressed him. After sobering up, Novarro apologized to Una Merkel, who was very gracious and told him he was the highlight to an otherwise dull evening. She also asked if he could attend her next party. Fortunately, Novarro's unusual behavior was witnessed in private by fellow actors who knew how to keep secrets, secrets which many of them understood.

A week later *The Barbarian* began filming with Myrna Loy cast opposite Novarro. MGM signed Loy to a contract in 1931 and put her in supporting roles until her first lead in *The Barbarian*, opposite Novarro. Just as with Garbo, Ramon became very close friends with Myrna Loy.

The Barbarian was a remake of Novarro's 1924 silent film *The Arab*, with a screenplay adapted by Anita Loos. Novarro performed the hit "Love Songs of the Nile," written by the team of Arthur Freed and Nacio Herb Brown, who also wrote "The Pagan Love Song."

Moviegoers at the time were tiring of the Latin-lover image and were flocking to films with men like Clark Gable and James Cagney, a new breed of tough guy. Novarro knew he could never fit into that mold and was glad for his upcoming concert tour. Even if he had done another film to equal his success in *Ben-Hur*, it would still have taken a backseat to his singing career, which was his first true love. Films were but a means to his eventual goal as a singer; in his native Mexico, opera was revered as a "true art," unlike filmmaking.

When filming was completed, Ramon entertained Myrna Loy and several friends at his Los Feliz house. The gathering was a bon voyage party for Ramon, who was leaving by train for New York and then going on to Europe to begin his concert tour. Myrna, who agreed to house-sit while he was gone, escorted Ramon and his party to the train station. Accompanying Ramon to Europe was his youngest brother Eduardo; his cousin and chauffeur, George Gavilan; and his secretary, Phillip Moreland.

"Eduardo will have a grand time viewing all the cathedrals and palaces, chateaus and castles of the Old World," Ramon told the press who gathered to see them off.[4] After several photos with Myrna, the entourage boarded the train for New York, where they sailed on the French liner *Paris* on March 24, 1933. Novarro planned to be away several months, singing in Paris, London, and other European cities.

Three days later Myrna was having breakfast at the Los Feliz house

Myrna Loy, Ramon's costar in *The Barbarian* (1933, MGM), sees Ramon and company off at the train station on his way to begin his European concert tour. While Ramon was away, Myrna house-sat at his Los Feliz home.

when she saw a disturbing article in the morning paper. It began, "Chatter in Hollywood: Only a few intimate friends know that Ramon Novarro and Myrna Loy have a tremendous yen for each other. Ramon, heretofore impervious to women with the exception of Greta Garbo, for whom he admitted a worshipful adoration, has fallen hard for the redheaded actress. Myrna returns Ramon's feelings and they have been seeing each other everyday. No one has ever associated the thought of marriage with Ramon, who has frequently talked of going into a monastery. But it may be marriage in this case, for it is his greatest romance."[5]

Myrna was outraged. The MGM publicity department wanted to introduce a little romance into Ramon's lagging publicity and used the unsuspecting Myrna. Myrna knew of Ramon's preference for men, and at the time she was seeing producer Arthur Hornblow, so the unlikely pairing of her with Ramon seemed preposterous. She stormed into the studio and made such an uproar that they never again tried to match her romantically with a costar.

The possibility that Ramon might be a success on the concert stage was well contemplated by the ruling powers at MGM. Ramon was still entertaining the idea of leaving films and devoting himself entirely to his music, but the studio had made him such a fantastic financial offer when he signed his last contract that he had decided to stay one more year. His love of music was still not enough incentive for him to quit. He wanted to secure the financial independence of his family before abandoning films for good.

Fortunately his concert tour was a complete success, in contrast to his 1929 aborted attempt. He gave 34 concerts in such cities as London, Paris, and Biarritz. Everywhere fans mobbed him. Souvenir hunters took more than 100 buttons from his coats, 22 scarves, and several handkerchiefs. After the first few times, he decided to return the affection and began snatching things from his fans, much to their surprise.

While Ramon was in Paris, French showman Leon Volterra invited him to the premiere of his latest revue, which starred the famed dancer Frederic Rey, who appeared on stage almost nude. Rey was a close friend and escort of the French music hall star Mistinguett and was often accused of being her gigolo. After the performance, Ramon went backstage to meet the young dancer, who had had a crush on Novarro since seeing him in *The Pagan*. When they met, there was an instant attraction and the two became inseparable.

That weekend Rey was to accompany Mistinguett to a wedding, but he politely declined when Ramon came onto the scene. When the chanteuse discovered that she had been stood up for a man, she called Volterra at his casino and told him to fire Rey. But since the dancer's revue was making the box-office coffers overflow, Volterra politely refused.[6]

Novarro and company returned to the United States from Southampton and Cherbourg on the *Olympic*, the sister ship of the ill-fated *Titanic*. His fellow passengers included Gloria Swanson and her husband, Michael Farmer; Lillian Gish; and composer Jerome Kern.

Gloria Swanson had been in Switzerland visiting her children, and Lillian Gish was in Baden Baden, Germany, for her yearly "cure," which included sleeping each night with a bandage saturated with brandy about her waist.[7] Jerome Kern was completing a new musical on the trip home and worked with Novarro on the production of *The Cat and the Fiddle,* which was his next project for MGM.

The *Olympic* docked in New York on August 1, 1933. From there, Ramon and his bevy traveled by train to San Francisco and then headed for Los Angeles. Family and friends met them at the station, congratulating Ramon on his successful concert tour. One reporter asked Novarro about the alleged romance between himself and costar Myrna Loy. "I don't believe it, do you?" he asked the reporter. "Miss Loy and I are the best of friends, but there has been nothing said of an engagement or marriage."[8]

Upon his return, Ramon began work on *The Cat and the Fiddle* (1934), based on the successful musical by Jerome Kern and Otto Harbach. The studio had recently signed the former Paramount star Jeanette MacDonald but was unsuccessful in finding the right vehicle for her. Mayer offered her two scripts and allowed her to choose; they were *The Cat and the Fiddle* and *The Merry Widow.* She wasn't thrilled with either but picked *The Cat and the Fiddle* after being pressured to select one.

Costar Vivienne Segal, who played the vamp, Odette, thought her role had been weakened by the lightened tone of the musical when it was translated to the screen. "That was the picture that ruined my career," she later said. "No one would cast me after that."[9]

According to Segal, it was Jeanette MacDonald who ordered the downplaying of her character. On the first day of shooting, MacDonald reportedly said: "Hello, Viv. Have you read your part? It's a real stinker!"[10] Segal was to sing "If You're for Me" as her big single number, but it was cut from the film shortly before the opening. After the picture was completed, Vivienne Segal returned to the stage and never worked in films again.

Although the relationship between MacDonald and Novarro was friendly, there was no camaraderie between the two. It was rumored that Jeanette liked to be amorous with her leading men, which did not interest Ramon in the least.

The Cat and the Fiddle premiered at the Capitol Theater in New York City on February 16, 1934, to mixed reviews. *Variety* said the stage script had been "so altered by the films adapters that the only thing of merit remaining is the music."[11] The *New York Times,* on the other hand, said that it came to the screen "with much of its original charm and spontaneity."[12] When *The Cat and the Fiddle* was to be reissued in 1937, the Hays Office rejected it because the two leads engaged in an "illicit sex relationship without compensating moral values."[13] MGM had originally planned to pair Novarro and MacDonald in a series of musicals but decided against it after the picture was released.

In September the actor opened up his Novarro's Teatro Intimo and gave his family, friends, and colleagues a taste of what he had done on his European tour. Novarro performed a vast array of songs to the largest gathering

On the set of *Cat and the Fiddle* (1934, MGM) with costar Jeanette MacDonald.

of movie stars ever seen at his small theater. Among his 60 guests were Irving Thalberg and Norma Shearer, Cary Grant, Myrna Loy, and Elsie Janis. Gloria Swanson also attended "with her hair curled up like the petals of a chrysanthemum about a tiny black velvet hat which had a conical top and was perched at a perilous forward angle directly over her right eye."[14]

Among the guest performers was French singer Jean Sablon, who became acquainted with Novarro in Paris and returned with him on the *Olympic*. Pianist Andre Renaud amazed everyone by playing two grand pianos at the same time. A reviewer praised the concert and said that Novarro "sang with new surety and beauty of tone; his comedy was delicious, untouchable by any singer I know of today."[15]

One close friend who could not attend that evening was actress Renee Adoree, who was suffering from tuberculosis. She was living at her home in Tujunga, just outside Los Angeles, and was hoping to return to her career as soon as she was well. On September 30, 1933, she celebrated her 34th birthday with a small gathering of family and friends. Five days later Renee Adoree died.

The Hollywood community was stunned, having thought that Adoree was recovering and would soon be back to work. Ramon was asked to be an honorary pallbearer at the funeral, which Marion Davies arranged at Hollywood Cemetery. After the service, Adoree's cremated remains were placed in a vault in the Abbey of the Psalms mausoleum.

That month the Mexican consulate asked Novarro to headline a benefit for the relief of victims of the recent Tampico storm disaster. Novarro sang Spanish, French, and English versions of his songs, accompanied by Juan Aguillar's orchestra. On the program with Novarro was his sister Carmen, who had her professional debut as an interpretive Spanish danseuse. Dolores Del Rio and a host of other Mexican celebrities rounded out the evening's entertainment. Because of his cooperation with the Mexican government, Novarro agreed to do a concert tour of his homeland.

He was still busy working on his play, *It's Another Story*, which he hoped to produce in London that fall. Besides writing and producing the play, Novarro also planned to star in it, and wanted actress Beulah Bondi for the principal character role. The Hollywood papers said of Novarro's new project: "And at the last moment, Novarro probably will decide to direct the play. He really ought to bring a song or two into it, and then, too, he might also design the sets and costumes! Maybe he's going over to London to show Noel Coward a thing or two about versatility. Anyway, those who like Novarro in London will have ample opportunity to view his talents."[16]

That reviewer's comments, though tongue-in-cheek, were not far from the truth. From the time he was a child producing marionette shows for the people of Durango to his concerts in his Teatro Intimo, it was always about control. Whatever force possessed Novarro to dominate a project still had a strong hold on him and would continue through the rest of his life. Although multitalented, he might have seen more success in his career had he limited himself. However, no manner of talent or control could have prevented the horrendous outcome of his next project for MGM.

Chapter Nineteen

Nothing to Laugh At (1933–1934)

I know there has been some comment and conjecture about this. It seems curious to the majority of people that a young man, placed so advantageously among so many young and beautiful women, does not fall violently in love once, if not oftener.

—Ramon Novarro[1]

In 1932, directors John Huston and William Wyler convinced Universal to buy the film rights to Oliver La Farge's Pulitzer Prize–winning novel, *Laughing Boy.* Huston was so intrigued by the story of the plight of the American Indian that he traveled to Navajo country in Arizona to do research and wrote a screenplay on his return to Los Angeles.

Universal turned down his treatment, however, when they had difficulty casting the title role. Huston suggested that they cast real Indians, but Universal was not interested, so they sold the rights to MGM. Ramon's brother Angel was asked to audition for the part, but the studio decided to go with his more famous brother. According to an MGM press release, it took two years to find the right actor; they should have searched longer.

W. S. Van Dyke, who directed *The Pagan,* was assigned to the film, and Mexican actress Lupe Velez was chosen as Novarro's costar. Producer Hunt Stromberg considered using Novarro's sister Carmen in the film and told screenwriter John Lee Mahin to look at her for the role of Laughing Boy's sister, Rosie. "I want to explain to Van Dyke," he told Mahin, "that I think it would be clever and sincere to have Novarro's sister play the sister, and if Van Dyke could get a scene where both are looking up, it might be effective."[2] Instead the part went to Carol Flores.

Lupe and Ramon had been friends for a long time, and on occasion, they would join Dolores Del Rio at their favorite restaurant, La Golandrina Café. It was Ramon who many years earlier introduced Lupe to Gary Cooper, which resulted in a torrid love affair. Lupe was now, however, on her honeymoon with former Olympic medalist and current Tarzan star, Johnny Weissmuller.

Indians living on the reservation near Cameron, Arizona, were employed to play parts in the film and provide atmosphere. The tribal chieftains of the Navajos and an audience of 700 Native Americans declared Novarro and Van Dyke honorary chiefs. Novarro was named "Chief Dine-Id-Loi," which means Laughing Boy, and Van Dyke was named "Chief No-Hikeh-Nagaih," or World Traveler. Unfortunately, Navajos do not confer laurels on women, so Lupe had to be content with a sheepskin parchment of honor from the tribe.[3]

The company left Arizona on Thanksgiving Day but spent the next three months filming retakes on the MGM back lot. Preview showings were inferior, and the New York Censor Board found the film objectionable. Editing and reshooting did nothing to improve it.[4]

Variety panned the film, saying, "For one thing, the simulation of Indian accents, notably by Ramon Novarro, leaves something to be desired. Most of the time the star sounds like Maurice Chevalier."[5] Van Dyke hated the picture, and Novarro disliked it so much that he said, "*Laughing Boy* nearly destroyed me; it was the worst picture I ever made, bar none."[6]

Because of the continual retakes for *Laughing Boy* and some additional scenes for *The Cat and the Fiddle*, Novarro was forced to cancel his concert tour of Mexico. Ramon and Jeanette MacDonald returned to the studio to film a special musical number (budgeted at $135,000) to accompany the dubbed French-release print of *The Cat and the Fiddle*.

Afterward, *Our Gang* producer Hal Roach asked to borrow Novarro for the part of Tom-Tom Piper in his new film, *Babes in Toyland* (1934), which costarred Laurel and Hardy. Because of reshoots, Novarro was not available, so Roach hired Felix Knight for the part.

On February 6, 1934, Novarro made a two-day personal appearance at the Capital Theater in New York for the premiere of *The Cat and the Fiddle*. He was paid $26,000 for two days, and as a result of the appearance, he signed a contract for concerts in Baltimore and Washington, D.C. He also finalized plans for a South American tour to begin in April.[7]

In an interview that made almost every paper in the country, Novarro declared that the actor who marries is a fool. "Novarro Boos at Marriages in

On the set of *Laughing Boy* (MGM, 1934) with costar Lupe Velez and her mother. Novarro hated the film so much that he refused to ever talk about it.

Hollywood," wrote the *San Francisco Chronicle.* "Fool to Wed, Says Novarro," proclaimed the *Examiner.* While Novarro was surrounded by a mob of screaming female autograph hounds in front of his New York hotel, a reporter asked if he would come back from his South American tour engaged or married.

"In Hollywood, the chances are 99 to 1 the marriage will be unhappy," Ramon shouted. "Women—phooey! Marry? Not me. There's not been a successful marriage in Hollywood. Beautiful women? Sure. And they're charming, too. But marriage—not so long as I'm still acting. I've never been in love though, and you can never tell. But if I do ever get married, I'll not stay in pictures. I'll write."[8]

Reporters and fans alike were questioning why Novarro never married. He was one of the handsomest men in Hollywood, and women were constantly making themselves available to him. It's hard to believe he never took advantage of a willing young lady, even if out of curiosity. He, of course, refused to marry just to hide his sexuality, as many of his contemporaries did, but he always had an excuse when the subject of marriage arose.

"It seems curious for a young man never to become engaged to be married, never to marry," Novarro would say. "But I haven't the time or the energy.

And love requires energy and the power of concentration. I know enough about it to know that I simply haven't had either the time or the power of concentration."[9]

"You never run out of clever answers, do you?" a reporter once asked.

"Not about marriage," Ramon replied with a smile.[10] Near the end of his life, he once more was asked why he had never married. "That's one mistake I never made," he replied.[11]

After his concerts in Washington, D.C., and Baltimore, Novarro returned to Hollywood to prepare for his South American tour. He leased his Los Feliz home to actor and friend Douglas Montgomery. Montgomery had costarred with Novarro in *Daybreak* when he was known as Kent Douglass. It was Montgomery's habit to nickname any house or apartment that he lived in, and for the sake of disparity, he called Novarro's modernistic home, "The Vicarage."[12]

In mid–April, Novarro left by boat for South America. His first stop was Rio De Janiero, where the Brazilian press highly publicized his visit. The next day, at Montevideo, Uruguay, thousands of females were waiting at the dock. As he left the ship, many broke through police barricades and rushed the actor, embracing and kissing him. Suddenly, they began to pull at his hair and tear at his clothing, demanding an autograph. Novarro panicked, but with the help of the crew, he broke away and locked himself in his stateroom. After an hour, the crowd dwindled and he departed with a bodyguard and was given a tour of the city.[13]

The scene repeated itself the next day in Buenos Aires, where an estimated crowd of 5,000—mostly women—were waiting on the dock to catch a glimpse of the Latin heartthrob. The police were ready this time and escorted Novarro to his hotel. Several thousand people followed, however, and the hotel had to close its doors.[14]

Almost 13 years before the infamous McCarthy witch-hunts, which blacklisted anyone who even appeared to be a Communist sympathizer, Hollywood was given a taste of the hysteria to come. In August 1934, police raided Communist headquarters in Sacramento, where the names Lupe Velez, Dolores Del Rio, and Ramon Novarro were found among the effects of Caroline Decker, secretary of the Cannery and Agricultural Workers' Union. She was one of 17 people in jail under indictments charging criminal syndicalism.

The man behind the investigation was District Attorney Neil McAllister, who asked for injunctions against the stars if they proved to be guilty of being Communist sympathizers. McAllister had recently cited actor James Cagney after his name appeared in letters to Caroline Decker from author Ella Winter, author of *Red Virtue*, a book on Soviet Russia. Cagney responded by saying: "I deny ever giving Communists any aid or that I ever intended to. It appears to me that McAllister's actions are a bid for personal publicity at the expense of my reputation."[15]

Novarro was in San Francisco at the time and was unavailable for comment, but Lupe Velez was outraged. At a press conference in Beverly Hills, she declared: "Me a Communist? Ho, I don't even know what the blazes a Communist is!"[16]

Los Angeles Chief of Police Davis announced that he would cooperate with Sacramento authorities to investigate Communist activities among Hollywood actors. "I intend to conduct a quiet investigation into reports that Communistic tendencies have been displayed in Hollywood," Davis said.

Cedric Gibbons was indignant and declared that his wife, Dolores Del Rio, was not interested in radical activities. "It's too silly for words," Del Rio added. "It's ridiculous. I never had anything to do with Communists. I don't even know any Communists and I've never contributed a cent to anything but worthy charities. Why doesn't this man in Sacramento find out about things before he talks so much?"

When Lupe Velez was asked if she had contributed money to any Communist organization, she replied, "I don't give my money to anybody. I need my own dough. What is the matter with this Sacramento man, anyway? I think maybe they should put him in the lockup tight."[17]

If the actors were found guilty of violating McAllister's proposed injunction, they would automatically be in contempt of court and subject to imprisonment without further court action. The next day Novarro released a statement through his attorney, Stanley Barnes, denying he was a member of any Communist organization:

> I belong to no Communistic organization or any similar organization, and in fact I belong to no political organization. I have in no way, directly or indirectly, aided either financially or otherwise any Communistic organization or any other political organization.
>
> My sole contribution to any organization for the past two years has been to the motion-picture actors' relief fund, the Los Angeles Community Chest and the various charities of the Catholic Church.[18]

It was later discovered that Cagney's alleged connection with the Communist organization was a contribution he had made to alleviate the suffering of the cotton strikers in the San Joaquin Valley, where a baby had died of starvation the year before. He was appalled at the conditions in which the people had to live and sent money to help relieve their misery. After being confronted by the denial of the four film stars, D.A. McAllister decided not to subpoena them.

After Novarro's "Red Scare," he and Dolores Del Rio were invited to Durango to celebrate the grand opening of a new opera house. Before arriving, he made a side trip to Mexico City along with Douglas Fairbanks and Joseph Schenck, president of United Artists. A military detail was necessary to keep back the throngs of women admirers who gathered to catch a glimpse of Novarro and Fairbanks. The trio were given a tour of the city's new police headquarters and were named honorary commanders by the head of the department.[19]

In Durango, Novarro and his brother Angel were mobbed by a tremendous crowd. Angel was still unemployed and planned to stay with relatives in Mexico City. "I have a good education, and while there maybe I can look for a job," he told his brother.[20] Ramon agreed, but Angel found the job opportunities in Mexico were practically nonexistent and what jobs there were paid next to nothing, so he returned to Los Angeles.

Filming began in October 1934 for Novarro's next picture, *The Night Is Young* (1934), which was MGM's first operetta. The studio signed English musical comedy performer Evelyn Laye to star opposite Novarro for her first and only American film. While filming a scene on a ferris wheel, director Dudley Murphy told Novarro that he could not come down between takes. Novarro had spent most of the day there, and his temper suddenly flared. He insisted on coming down, causing a verbal jousting match with Murphy that was uncharacteristic of Novarro. This was only the beginning of signs that something was wrong.

During filming, Evelyn Laye married her longtime beau, actor Frank Lawton, and eloped to Yuma, Arizona. Laye, who was scheduled to do another film with Novarro, became very good friends with the actor. "He was a very good, a very fine person," she said. "He was a Catholic, which I am not, but we had a lot of the same ideas about life. He would always do the right thing, which is a very difficult thing to do in a world as lopsided as this one is."[21]

Lopsided or not, this was the world that Novarro chose to live in, and regardless of what Evelyn Laye thought, he did not always do the right thing. Unknown to him, his days at MGM were numbered. Novarro's need for control did not apply to his private life, where his drinking and sexual appetites spun out of control and became too much for the studio to handle. One by one, things were falling into place to bring about his eventual departure from MGM.

Chapter Twenty

Farewell, MGM (1934–1936)

But I may not do another picture for a while, because I am
fed up with the kind of stories in which I've been playing.
Of course there has been something vitally wrong with my
career. And do you know exactly what? There has been no
progress. I have been at a standstill for a long, long time.
For the past five years I have done nothing on the screen
which was worth the doing!

—Ramon Novarro[1]

Near the end of 1934, MGM was in the planning stages of another musical for Novarro to star in called *Love While You May*, again with Evelyn Laye. Suddenly, things were put on hold, and by the new year, Novarro's contract was canceled. The official reason for the split was "artistic differences," but one rumor circulating around the studio hinted that Novarro had been caught in a compromising situation.

Another rumor said that Mayer had again encouraged Novarro to find a wife—almost issuing an ultimatum—and when Novarro did not comply with his wishes, the two mutually agreed to end his 13-year relationship with Metro-Goldwyn-Mayer.[2] In an interview years later, Novarro gave a different explanation for leaving the studio. "That last big movie," he explained, "that last one, *The Night Is Young*. After we made it, Eddie Mannix, the boss at

Metro-Goldwyn-Mayer, called me into his office and he said, 'It wasn't very good,' and I said 'shake.'"[3]

Months before the split, Ramon's brother Angel noticed that something was bothering him about his work. "What can I do to help you?" he asked Ramon. "I know that you are not happy.... You're unhappy about something."[4] Unfortunately, Ramon chose to keep his problem to himself and not share it with his brother.

The Night Is Young was not set for release until January 11, so it was agreed to wait until February 7, 1935, one day after Ramon's 36th birthday, to release a simple statement saying, "While there was no disagreement, Mr. Novarro requested release from his contract at a time when the studio had a story in preparation for him, but not ready for production."[5]

Publicly, Ramon told the press, "I have been playing the same part in different costumes, with different people, all the time! I don't want to hang on to the yesterdays. I don't want to keep remaking the same stories. Viennese romances, football pictures! I left MGM amicably, but that's the reason. What was the use of making another film with the same old theme?"[6]

The stress from the entire incident affected Ramon deeply. Shortly after leaving the studio, he had another nervous breakdown. On doctors' orders, he closed up his Los Feliz house and moved back in with his family on West 22d Street. He had his quarters redecorated, adding a music room. In an effort to recover, he completely changed his lifestyle, dismissing his secretary and taking dancing lessons in preparation for a European concert tour he had planned for the summer with his sister Carmen.

"My freedom means more to me right now than all the money in the world," he said. "For 13 years I have been tied down. Now I can do as the mood strikes me. I can sit for hours at a time with my thoughts, or I can dash to a movie. Do whatever I wish. I never even had a chance to play tennis on our court before."[7]

Ramon also continued with two writing projects: a screenplay for a Spanish-language film that he planned to produce and direct, and his play *It's Another Story*, which he hoped to have produced at the Old Vic Theater in London that coming fall. "I have written a play about love called *It's Another Story*," Novarro told reporters. "Naturally, it is founded on my own experience of the cruelties and insincerities of the film trade—and my hero dies a happy, sweet death after the torments of being a star."[8]

Although he denied it, the story was somewhat autobiographical. The hero was a man who had been a romantic movie star for ten years. The play opens on his last day at the studio, and he leaves Hollywood for London, where he hopes to star in a play of his own authorship. Novarro wanted to produce the play in English, French, and Spanish before filming it.

His screenplay, titled *Contra la Corriente* (*Against the Current*), was based upon an incident at the 1932 Olympic Games, which were held in Los

Angeles. Novarro formed his own company called RNS Productions and invested $200,000 of his own money into the project. *Contra la Corriente* (1936) was to be the first of six productions planned by Novarro, but the other five never materialized. Filming began on March 14 at the Talisman Studios on Sunset Boulevard and continued over a 16-day shooting period.

The project was another family affair for the Samaniegos. Ramon hired Antonio as his assistant director, and Eduardo designed the sets. His uncle Ramon Guerrero and sister Carmen both performed. Angel, who was the paymaster, was hired by Shell Oil Company during the filming and broke the news to Ramon, who wished his younger brother success. Angel moved to northern California until his retirement in the early 1960s.

Ramon cast actress Luana Alcaniz as the heiress and Jose Caraballo as the Argentine swimmer who wins the world championship before he wins his bride. Location shooting continued around Los Angeles, and by mid–July, principal filming was completed. Ramon supervised the editing and final dubbing.

Ramon did not act in the film, but he appeared in a prologue in which he gave a tribute to Rex Ingram and encouraged people to support the film. *Contra la Corriente* was scheduled to be premiered in Ramon's hometown of Durango, but there is no proof that the event took place. There was a private preview in August, but the film did not have its official premiere until March 1936 in New York City.[9]

The *New York Times* said, tongue-in-cheek, "When Ramon Novarro transferred his activities from acting to writing and directing, it did not signify any epoch-making changes or improvements in the world of motion pictures."[10]

In Los Angeles the film was a success and packed the theaters for weeks. The *Los Angeles Times* said: "Hailed as a pioneer in the Spanish film field, the picture is an all–Novarro production. His personality is dominant in the story of the penniless youth which he wrote, in the music he synchronized, the players he chose and in the sets he designed."[11]

Novarro's stage play, *It's Another Story*, was not produced for reasons that were never explained. Instead, he left for England in August to star in a musical play called *A Royal Exchange*, along with his sister Carmen. The musical was about a film actor who pretends to be a prince and falls in love with a princess. It starred Doris Kenyon and Eddie Foy, Jr., and opened on December 6, 1935, at His Majesty's Theater. The theater critics hated the play.

The *London Times* said, "A pretty mess it is, when all's done. Mr. Novarro has a small, not unpleasing voice, and a certain mousy precision of manner— a certain modesty, too, which prevents him from pretending to be what he certainly is not; but as a romantic hero in glittering uniforms on the stage of His Majesty's, he is almost pathetically misplaced."[12]

After the performance, the cast lingered to give speeches, much to the

chagrin of the audience. Some members of the audience actually booed Novarro during his speech. Novarro called them radicals and rationalized the incident by saying, "The audience was really very nice to me, but you find people like those who caused the disturbance in many places."[13]

There were three curtain calls, and in two of them the curtain fell on Novarro's head, leaving the entire evening an embarrassment to everyone. To Novarro, the experience ranked with the film *Laughing Boy* and he would never discuss *A Royal Exchange* again.

"You know," Novarro once said, "I'm not sorry for anything that has ever happened to me. It has all been an experience, not wasted time. The only profitable emotion is suffering, anyway. After the grief passes, you comprehend so much more."[14]

While in London, he took the opportunity to record some of his former movie songs including "The Pagan Love Song," "Love Songs of the Nile," and "The Night Is Young." He also prepared for his next concert tour with Carmen, which began at the London Palladium and covered parts of Europe and Scotland.

The 20-week tour was highly successful but had its difficulties. In Budapest a theater owner did not pay him as agreed, so Novarro walked out. In another city, labor troubles with the theatrical employees caused a disruption in his performance. In Paris there was a misunderstanding over the extension of his contract, and he and Carmen were stranded without funds. And in Scotland he came down with a severe illness which put the entire tour on hold.

After returning to the United States, Ramon and Carmen performed their song and dance act at Toronto's Shea Theatre and stopped off in Chicago for a week of sold-out concerts. On June 10, 1936, they returned to Burbank and were greeted by their family, as well as Rex Ingram and Alice Terry, who had just returned to Hollywood after living abroad for many years.

At the airport, Alice, who was very fond of sweets and had gained several pounds, was resistant about appearing in photographs with Ramon. After much coaxing, she relented and gave Ramon a welcome home kiss for the shutter-bugs.[15] Novarro told reporters he would either accept an offer to tour the Orient or would direct and act in motion pictures. In the meantime, he rented a white farmhouse in Monterey which overlooked a valley near the sea and continued to study music and read scripts. He was in no hurry to make another picture. After almost two decades of endless work, he was having his first real holiday.

"I have been advised to make a picture immediately, tomorrow," Novarro

Opposite: **Novarro with his sister Carmen, en route to their European concert tour, 1935.**

Novarro is greeted at Burbank Airport by his former costar Alice Terry, June 1936, as he returns from his European concert tour.

told a friend. "They tell me it is fatal to be off the screen so long. Make anything! But I don't agree. You let your friends down when you play just any part. I'm going to wait for the right one!"[16]

Shortly after his return, Novarro came down with a serious case of jaundice, which it was assumed he had contracted overseas. During a crucial six-week period, he recuperated at the Santa Monica home of Dolores Del Rio. Doctors were not sure if he would make it at one point, but he pulled through and stayed with Dolores for the next nine months.

After recuperating, Novarro was ready to do another film and decided to go back to acting. Even though he was successful with his directing on *Contra la Corriente*, the work did not satisfy him. "The experiment only proved that directing was not my field," he later said. "I liked it, yes—but acting was my true métier."[17]

Novarro wanted the experience of directing because he had worked with at least four wonderful directors and believed it was a natural progression, but when it came to film work, he thought acting was more satisfying. Other than briefly taking over the directorial reigns of another film, Novarro never again sat in the director's chair.

After two years away from the daily grind of moviemaking, Novarro was bored. It was this boredom that prompted him eventually to sign with a studio that he believed was inferior. Republic Studios was known for Westerns and serials, but could it produce something to satisfy the whims of a former Latin heartthrob looking for employment?

Chapter Twenty-One

The Republic Years
(1937–1941)

Ramon Novarro's "comeback" is attracting quite a lot of attention. It's hardly surprising, of course. Few stars have ever attained the popularity he enjoyed for so many years and, in spite of his absence from the screen, most people have remembered him.

—Robert Coote[1]

Even though he wanted to work again, Novarro did nothing to help himself find a role. He would not ask for a job; he did read several scripts, but nothing interested him. He told a few friends about his desire and waited, hoping that something would come up.

Finally he received an offer from Republic Studios, which without his knowledge had a script written specially for him called *The Sheik Steps Out* (1937).[2] Republic thought the Novarro name would lend some prestige to the fledgling studio. Novarro read the scenario and liked it. He met with executives at Republic, and signed a contract to do a total of four pictures.

The Sheik Steps Out was a parody of the sheik films, including two of Novarro's—*The Arab* and *The Barbarian*. He liked the idea of satirizing his so-called "Latin lover" image, plus the role would allow him to sing a few songs, which were written for him by his friend Elsie Janis.

When it was announced that Novarro was making a comeback, the press speculated whether he would be successful. It had been more than two years since he had appeared before the camera, and secretly Republic crossed its fingers, hoping that filmgoers were interested. The studio was unaware that Novarro still received bags of fan mail each week demanding his return to the screen.

"Novarro was instantly friendly," recalled costar Robert Coote, "and particularly interested when he found I was English. He talked a lot about England, was very sorry, but very gracious, about the failure of his play in London. There was no trace of bitterness, and he told me that he hoped to have another try some day."[3]

The Sheik Steps Out was not the type of film Novarro was accustomed to making when he was at MGM; it was inexpensive and was shot in less than two weeks. In the hopes of insuring the film's success, Novarro gave unsolicited advice to both the director and his costars. His days as a romantic lead were nearing an end, and he knew if the film were a hit, he could work long enough to have a smooth transition as a character actor.

The film did well at the box office, and for the most part, critics were kind. Many reasoned the picture's success resulted in part from his fan's curiosity. *Variety* said, "Novarro speaks English distinctly and there is no reason why he should not regain some standing in films, if given a part in a major production where he would be assisted by competent actors."[4]

"I am so glad that the jury's verdict was for and not against *The Sheik Steps Out*," Ramon said. "Although you cannot fool me much, I am grateful and looking forward to doing in the near future, something that in my estimation will be deserving of your praises."[5]

Shortly after the holidays, Novarro gave a cocktail party in honor of Republic mogul Herbert Yates at his Los Feliz home. He announced that his next picture for Republic would be *A Desperate Adventure* and that he hoped his leading lady would be former MGM costar, Madge Evans. Someone suggested that he do another costume picture, as in his early days at MGM. He liked the idea but explained, "Republic feels that I should do a modern comedy first, and I seem to agree with them about it, because the most successful pictures at the present moment are just that and naturally, they want me to have a strong hold at the box office before they can afford to give me an expensive production."[6]

In March of 1938, Novarro and his sister Carmen took their concert act on the road again. In Chicago they played to a packed house at the State-Lake Theater, where Carmen performed her traditional "skirt" dances. Ramon sang his repertoire of movie songs, including "The Pagan Love Song," which became his signature piece. "I would like to sing 'Pagan Love Song' for you," he told his audience. "That is, of course, if you don't mind."[7]

Of course his fans were always agreeable. They were thrilled to hear him sing the love song which most of them imagined that he sang only for them.

He later wrote to his friend and pen pal, Eddie Zubbrick, "I had a wonderful week in Chicago and I feel grateful for the loyalty of your city."[8]

After Chicago the pair played a week in Detroit, where Ramon caught a bad cold, and then they returned to Los Angeles. Novarro was to begin *A Desperate Adventure* (1938), but because of script problems, the film was delayed until June. Because of the delay, Madge Evans was unavailable, so the role went to actress Marian Marsh.

A Desperate Adventure was a big disappointment to everyone. One reviewer said, "A picture that does not live up to its promises. Ramon Novarro is a graceful, charming, romantic actor with qualities that are rare to the screen. [Novarro] is deft and pleasing as an artist. Please Mr. Republic, give Novarro a real role."[9]

Unfortunately, Mr. Republic did not get the chance. After this letdown, Novarro asked to be released from his contract, even though the studio had a pirate story ready to begin filming. To him, working at Republic was an embarrassment, so Yates gave him his freedom and once again Ramon was unemployed.

Novarro's problem with alcohol was still a constant battle, with weeks, sometimes months, of sobriety but an eventual return to the bottle. He once had been very discreet about his drinking habits, but now he became careless, mixing his drinking with driving. On one such occasion, Novarro left the home of a friend and was driving down Sunset Boulevard when he struck a pedestrian crossing the street. Fortunately, the man was not badly injured, but police were summoned and Novarro was cited for reckless driving. At the trial, Novarro claimed that the man had become confused and was returning to the curb when he was struck. "I hit him unavoidably," Novarro told the judge, who ruled for the plaintiff.[10] The friend Novarro had visited later said that the actor had had a few drinks, but fortunately for Ramon, that did not come out in the trial.

Novarro also never had a long-term monogamous relationship, which may have compounded his drinking. His dalliances, however, were usually not with well-known men. One exception was Richard Halliburton, the author of best-selling books on travel and exploration such as *The Royal Road to Romance* and *The Flying Carpet*.[11]

In 1933, Hollywood asked Halliburton to star in a film called *India Speaks*, which was based on his adventures. Mary Pickford introduced the explorer to Novarro at a party at Pickfair, where a mutual attraction took place. They were soon involved in an affair.

Halliburton was a handsome, rugged individual, and no one suspected he was a homosexual. On many occasions he would take Novarro on excursions in his airplane called *The Flying Carpet*. When *India Speaks* was finished, Halliburton left Hollywood, but their relationship continued.

In March 1939, Halliburton left from China on a junk called the *Sea*

Dragon with a ten-man crew headed for San Francisco, where Ramon planned to meet him.[12] Several days into the journey, a typhoon arose in the Pacific, and the *Sea Dragon* was reported lost at sea. The U.S. Navy searched for survivors, but no traces were ever found of the explorer or his boat. He was declared legally dead the following October.

Early in 1940, Novarro was offered a role by famed French director Marcel L'Herbier. The film, titled *La Comédie du Bonheur* (1940), was a French-language film made in Rome. Shortly after his arrival, Novarro received word of the death of his uncle Ramon Guerrero from bronchial pneumonia. Guerrero was a linguist by trade and had done the Spanish translation for *Call of the Flesh;* he had also appeared as an actor in Ramon's production of *Contra la Corriente.* He was adored by the family and was laid to rest next to Novarro's brother Jose in the family plot at Calvary Cemetery.

La Comédie du Bonheur had a cast of French actors, including Michel Simon, Micheline Presle, and 20-year-old Louis Jourdan in his second film role. The story, with dialogue by Jean Cocteau, was about a man who escapes a mental institution and moves into a boardinghouse where he hires a troupe of carnival players to cheer up the unhappy tenants.

One day during shooting Novarro didn't show up on the set. The actor had not been paid in weeks and told L'Herbier that he would not work one minute longer. The director called the producer, who rushed over to Novarro's hotel and handed him a check. "Now, Mr. Novarro, let's go to the studio," he pleaded.

"Excuse me, signor," Novarro replied, "but we'll first stop at the bank."[13]

At the time, Europe was on the threshold of war, although life in Italy did not appear to reflect the impending events. "Theaters were open," Novarro recalled. "Cafes were gay as ever. And outwardly, life seemed to be going on as usual. Not until I learned that loudspeakers were being installed in all public places in Rome did I sense that the situation was ominous. I knew that they were being installed for some fateful message from Mussolini."[14]

Suddenly, L'Herbier was called back to France with the picture unfinished. The producer knew Novarro had experience as a director and asked him to finish *La Comédie du Bonheur,* which he did. The producer was pleased with Novarro's work and offered him other pictures to direct in Italy. The world situation interfered, however, and by June the entire cast had to flee the country. Novarro barely had time to board the refugee liner *Manhattan* and sail for New York.

On his return home at Burbank airport, Novarro told reporters that Americans should protect their freedom of speech at all costs. "Only by a free press," he said, "can this nation keep the world honestly informed of events today taking place over the globe."[15]

As for *La Comédie du Bonheur,* the film lay dormant for several months until a fire destroyed some of the negative. Marcel L'Herbier did his best to

Novarro on stage during one of his concert appearances at the State-Lake Theater in Chicago in 1940 (courtesy of Edward Zubbrick).

refilm it, but two of the cast members were already dead. When it finally premiered in Europe, it was very popular but was never shown in the States, mainly because of the war.

After Novarro returned from Italy, he read that Norma Shearer was starring in a film based on the best-selling novel *Escape* by Ethel Vance. Novarro was familiar with the story about the Nazi's persecution of the Jews and thought he would be perfect for the part of the Nazi general. He called Norma, who agreed with him and said that she would recommend him.

Novarro waited and waited until he eventually learned that Conrad Veidt was cast in the role. Norma never told Ramon why he didn't get the part, and their relationship grew cold. Sadly, he never spoke to her again.[16]

A few months later Novarro was contacted by New York agent Alan Brock about appearing in summer stock. Several theater managers urged Brock to sign Novarro, and after some careful thought (his last attempt at stage acting had been a failure), the actor agree. He was paid $200 a week (the same as Ethel Barrymore and Ina Claire were receiving) to star in the play *Candlelight*, which had been a New York stage success for Leslie Howard.

Brock never met Novarro in person until 12 years later, but he received good reports from the theater managers and each one praised Novarro, not only for his talent, but for being gracious and cooperative offstage as well.

When his stint in summer stock was over, Novarro returned to the concert stage and played a week at the State-Lake Theater in Chicago. A local reviewer noted that Novarro had poise, dignity, and vocal ability and did not resort to any "south of the border" sentimentality. "Anyhow his listeners applaud politely rather than vigorously," the reviewer continued, "and the matinee girls don't seem to lose their heads as they would for Valentino."[17]

Death overshadowed Novarro's life once again when his father passed away on November 15, 1940. Novarro was in New York at the time and returned home one day after his father's burial. Dr. Samaniego, who was 69, had undergone a prostatectomy the previous year. Death was attributed to myocardial degeneration or inflammation of the heart.[18]

A month after his father's death Novarro was involved in a head-on collision at the intersection of Sunset Boulevard and Havenhurst Avenue. The driver of the other car was injured, and Novarro received a concussion and two fractured ribs. In a letter to a friend, he wrote: "but fortunately and truly, by the grace of God, I came out with only minor injuries. However, I was in the hospital for almost three weeks and spent my Christmas there, but God is everywhere and He was there, so I was very happy."[19]

Novarro, who gave his occupation as a concert singer, was arrested and charged with driving over the center line and failing to make a proper turn. He pleaded not guilty and was ordered to stand trial, but he later changed his plea to guilty and was fined $23.

Novarro would accumulate several more offenses over the next two decades, but the court's punishment was seldom more than a fine. But on those rare occasions, when it was necessary, Novarro knew all the tricks to get around a suspended license. He was about to meet a young man who would become a witness to Novarro's dark side and could have been a stabilizing force in the actor's life, if only Ramon would have allowed him that role.

Chapter Twenty-Two

The Loss of Stardom
(1941–1944)

I will say this, his days of stardom were over when I first
met him. Those days were behind him. He was drifting
steadily downward in alcoholism—he was enslaved by
alcoholism. And this was basically his downfall.
                                            —Don Atkins[1]

By the early 1940s, Novarro very seldom saw anyone from his MGM
days, except maybe Rex Ingram and Alice Terry and, on occasion, Gloria
Swanson. Most of his time was spent with his family or with friends who
were not in the business.

One such friend was Don Atkins, who became acquainted with Novarro
through an unusual incident. Early in 1940, Atkins went to the Hollywood
Women's Club to see Norvel, who was known as the "astrologer to the stars."[2]
Don was impressed by the soothsayer's performance and made an appointment the following day for a personal reading. "You're going to meet an older
movie star," Norvel told him, "and this will be the start of a very close relationship. I keep getting the letter 'R,' the letter 'N.' 'R ... N.'... It's Ramon
Novarro! You're going to meet him and he will be a very important person in
your life."

Norvel also told Atkins that he would meet Novarro through a woman.
Don was intrigued but put the matter behind him. He had better things to

do because he had recently inherited a large sum of money and by his own admission was "frittering away his time." Months later he received a call from his friend, Juliette Marglin, who had a beauty shop on Sunset Boulevard with many star clients. "Paulette Goddard and Ramon Novarro are coming over," she told Don. "I want you to meet Ramon. I think you'll like him."

"I certainly will be there," he told her. Since he had never mentioned Norvel's prediction to her, or anyone, Don found her invitation fascinating. When he met Ramon, they became instant friends, just as Norvel had predicted. Don immediately began calling his new friend, "Ramonito."

"I had a crush on him for a long time," Don said. "Ramon had lustrous blue-black hair and beautiful alabaster skin. He was always impeccably dressed, except when he was drinking."

It wasn't long before Don learned that alcohol was a major part of Ramon's life. By now, Novarro was a compulsive drinker. There were periods of sobriety, but any problem would bring on a relapse. Novarro's depression was caused by many things, including the fact that his stardom had faded. Also, he could not reconcile his homosexuality with his Catholicism, a very important part of his life. Ramon always invoked the Virgin Mary and repeated the Rosary, which immensely annoyed Don, who was not devout in any religion.

To insure their privacy, Ramon bought a three-story house on North Catalina Drive, one block north of Los Feliz Boulevard. When Ramon would visit, he would enter by a side door where he would not be seen by anyone on the street. Even though they had a small circle of friends, both men were loners and were more comfortable in one-on-one situations.

Many times Ramon would relax on the second floor, reading or listening to music. Other times he would nervously pace back and forth, eventually leaving and telling Don he had to do this or that. Later, friends would tell Don that they had seen Ramon cruising on Sunset Boulevard, something he did quite often.

Ramon and Don had an open relationship. Don knew that Ramon could not commit completely to one person; he could not give of himself to that extent. He needed unattached relationships that allowed him his freedom. "We were very close friends," Don said, "but was I the love of his life? No, I was not."

It was Novarro's drinking that most bothered Don, especially when he would drive. Don would often take the wheel, but many times Ramon insisted on driving. On October 28, 1941, they were driving on Hollywood Boulevard in a car Novarro had borrowed from his agent, Rebecca Ravenswood. Ramon had been drinking heavily and stalled the car as they approached Cherokee Street.

Two policemen approached, and suspecting that Novarro was inebriated, they tried to pull him, from the car. Don's temper got the best of him, and he began to berate the officers. Even though he was sober, he was arrested along with Novarro and taken to the Hollywood police station. Don lied and gave the police a fake name; he was placed in the drunk tank with Novarro. The next morning Novarro called his attorney, Stanley Barnes, to bail him out.

"Fifty dollars or 20 days," the judge demanded. As Barnes stepped forward to pay the bail, Novarro pointed to Don and said, "Pay his fine too." The press was waiting for them as they left the station.

"The police arrested me when I had trouble with the engine at a boulevard stop," he told reporters. "They said I was drunk. I had taken some drinks, yes, but what could I do? I pleaded guilty: it is so much easier and quicker."

After they left, reporters asked Stanley Barnes if Novarro was down on his luck. "Novarro is not broke," Barnes replied. "He has ample funds in trust with which he can live in comfort for the rest of his life. This is just an unfortunate accident."[3]

Knowing Novarro was not going to change, Don gave him a piece of advice. "Ramonito, put a $100 bill in your wallet over your license. If we're stopped again, hand the officer your license and the $100 bill. I'm sure it will take care of itself."

Sometime later they were stopped again for erratic driving. Novarro gave his wallet to the officer, along with the $100 bill. After toying with it for a few minutes, the policeman handed the wallet back and warned Novarro to be more careful. The $100 bill was, of course, gone.

Don thought Ramon was one of the most charming and gracious men he knew, but he became a different person when drinking. His moods changed by the hour. One moment he would be depressed, then he would have a period of great euphoria that would end in a fit of anger.

The one person Ramon felt comfortable around was his cousin, Dolores Del Rio. With her, he opened up and seemed much happier; she could put a smile on his face and change his moods. Don also enjoyed his visits with Ramon to Dolores' art deco home near Santa Monica. Many times the three of them would drive to La Jolla for a picnic, where they would build sand castles, tell dirty jokes, and splash each other, just like kids. During these times, there was no drinking or fighting, and he was very happy.

Dolores knew about Ramon's sexual preference and openly joked about it. Of his days at MGM, she said, "Mr. Mayer could not believe my cousin was homosexual. He did not really know what a homosexual was. He felt if he forced Ramon to marry, he could convert him."[4]

Ramon felt no condemnation in her presence. Unfortunately, it was not the same with his own family. Even though they loved him, the same spirit of acceptance was not felt on West 22d Street. Whenever Don dined there, Novarro would warn him, "You are not to bring up any of our friends or any of the places that we go."

Don was certain that Ramon's family knew about his homosexuality, even though the subject was never discussed. Dinner at the Samaniegos was always uncomfortable. Don remembered Ramon's mother as being very gracious—not extremely friendly—but he liked her. She had fine features and was always dressed in black, with her hair pulled back in a bun.

Even though the family was always polite, Don felt a coolness in their behavior towards him. Most evenings there was very little conversation, but when someone did speak, it was usually in Spanish, which was their way of excluding him. "I always felt slightly ill at ease," Don said. "They didn't deliberately make me feel ill at ease, but I didn't feel I was part of it."

"During dinner," he added, "I would look at Ramon and he would look at me. All that time I kept thinking how I wanted to get out of there."

One evening when the family was out, Don was invited to an intimate dinner. Ramon decorated the garden with hanging lanterns and ordered several boxes of fireflies to be released during dinner. Later Ramon sang and played the piano and recited poetry, which was an example of a sober Ramon Novarro. "He was a sweet and loving person," Don remembered, "and helped many people." Unfortunately, Novarro's periods of sobriety were fleeting.

In April 1942, Ramon was again arrested for drunk driving. At his trial, he was ordered to surrender his driver's license for six months and advised to see a psychiatrist. He was placed on a one-year probation and told if he took a drink during that time, "he must go to jail."[5] Novarro was clever enough, however, to devise little tricks to get around the law. If he could not borrow a friend's license, he would use one of two licenses that he had; one for Ramon Novarro and the other for Ramon Samaniego.

Don hoped that going back to work would help Ramon and encouraged him to do so many times. Often Ramon would tell him, "I want to do another *Ben-Hur*."

"You know, Ramonito," Don told him, "the perfect movie for you would be *The Mark of Zorro*." As early as 1932, it was proposed to Irving Thalberg to cast Novarro as Zorro. "Acquire it for your own use, for it's a honey," wrote one critic. "'Zorro' would bring into play your deft and charming talents as none of your recent pictures have done."[6] Years later Novarro's friend from Chicago, Eddie Zubbrick, proposed the same thing to him while he was at Republic. "Your suggestions about 'Zorro' are excellent," Novarro replied, "but Republic has done a new version in serial form with John Carroll in it, and I hear it is very good."[7]

Don believed that Ramon's accent was very much against him and that Zorro would have been the ideal role. Ramon's personality and demeanor suited the character perfectly. His agent, Rebecca Ravenswood, petitioned the

Opposite: **Novarro being released from the Hollywood jail after one of his many drunk driving arrests, October 1941.**

Novarro with his cousin, actress Dolores Del Rio.

studios, but Twentieth Century–Fox had just filmed a successful version of *The Mark of Zorro* (1940) two years earlier with Tyrone Power, and she was told it was too soon for another version. Don thought that Rebecca Ravenswood was useless to Ramon's career. "Ramon had a group of losers around him," he said, "who promised everything and delivered nothing."

Because World War II was escalating in Europe and the South Seas, everyone was urged to do their part for the war effort. In August 1942, Novarro surprised everyone when he announced that he wanted to serve America as a soldier, even though he was too old for the draft. There was another problem; Novarro was not an American citizen, and according to the Mexican constitution, he would lose his birthright if he enlisted in a foreign army. He telegraphed a formal petition to the permanent committee of the Congress of Mexico, asking permission to join the United States Army. He asked for written assurance guaranteeing him his Mexican citizenship. The committee, which has the power to make exceptions in special cases, surprisingly granted Novarro's request a week later. It was the first time the government had given such permission; it had previously refused 5,000 similar applications.[8]

Was this a fantasy on Novarro's part or at the very least a publicity ruse? Maybe he assumed the Mexican government would deny his request because it had never given its permission before. In any case, a month later he boarded a plane for Mexico City and told reporters that he would first offer his services as a soldier to his native Mexico.

Upon arrival in Mexico City, he met with President Manuel Avila Camacho who graciously told him he would be rendering Mexico as much service by aiding its film industry as by entering the armed services. So Novarro agreed to perform in a film which would be made entirely in Mexico. It would take about a year to find a suitable project and finish all the preproduction; in the meantime, Novarro returned to Los Angeles.

Around this time, Novarro met Samson DeBrier, who in later years became quite an oddity in Hollywood.[9] DeBrier had interviewed Novarro in 1937 at a Brooklyn theater for radio station WMCA in New York. He found Novarro to be gracious but thought his appearance at this little theater was quite a step down from his glory days at the much larger Capitol Theater.

They corresponded over the next few years until DeBrier moved to Los Angeles in 1942. Sometime later, on June 14, 1943, Novarro was stopped by police and was asked to perform a field sobriety test. Several times he failed to walk a straight line, and he was arrested for drunk driving. Two days later Novarro appeared at his arraignment and pleaded not guilty, asking for a jury trial, which the judge set for June 30. DeBrier read the account of Novarro's arrest in the newspaper and wrote to him asking if he could be of any help.

"Thank you so much for your fine letter," Novarro wrote to DeBrier. "My trial, as you know, has been postponed for July 29, but I have great hopes that it might be arranged before that. If that is the case, I will be leaving for Mexico to do a picture and won't be back until the end of October."[10]

Meanwhile, Novarro's relationship with Don Atkins was deteriorating. They continued to argue more every day, mostly over money. Don's inheritance had been spent, and Ramon would give him money to cover the bills. Finally, Ramon sold the North Catalina Drive house, and Don moved to a large two-story house on Hollywood Boulevard. The new house was not as private, which bothered Ramon because there was a chance he might be seen.

Because Don had to rent out the extra rooms to cover expenses, there was no longer the privacy they had once enjoyed. The two continued to drift apart, and Don began seeing other people. Ramon was usually drunk when he did visit, and the evening would end in an argument. Eventually, Ramon no longer visited. A few years later Don moved to New York City and never saw Ramon again.

Soon Ramon would travel to Mexico to begin work on *La Virgen que Forjó una Patria*, his contribution to Mexico's film industry. The remainder of the decade would be relatively quiet until he finally saw a resurgence in his career that almost rivaled his days at MGM.

Chapter Twenty-Three

Comeback (1944–1951)

I am just living my life backwards. I worked when I should have been in school…. Now I'm studying when I should be working.

—Ramon Novarro[1]

In October, Novarro left for Mexico City to begin filming *La Virgen que Forjó una Patria* at Clasa Studios.[2] One day he visited actress Lupita Tovar, who was shooting a film on a neighboring soundstage. Lupita first met Ramon in 1929 at a benefit at his Los Feliz home that was arranged by the Mexican counsel. "I liked him very much," Tovar recalled. "He was a very, very nice person, beautifully mannered and well-educated."

After lunch, however, Ramon was so drunk that he could hardly stand. "I guess the fact that he lost his career was hard to take, and he started drinking," Tovar said.[3] That was the last time she ever saw him.

La Virgen que Forjó una Patria was so successful in Mexico and other Latin-American countries that President Camacho decorated Novarro, saying his performance contributed to religious patriotism. Critics in the United States gave the film favorable reviews but said the plot unfolded so tediously that it had a slim chance in America except at art houses. But they were certain about Novarro's part in the film. "Ramon Novarro is forthright as the peon who sees the saint," *Variety* said, "displaying some of his old screen skill. It's a difficult role, but he does it well."[4]

After finishing *La Virgen que Forjó una Patria*, Novarro became somewhat reclusive, spending most of his time dabbling in real estate. He commissioned his brother Eduardo to design a business structure on the northeast corner of Van Nuys Boulevard and Gilmore Street. Upon completion, the J. C. Penney Company occupied the building for more than 25 years.

Once again Novarro considered entering a monastery, and he made several visits to Trappist retreats in Ohio and Indiana. The priests were honest and told him that it was a hard life and he simply did not have the vocation. "I tried to become a Jesuit, but they said I was too old," he recalled, "and of course they were right. And then I contemplated the life of a Trappist monk. Imagine, an actor taking a vow of silence."[5]

It had been 10 years since Ramon Novarro had acted in an American film. Novarro was 49 years old, and his days of stardom were far behind him. The only acting he had done recently was two seasons in summer stock starring in *Command to Love, Tovarich*, and a French play called *In the Shadows of the Harem*.

However, a new career as a character actor was about to open up to him. Director John Huston asked Novarro if he would accept a small role in his upcoming film for Columbia, *We Were Strangers* (1949), which was to star John Garfield and Jennifer Jones.

"It was a small but important role, the chief of a Cuban revolution," Novarro said. "Something I had never done before, but a chance for real acting. Huston gave me the part without making a test. He was very gracious."[6]

Novarro's looks had changed drastically over the previous five years. He had gained more than 20 pounds, and his now gray hair was thinning. For the part, he grew a scrubby beard, wore pince-nez glasses, and spoke in a high-pitched voice. When the film premiered, *Variety* said, "Ramon Novarro is totally unrecognizable from his youthful, romantic stints. Novarro works in an effective metallic, fast-talking quality in the part of a rebel chief."[7]

Novarro was thrilled with the results of his part in *We Were Strangers*. "This role was in a sense a test," Novarro claimed. "Out of it came a bigger part in *The Big Steal*—that of Colonel Ortega, a Mexican police official who is very proud of his knowledge of the English language."[8]

Novarro's publicist, Leonard Shannon, was responsible for getting Novarro the part in *The Big Steal* (1949), which was made at RKO and starred Robert Mitchum and Jane Greer. The story was a standard chase mystery with Novarro as the chief of police of a small Mexican town.

At the time, Novarro's mother was very ill with a malignancy of the colon. After a preliminary colostomy operation, she was scheduled to have another operation two months later. Since Ramon would soon be going on location to Mexico for filming, he moved his mother into a bungalow of an apartment building he owned on Riverside Drive. There Carmen and her husband, George, could look after her.

When George Raft had to bow out of *The Big Steal*, RKO signed Robert

Mitchum, even though he had been arrested on August 31, 1948, for possession of marijuana at the Laurel Canyon cottage of actress Lila Leeds. Massive newspaper coverage of the event led RKO to release a statement hoping that Mitchum's prominence in the film industry would not "deprive him of the rights and privileges of every American citizen to receive fair play."[9]

Novarro came in for a sound and photo test on January 18, 1949, and filming was hurried into production on January 26. Originally, Lizabeth Scott was to play the female lead, but she only worked for three days and then left the picture. Many claimed it was because of Mitchum's arrest. At any rate, former costar Jane Greer was signed to replace her. Years later Greer recalled how Novarro would "bring in scrapbooks on his career and regale us with stories from his MGM days."[10]

On February 12, the cast left for Tehuacan, Mexico, for principal filming. When they returned ten days later, Novarro suffered a devastating loss. Mrs. Samaniego died suddenly of a blood clot at California Hospital. Ramon was grief stricken; his mother, the woman whom he idolized, was gone. After a requiem mass was said at St. Agnes Church, Mrs. Samaniego was laid to rest next to her husband at Calvary Cemetery.

Two months later Novarro and the rest of the cast returned to Tehuacan and filmed several scenes with interiors shot at Estudios Churubusco. Ten days later filming was completed, and the cast returned to Los Angeles. One day a reporter interviewed Novarro at the RKO commissary and asked him about the old days.

"When I was a leading man," Novarro told him, "every part was the same. I was always the hero—with no vices—reciting practically the same line to the leading lady."

When asked how pictures differed from his time, Novarro said, "The current crop of movie heroes are less handicapped than the old ones. They are more human. The leading men of silent films were always Adonis's and Apollos—no one really is, of course."

During the interview, the waitress set a large piece of apple pie before him. "And, ah," Novarro added, "in the old days I couldn't eat much dessert. I had to watch my figure. Is it not better to be a character actor?"[11]

Novarro earned $8,000 for his role in *The Big Steal* and some of the best reviews of his career. *Time* magazine said, "As the gentle, humorous, sly Mexican army colonel, he steals the show."[12] Novarro's performance as Colonel Ortega drew more praise at previews than anyone's, including Mitchum's or Greer's. RKO offered him a series of films with Colonel Ortega as the central figure. Novarro was flattered, but politely turned the studio down. "I don't want to be typed," he said. "I belong to no studio; it is better just to take the parts as they come along. I want the right to say yes or no to them all."[13]

With his mother now gone, Ramon sold his Los Feliz home and the family home on West 22d Street. Also gone was Novarro's Teatro Intimo, which had been sitting dark for many years. "What would my youngest brother and I do in a house of 17 rooms?" he asked. "I would be a slave to my possessions—and I don't like that."[14]

Besides, Eduardo was getting married in July in Mexico and Ramon would be alone, so he moved into the apartment building he had built 10 years earlier.[15] In the living room of his fourth floor apartment, Novarro kept religious icons and memorabilia of his career, including the sword he wore in *The Prisoner of Zenda*. He continued to live there for the next 15 years.

Novarro divided his time between his North Hollywood apartment and a 49-acre ranch he purchased at Pala, California, that he named *El Rosario*. When asked what he grew there, he replied: "Now only good wishes for everybody. Later I intend to plant avocados—if the movies don't interfere."[16]

But the movies did interfere—for the next two years anyway. In the fall of 1949, Novarro returned to MGM Studios for a part in his first Western. Even though *The Outriders* (1950) was filmed mostly on location, one can only wonder what went through his mind as he stepped back onto the lot for the first time in 15 years. Did Louis B. Mayer, who was nearing the end of his reign at the studio, welcome him with open arms? History, unfortunately did not record the incident, but, regardless of Louis B. Mayer's reaction, the *Hollywood Reporter* was enthusiastic about his return, writing, "Ramon Novarro's emergence as a character actor continues to be one of the joys of present day filmgoing."[17]

On December 20, 1949, Novarro attended a get-together of Hollywood "old-timers." The event marked the opening of a branch of the California Bank at Selma and Vine streets. The site was the original location of Famous Players–Lasky, where Novarro had made his debut as an extra. Cecil B. DeMille presided over more than 50 stars who had at one time worked on the old movie lot, including Blanche Sweet, Francis X. Bushman, Mae Murray, and Theda Bara. When Novarro was asked what he thought of the modern heroes of film, he replied: "Today the hero can even take a poke at the leading lady. In my time, a hero who hit the girl just once would have been out. Sometimes, though, I think today's leading men get a little too rough in their treatment of the ladies."[18]

Novarro took a small part in another MGM film called *Crisis* (1950), which starred Cary Grant and was written and directed by Richard Brooks. Novarro replaced Mexican character actor Rudolph Acosta in the role of Colonel Adragon. Gilbert Roland, a friend of Novarro's for 25 years, also costarred.

This part was different from any Novarro had ever played. Adragon was a merciless tyrant who would do anything for the cause of the dictator, played by Jose Ferrer. Novarro was excellent in an otherwise disappointing film.

Even though Novarro was again working on the back lot at MGM, the experience was less than joyful for him, mostly because of director Richard

Novarro relaxes at his ranch, El Rosario, near Pala, California.

Brooks. Novarro worked on the film for six weeks, and during that time, Brooks made it clear that he didn't want Novarro around. Gilbert Roland saw what was happening, and when Novarro was not provided a cast chair, he stepped in to defend his friend. Roland thought Novarro was not given the consideration that a star of his stature deserved, and he created an uproar all the way to Mayer's office.[19] Even though Novarro was treated better after the incident, it affected him negatively. After filming was completed in February, he checked into Scripps Clinic for a rest and to dry out.

When *Crisis* was previewed at the Picwood Theater, one theatergoer proclaimed, "Ramon Novarro—excellent!" Another asked, "Why not give Novarro bigger parts?" When asked how he liked his part as the bad guy, Novarro replied, "Heroes were fun to play ... but heels take a bit of doing."[20]

Over the years Novarro had continued his friendship with Rex Ingram and Alice Terry. The Ingrams were now retired, and Rex spent most of his time traveling around the world and sculpting, while Alice took up painting. Ingram contracted malaria on one of his travels, and his health never fully recovered. On July 21, 1950, the day after he checked into a hospital for X-rays, Rex Ingram died suddenly at the age of 58. Ramon accompanied Alice to Ingram's funeral at Forest Lawn Cemetery, where the director's body was cremated.

Even though Alice Terry had been retired for twenty years, Novarro's career was experiencing a new resurgence. He had appeared in almost every major entertainment medium: vaudeville, theater, concert stage, motion pictures—both silent and talking—and, on occasion, radio. However, he was about to enter into a medium that was in its infancy and would give him major exposure for the remainder of his career.

Chapter Twenty-Four

Ramon Novarro Film Club (1952–1959)

I had represented at least fifty percent of the already famous stars of stage and screen. Few of them could approach Novarro when it came to dedication and a basic knowledge of his own special talents.

—Alan Brock[1]

Beginning in February 1952, Novarro was asked to make appearances on television. His first was on the *Ken Murray Show*, which was produced in New York. Alan Brock, who had scheduled his appearances in summer stock in 1940, made all the arrangements. Until then, the two had never met, but they were finally introduced at New York's Warwick Hotel, where Brock had his offices. After several visits, the two began a close friendship. Brock thought that Novarro was real, direct, and warm. "Nothing phony, nothing theatrical," Brock recalled. "He appeared naive, but underneath he was sharp and knowing."[2]

In the winter of 1954, Ramon began making yearly trips to Europe on his favorite ship, the Italian liner *Andrea Doria*, until it collided with a Swedish liner and sank off the coast of Nantucket. His first stop that year was Barcelona, where he visited his sister Rosa, who was mother superior at the Order of Sisters of Charity in Teruel, Spain. Ramon was thinking about selling his ranch, *El Rosario*, and needed time to sort things out.

"The deer eat all that grows above ground," he said, "and the gophers eat all below."[3]

Ramon's next stop was London, which he had not visited since his disastrous experience in the play *A Royal Exchange*. At a small press conference in his room at the Savoy, someone brought up the subject of marriage. Ramon laughed and said, "I have often been in love, but never married. You see, I was too frightened of divorce."[4]

While in London, Ramon threw a party at the Savoy for 18 members of the Ramon Novarro Film Club, most of whom had never before met their idol. For more than 25 years the club had remained faithful to the actor and his career. After welcoming the ladies, Ramon prepared cocktails—a fiery concoction he invented that was named after the Mexican volcano, Popocatepetl. After dinner, Ramon told stories about his films and famous costars. Someone asked what had become of his leading ladies, especially Alice Terry, Barbara La Marr, and May McAvoy.

"Barbara is dead," Ramon replied, "It was T. B. You know they had to keep thin in those days. Alice I often see. She lives nearby in a nice house. May, she is doing extra work in the studios. It's a crime."

As the evening wore on, Ramon told them: "This party's getting dull. Let's have some liqueurs." The conversation soon loosened up, and everyone positioned their chairs around Ramon to hear more stories of Hollywood. Someone asked Ramon who his favorite stars of the present day were. He told them that Richard Burton was a great actor and Anna Magnani was an equally great actress. He talked about Garbo, who he said was more than beautiful and had "something indefinably superior."[5] When an admirer asked if he would write his biography, Novarro replied, "No, I would be the only one to read it and it would bore me."[6]

One by one the ladies left to return to their husbands, but at midnight, seven still remained to listen to Ramon's stories of the Golden Era. The following day he continued his vacation to Paris, and then he went to Rome, where he wrote a letter to the Film Club.

"Just a line to let you know I am wanted at home to decide what to do with the ranch and other things, so I think it prudent to return, and I'm sailing on the *Andrea Doria* from Naples on March 11. I go back with sweet memories, and deeply grateful for them. By that I mean London. God bless you all. Ramon."[7]

He arrived back in California on April 13 and drove to El Rosario the following Tuesday. Novarro decided to keep the ranch, using it to meditate, raise strawberries, and tend to five cats and his dog named Chepo. Ramon would volunteer at the local Pala Mission, giving of his time and money to those who were in need.[8] "All I have down here now in my own house is a lot of things I didn't need in my San Fernando Valley residence," he told friends.[9]

Novarro gives a party for members of his Ramon Novarro Film Club at the Savoy Hotel in London, 1954. Surrounding Novarro from left are, Mary Greenhill; Margaret Neville; Audrey Homan, president; and Molly Sutcliffe.

It was while living at El Rosario that Novarro began a film project based on Owen Wister's *Padre Ignacio*, the story of a remarkable California mission priest who was once an operatic singing star. He bought the film rights in 1938 after the story was brought to his attention in England by William Hutchinson, who was then the youngest member of Parliament. "The story haunted me constantly through the years," he recalled, "and I began to dedicate myself to preparing it for pictures when I took up my residence on my ranch at Pala."

Over the next five years, Novarro made several unsuccessful attempts to have the film made. Once again he tried doing everything himself, including producing, writing, and starring in the picture. The estimate to produce his screenplay, which he called *Just Passing By*, was $500,000 if he shot it on location in Spain. "While the locale is lower California," he told a friend, "it is odd, but I believe we will be able to make the film very successfully on location in Spain. We can effect great economy in our operations there."[10]

Unfortunately, things failed to materialize, and the deal fell through. Novarro would try again the next year, but that effort also failed, so he put it on the shelf. Several times over the years he would dust it off and consider having it made, but it never came to pass.

In April 1956, Novarro attended a special party of more than 200 silent film stars given by Mary Pickford and her husband, Charles "Buddy" Rogers, at Pickfair. At the party, Novarro ran into Alan Brock, who disclosed a plan to open an office representing a few of the former stars who were present at Pickfair that day. Brock recalled, "We were both aware of the many new producers of TV, motion pictures and stage who were either too young to know many of the top stars of the twenties or else too uninformed."

Before the afternoon was over, Brock had won Ramon over. "Alan, it would give me great pleasure to be able to help you finance this project," he said. "I would feel honored if you would allow me to help."[11] That day the entire operation was founded on the cooperation of six former film stars who agreed to be represented by Alan Brock for all stage, TV, and motion picture appearances on the East Coast, each one helping with office expenses.

While on another trip to Europe, Novarro stopped in London to visit with British actor Patrick Brock. Brock told him that Joan Crawford was in town filming *The Story of Esther Costello* (1957) and was staying at his hotel. "We rang her apartment in the hotel and found her quite alone and free," Patrick recalled, "the surprising position of a big star."

Crawford was overjoyed at seeing Ramon again after all these years. The two talked all evening, catching up on old times. A few days later Brock and Novarro drove outside London to visit Crawford on the set. Again, she greeted them warmly and introduced Novarro to the entire cast and crew, many of whom remembered him from his MGM days. On the drive back to town, Brock asked Novarro, "Do you find her much changed?"

"No," he answered sweetly. "She was a little plumper then."[12]

Talking to Joan Crawford brought back a lot of memories from the old days. It had been more than 30 years since Novarro had sat on the podium at Metro-Goldwyn-Mayer and observed the opening ceremonies of the studio which became one of Hollywood's biggest and best. By the late fifties, however, the lion's roar was beginning to weaken, and the once mighty studio was seeing a decline in its past glory.[13] Television was beginning to rival feature films as people stayed home to watch their favorite shows. The studios saw a way, however, to make money on this new medium by selling their inventory of old films to television.

In November 1957, Novarro and several other Hollywood celebrities were honored by the George Eastman House. When he arrived in Rochester, New York, Novarro was surprised to learn that director Frank Borzage and singer Maurice Chevalier were on the same plane. Chevalier was introduced to Ramon and immediately grabbed his hand and exclaimed, "I've been wanting to meet you for years—ever since I saw *Ben-Hur!*"[14]

The following spring Ramon was not feeling well and went for a physical checkup, where it was discovered that he had low blood pressure. "You don't like what you're doing," the doctor told him. "Why not go back to the entertainment world?"

It had been six years since Novarro had been in front of a camera. When he was offered a role in *The Nine Lives of Elfego Baca* series for *Walt Disney Presents*, which was made for both television and theaters, he accepted. Shortly after filming began, Ramon said of his doctor's advice: "He's right. I was bored. I haven't felt this healthy in years."[15]

On January 3, 1959, less than a month after the episodes aired, Novarro was driving on Hollywood Boulevard and ran a red light at Highland Avenue. He was stopped by police officers who reported that Novarro had become abusive and had insisted he was not drunk. "I only had a bourbon and soda—or maybe three—at my sister's," he told them.[16]

Novarro failed a field sobriety test and was arrested. He was freed that day on $263 bail and ordered to appear in municipal court. At his arraignment, Novarro pleaded not guilty and asked for a jury trial, but he later reversed his plea and paid the fine.

Ironically, MGM's glory days would be book-ended by the same film. In 1958 the studio announced it was going to remake *Ben-Hur*, with principal filming again in Italy. The production problems that plagued the studio more than 30 years earlier were but a memory. Cedric Gibbons and J. J. Cohn were among the few at MGM who remembered the first fiasco.

The film premiered in November 1959 at Loew's State Theater in New York City to an audience of more than 1,800. Charlton Heston starred in the role originally played by Novarro, with Stephen Boyd as Messala. Novarro was invited as a guest to the premiere, along with Carmel Myers, who played Iras in the original.

"A curious thing happened," Novarro recalled. "The audience was rooting out loud for Messala to win the chariot race. The anti-hero was already in then, and he is even more so as time has passed. I think had I been Charlton Heston, I would have wanted to play Messala."[17] Afterward, Novarro and Heston met and shook hands for photographers.

Ben-Hur proved to be a critical and box-office success. The following year the film won a record 11 Academy Awards, including Best Picture. At the Golden Globe ceremonies that same year, *Ben-Hur* was once again a big winner. In recognition of Novarro's contribution to the legend of *Ben-Hur*, he and fellow actor Francis X. Bushman were given a special Golden Globe award for their part in the silent film classic.

It is surprising that Novarro still got noticed after 40 years in the business, albeit not always in a good way. Unknown to him, he was about to accept what would become his last movie role and to have another embarrassing scrape with the law that would bring him the most widespread publicity he had received in almost 25 years.

Chapter Twenty-Five

Broadway (1960–1965)

John Barrymore once told me that if I ever got a chance to appear in a film directed by George Cukor it would be an experience I'd value—and I did greatly enjoy every moment working for Mr. Cukor.
> —Ramon Novarro[1]

When director George Cukor began work on *Heller in Pink Tights* (1960), he called Novarro and asked if he would take a small but effective part in the new Paramount production. It had been almost ten years since Novarro had appeared in a motion picture, so he gladly accepted the director's offer.

Anthony Quinn and the Italian beauty Sophia Loren starred, along with former child actress Margaret O'Brien, who remembered Novarro as "very kind and charming, though he stayed mostly to himself during filming."[2]

Paramount almost didn't use Novarro because of his recent drunk driving arrest and the rumors of his sexuality. Fortunately, Cukor fought the studio on this issue. "Novarro was still good-looking," Cukor recalled. "He was an exotically beautiful young man. In the twenties, he was almost as popular as Valentino, but he had far more class."[3]

Cukor was also a homosexual and related to Novarro's problems. "Poor Ramon," Cukor said. "He was a very unhappy and sensitive fellow, and a rather lost one."[4]

Three months after *Heller in Pink Tights* premiered, Novarro was arrested twice for drunk driving within a 48-hour period. The first offense occurred after his car ran into the rear of a bus on Hollywood Boulevard. After failing a field sobriety test, Novarro was taken to the Hollywood jail, where he told the arresting officers, "I just had a glass of sherry."[5]

Two nights later, on May 28, 1960, Novarro was driving through North Hollywood Park, which was notorious for its cruising, when he struck a parked car on Westpark Drive. He again failed the sobriety test and was arrested. This time he told officers he had had only "two gin drinks."[6] In both cases he was released on bail pending an appearance in court.

Six weeks later at the trial the jury deadlocked on a more serious charge and convicted Novarro of driving while under the influence of nonnarcotic drugs. He was fined $250. The actor explained that he was an extremely nervous man and took tranquilizers. "I always have a little wine or a cocktail with my evening meals," he explained. "The pills and the drinks did not mix. So I got arrested. My lawyer advised me it would be better to plead guilty rather than go through a headlined trial. I suppose he was right."[7]

Nearly two years later, on February 20, 1962, Novarro was driving through the intersection of Sunland Boulevard and San Fernando Road when he ran a red light and hit another car. After a sobriety test, police arrested him for driving under the influence. "I am old and I just want to die," he allegedly told officers. Unfortunately, his statement was picked up by the press, but Novarro denied having said it. "I speak with an accent still—I've never been able to lose it," he explained, "and, naturally, on such an occasion, I was nervous. They must have misunderstood—or maybe it made a better story to misunderstand."

He said he was concerned about the notoriety and the possibility that people might think he was a common drunk. He admitted being arrested before on the same charge and claimed that he had in fact said: "I'd sooner die than have this happen again. Actually—and this is very true, I haven't had more than two drinks in any one day in more than 20 years."

This was not true, but it made his explanation more plausible. Before he could deny making his "death wish," he began receiving mail from around the world. Some were letters of encouragement from fans, and others scolded him for thinking his life was over. One woman wrote to say he should not think such thoughts but added: "If you still decide you want to die, please do me one favor. Before you do anything about it, please call me, reversing the charges, and sing 'Pagan Love Song' once more to me."[8]

His new secretary, Edward Weber, helped Ramon answer the letters, explaining that he had been misunderstood. Syndicated columnist James Bacon interviewed Novarro for his column, and once again letters arrived from fans and friends, including Antonio Moreno and May McAvoy. Even Garbo dropped him a line of encouragement. If anything good came out of the incident, it let Novarro know that he had not been forgotten after all these years, as he had thought.

Despite the adverse publicity—or because of it—he still received several job offers. Actress Ida Lupino asked him to appear in a *Thriller* episode she was directing called *La Strega*. Because of his admiration for her, he agreed to do it.

He did, however, turn down a play to be produced in Madrid called *Marriage Go Round*, which would have costarred his cousin Dolores Del Rio. Although he would have enjoyed working with Dolores, the producers insisted on two performances a day, which would have been too much work at his age.

Broadway was another matter, however, and had always been a dream, so in March he agreed to appear in producer Gene Wesson's play called *Infidel Caesar*. It starred Michael Ansara, John Ireland, and James Earl Jones in a reinterpretation of Shakespeare's *Julius Caesar*. Instead of ancient Rome, the story took place on a modern-day island in the Caribbean with Ansara as a bearded dictator, much like Fidel Castro. Wesson had been working on the idea of the parallel's between Julius Caesar and Castro for more than two years.

Before Novarro could begin work on the play, there was the little matter of his day in court. On March 27, Novarro was convicted of misdemeanor drunk driving and April 13 was set for sentencing. Because of his prior convictions, his attorney, John Frolich, was concerned Novarro would face a possible jail sentence, so he made plans to appeal the judge's verdict.

Novarro left three days later for New York and rehearsals for *Infidel Caesar*. The play was to open at Broadway's Music Box Theater on Friday, April 27, but it closed after only two preview performances. Wesson realized the play could not survive, and instead of subjecting it, and the actors, to the scorn of the New York critics, he shut the production down. Some critics said, "Poor Novarro. What a shame for him."

The actor responded by saying: "Poor Novarro indeed. It would have been 'Poor Novarro' if we had opened. I'm so glad we closed when we did. It was a good enough idea—*Infidel Caesar*—but it just didn't work. This way nobody knows how really bad it was except we of the company and that poor preview audience."

Meanwhile, Novarro's attorney was denied an appeal on his drunk driving conviction, and the actor was sentenced to 15 days in jail beginning in October. Novarro believed that his arrest the previous February was a miscarriage of justice and a violation of his constitutional rights, and he was prepared to fight. "That's all my lawyer will let me say for now," he told a reporter, "but we won't give in and sometime the real story will come out."

In the meantime, Novarro appeared in a summer stock production of the musical *The Desert Song* in Fort Worth, Texas. He had originally turned it down, saying: "It is such hard work, and I really have nothing to prove. Many people, you know, think I am down and out. I'm not."[9] The play opened on June 4, 1962, and was followed two weeks later with *The Flower Drum*

Song, both at the Casa Manana Theater. Critics were unanimous in their praise of Novarro's acting skills. "Novarro was a nostalgic plus as General Birabeau, heart warming in his role and handling it in high fashion," said the *Fort Worth Telegram*.[10]

The *Dallas News* said, "Novarro owns a commanding presence and an imperial manner."[11] He toured on the National Summer Theater circuit and was met with the same praise. "I am returning to the singing stage after 25 years," he declared, "and I love it."[12]

When Novarro returned to Los Angeles, his request for an appeal was denied again, so he surrendered to authorities on October 3, 1962, to begin his 15-day jail sentence. The next day Frolich successfully convinced a federal court judge to agree to another hearing and requested leniency for Novarro. "He has solved any psychological problems he may have had and has not driven a car or taken a drink for several months," Frolich informed the court.[13]

The judge signed a writ of habeas corpus and ordered Novarro released from jail after he had served only one day of the 15-day sentence. At Novarro's new hearing, Frolich argued that authorities had violated due process of the law and failed to give him equal protection under the law. He also claimed that the misdemeanor drunk complaint was illegal because it was signed by a court bailiff instead of the arresting officer.

The court, however, did not agree, and the appeal was eventually taken all the way to the U.S. Supreme Court on the grounds that the actor had been deprived of his constitutional rights. The case was still pending at the time of Novarro's death.

While all the legal appeals were taking their due process, Novarro bought a Spanish-style house at 3110 Laurel Canyon Boulevard, in the hills above the San Fernando Valley, not far from Alice Terry. To help him relax, he agreed to take painting lessons with Alice, and the two spent hours composing still lifes of bottles and pottery. Ramon sent a photo of his paintings to Audrey Homan of the Ramon Novarro Film Club in London.

"Although I haven't been consistent in my painting lessons as I should have," Ramon wrote, "I have managed to finish two canvasses. My teacher feels that I am improving but I still don't see it myself."

It was around this time that he also decided to write his memoirs. "We haven't tackled it yet," he explained, "as it would be too much for the present. I will have to get myself a tape recorder and start telling my story from my birth, and that will take some time."[14]

In mid–January, Ramon caught a cold that he had difficulty shaking off, so he decided to see a doctor and found that his heart and lungs were on the weak side. After Ramon was admitted to the hospital for more tests and a complete checkup, the doctor advised him to slow down and simplify his life as much as possible. To help build his strength, he returned to singing and

playing the piano and also started Yoga exercises. "Yoga gives me the state of tranquillity towards which we should all strive," he said. "I think I am on the road toward attaining it."[15]

Through it all, Ramon remained intensely religious. He attended mass at St. Charles Church in North Hollywood and spent many weekends on religious retreats. The thought of the priesthood never left him. "I still think about it," he admitted, "but I'm afraid I'm too old for that now."[16]

Over the next few years his health continued to decline, as he developed emphysema and showed symptoms of cirrhosis of the liver. He also suffered from blood dycrasia which would not allow his blood to clot normally.

Despite his doctor's orders to slow down, Novarro became more involved in television. While in New York on a visit, he appeared on the radio program *Luncheon at Sardi's*, produced by Marvin Paige. At the time, Paige was casting an episode of *Combat* starring Mickey Rooney, and he convinced Novarro to take the part of a Frenchman. The series was filmed at MGM, marking his first visit there in almost 14 years. He became one of the few stars who had worked at the legendary studio in silents, talkies, and now television.

Ramon found the basic art of silent pictures—pantomime—to be very helpful in his new work. With the intimacy of television, sometimes a look or a gesture was more effective than a speech, and Novarro proved it in the *Combat* episode, which required very little dialogue. "He had no illusions about himself," Paige claimed. "He was such a pro. Everyone on the *Combat* set said he made the show just beautiful."[17]

His role on *Combat* led to guest starring roles in *Rawhide* and in *Dr. Kildare*, in which he appeared in a three-part episode with Richard Chamberlain. Novarro enjoyed his newfound career but claimed that the old Hollywood had more security. "When you arrived, you *had* arrived," he said, "and weren't frantic if a picture turned out not quite so good as its predecessor. But those days are over."[18]

In April, Novarro attended the Academy Award ceremonies in Santa Monica and continued working on his new home. He landscaped the property and added a music room which cost him more than $5,000 to build. He was so amazed by its cost that he made a point of telling everyone who visited, including Betty Lasky, who interviewed him for *Players Showcase*. Lasky was the daughter of Jesse Lasky, one of the founders of Paramount.

"I started out as an extra working for Jesse Lasky, at the old Lasky Company," he told her.[19] At one point, she asked about his alleged romance with Myrna Loy during the filming of *The Barbarian*. "Suddenly Ramon became angry and began scolding me," Lasky claimed. "He told me that I should not be asking such things."[20]

Opposite: Ramon with his brothers and sisters (from left) Eduardo, Jose, Luz, Carmen, and Mariano (courtesy of the Academy of Motion Picture Arts and Sciences).

His next television appearance was in *Bonanza* opposite Lorne Greene and Michael Landon. Novarro turned in a bravura performance as a lonely old man who gets himself into trouble spinning fanciful tales. He was more relaxed in his television performances because he did not have the responsibility to carry the production. "In television I just go to the studio to act," he recalled. "I have none of the worries of being a star, and all of the fun."[21]

Once again the producers of *Combat* would call on Novarro to appear on their show. This time he would costar with a two-time Academy Award–winning actress who hadn't appeared before the camera in almost 20 years.

Chapter Twenty-Six

Final Years
(1965–1968)

As for me, well, I don't reminisce unless people want me to. After all, my idea of hell is to be a star all your life.
—Ramon Novarro[1]

The producers of *Combat* invited Novarro to appear in an episode with the legendary actress Luise Rainer, hoping to increase the sagging ratings. Costar Kurt Kreuger remembered Novarro as being very distant, but polite. "He didn't mingle with anyone," Kreuger recalled. "You could hardly talk to him, and he had the aura of a former star around him. When he was through with a scene, he would retreat to his dressing room."[2]

This behavior was very unlike Ramon, but unknown to the cast, he was in extreme pain from pleurisy. "I haven't been too well of late," he wrote to a friend. "Nothing to worry about, but I have to take care of myself from now on, and that I am doing already."[3]

Kreuger said he would have enjoyed talking with Novarro but never had the chance. He was also unaware of Novarro's alcoholism and said that it never manifested itself on the set. "He was very professional about it," Kreuger commented. "When someone is a true alcoholic, they never let on."

Kreuger had only one scene with Novarro, but he liked him, which, unfortunately, he could not say of his other costar, Luise Rainer. "She was a strange one," Kreuger remembered. "I didn't like her. She came into my dressing room and wanted to give me direction."

This was Rainer's first performance before the camera in almost 20 years. "All of a sudden she behaved like she was doing a very important film," Kreuger said. "It was only television. Let's face it. She wanted to sit with the director and discuss it. I think she didn't get anywhere with Novarro, so out of desperation and frustration she called a meeting and said, 'We have to discuss this scene,' like we were doing an Academy Award film. The director was a little annoyed at it because there was the pressure of time."[4]

Novarro did not appear at the wrap party, nor did he say good-bye to the cast and crew. After filming was over, he checked into a hospital for treatment. Because of his illness, Novarro again became very reclusive. He rarely went out except to attend church or to go to the unemployment office. He would care for his garden, play solitaire, or paint with Alice Terry. He and Weber began work on his autobiography that he called "R–3" which referred to the laundry mark his mother used on his clothes. "When I hit it big in the movies," Ramon recalled, "I put my mother and family in a big mansion, but my mother, God rest her soul, always insisted that she do my shirts."[5]

Around this time Novarro began using a Hollywood escort service that provided young men in the guise of massage therapy. Novarro was lonely and used the service often. Sometimes there would be sex involved and other times just conversation, dinner, and drinks. Because of his kindness and the fact that he paid very well, Novarro became very popular among the local male prostitutes. One young man that he met through the service was Larry Ortega, but they soon became just close friends.

In October, Ramon invited Audrey Homan, secretary of the Ramon Novarro Film Club, to visit him in Los Angeles. "I visit those loyal ladies every time I go abroad," he told a friend. "When they swoon over me now somebody has to help them get up."[6]

Audrey brought Ramon a bedspread embroidered by members of the club. In the center was inscribed "A Tribute to Ramon Novarro, Star of the Silver Screen from the R.N.F.C." Ramon was delighted with the gift and placed it on his bed. It had been six years since Audrey had last seen Ramon, and she was shocked at how much older he looked. "Time does not stand still for any of us," she wrote. "But the brown eyes still gleamed from a slightly fuller, clean-shaven face."

Ramon gave his guest a tour of his home, which was furnished in a Mexican-Spanish motif and included fine mirrors of gilded carved wood, straight-backed chairs in natural hide with brass studs, and a red tile floor in the main living room. In the dining room, Audrey recognized a mirror-top table that was featured in an old movie magazine when Ramon lived in his Los Feliz home. Several days later they drove up to the Hollywood Hills to see the copper-ornamented building designed by Lloyd Wright. Audrey peered over the hedge into the pool while Ramon rang the doorbell, but no one was home. "Perhaps it's better so," he told her. "It doesn't do to look back."

Novarro was a gracious host; his first thought was always the comfort of his guest, whether it was leaving a glass of water on Audrey's bedstand or making sure her room had fresh roses every day. He saw to it that they visited the usual tourist traps, and on Sundays, they would go to St. Anne's Catholic Church, which was designed by Eduardo. "Many of these thoughtful gestures that he would do," she said, "showed me the kindness of his nature."

As her trip ended, Audrey wrote to the other club members, "I have memories, which I have tried to pass on to you, as well as many photographs and souvenirs, of a wonderful, generous man who did not permit me to spend a single penny from the beginning to the end of this unforgettable Journey to a Star."[7]

When his health permitted, Ramon worked on his proposed autobiography with Weber. He roughed out the first part dealing with his childhood in Mexico and the beginnings of the revolution. It took a great deal of concentration for him to remember all the facts of his life. Weber was not a film buff, so he was not much help in recalling dates and information. "When dealing with facts, one must be accurate," Ramon said.[8] He was adamant that the book not be published until after his death, saying, "It's very honest—and honesty can sometimes offend, I regret to say."[9]

Ramon's health continued to decline. His drinking persisted, with some periods of sobriety, but he always returned to the bottle. His family became concerned, and brothers Mariano and Antonio sometimes expressed their disapproval. "Ramon had a problem with alcohol," his brother Angel said. "He tried to lick it several times, but just couldn't do it. And Antonio said some mean things that hurt Ramon."[10] Evelyn Laye once said, "He was always aware of the weaknesses in himself; we all have weaknesses, but Ramon tried to overcome them more than many of us do."[11]

Novarro did stop drinking by the summer of 1966, and his health improved somewhat. He felt well enough to make public appearances and do guest shots on television. In fact, his health improved enough that he scheduled a trip to Europe. While Novarro was in London, Patrick Brock visited him at his hotel and found him slumped over the bed in great pain. Brock notified the front desk, and an ambulance took Novarro to University College Hospital, where he underwent surgery for acute peritonitis.

In gratitude, Novarro gave Brock a copy of *The Imitation of Christ* and inscribed it, "To my good friend Patrick, who saved my life." Brock knew his friend had a drinking problem, but unlike some in Hollywood, he did not know about his propensity for men. "I never saw or heard anything to indicate Ramon's deviation," Brock recalled. "But I knew there had been an arrest for drunken-driving when his career slipped and the roles were no longer being offered."[12]

By the summer of 1967, Ramon had been sober for a year and hired a live-in male nurse to care for him. His health continued to improve, so he accepted a guest-starring role on *The Wild Wild West*. In December he appeared on the *Merv Griffin Show* and met with Broadway managers Ed Padula and Michael Ellis, who were considering creating a play for him.

Film historian DeWitt Bodeen contacted Novarro about an interview for *Films in Review* magazine. Novarro was cordial and agreed to set up a time for them to meet. "We had many mutual friends, but had never actually personally met," Bodeen wrote. "He had been ill in a sanitarium with a respiratory problem, and I had been told by a friend who knew him well that he was no longer drinking, that he had even given up cigarettes, and was systematically dieting to lose weight."

Ramon surprised Bodeen by how much he remembered about his career. "It was hard to believe," Bodeen said, "that this small, frail, aging man was the same handsome, impassioned, virile hero of such film classics as *Ben-Hur*, *The Student Prince*, *Scaramouche* and *Where the Pavement Ends*."[13]

On February 18, 1968, Novarro dismissed the live-in nurse and booked a cruise to Australia and the Orient aboard the ocean liner *Canberra*. He had been dry for almost two years and wanted time away to finish his autobiography, or so he said. Actually, all he had of his life story was a collection of jumbled notes and assorted anecdotes of his career.

On March 24, 1968, while Novarro was in Australia, an episode of *The High Chaparral* was broadcast in which he appeared as a priest. This was a part he had always wanted to play in real life but never did. Ironically, it would be his last appearance before the camera.

Ramon was 69 years old, overweight, and in ill health. He was becoming uncharacteristically bitter about life. He told a reporter on the *Canberra*, "One of the things I want to tell about in my book is how hard it is to grow old, when you've been at the top."

"I'll tell you a real truth," he continued. "You find out that some of the people you thought were your friends are not your friends."[14]

Besides Alice Terry, Gilbert Roland still visited regularly, as did Gloria Swanson. He also saw a group of former film stars who came by to play canasta, including Mae Clarke. Clarke became acquainted with Novarro at St. Charles Church in North Hollywood, where they both worshipped. At first Ramon appeared standoffish to the actress, but it was eventually he who approached her. They soon became friends.

Many afternoons Mae would stop by Ramon's Laurel Canyon home to play canasta, along with Alice Terry, Lila Lee, May McAvoy, and occasionally some others. At the end of the afternoon, without being rude, Ramon would give the impression that his guests should finish their drinks and leave because other friends were expected. There were never any names mentioned, and no one was invited to stay. Not much was thought of it at the time, but after his death it was the only indication to his friends that Ramon had had a "secret life."

Novarro in one of his last guest-starring roles on the television show *The Wild Wild West* (1967).

For some reason, in the summer of 1968, Ramon broke his two years of sobriety and began drinking heavily. On August 30, he was slightly injured during a dinner party when a guest became enraged and hit him on the head. He was not seriously hurt, but the incident had a traumatic effect on him and he checked into the hospital for a rest and to dry out.

When he returned home, he had his lawyer add a third codicil to his will. In it, he deleted his brother Antonio from the trust he had set up for his siblings but gave no reason for his decision. It was signed and witnessed on October 9, 1968.

A week and a half later the Ramon Novarro Film Club held its 500th consecutive monthly meeting. Ramon had hoped to fly to London for the occasion, but his health would not permit it, so Audrey Homan called and wished him a speedy recovery.

Ramon had cut Edward Weber's hours down to a few days a week, and Angel was concerned that he was spending too much time alone. On Saturday, October 26, he tried to convince his brother to hire a part-time maid. "Ramon, it's not right for you to be alone so long," he told him. "You know, something could happen to you and you wouldn't be able to get help."

Angel suggested that he use the woman who helped with the rentals at his apartment building to do some cooking and the laundry. Ramon was at first hesitant, but finally relented. "Good," Angel said. "A week from today, I'm going to bring her over."[15] That was the last time Angel would see his brother alive.

On Monday, Weber took Ramon to pick up his $65 unemployment check. Wednesday, October 30, was Weber's day off, so Ramon tended his garden and caught up on some reading. After lunch, Ramon received a call from a young hustler named Paul, who wanted to visit that evening. Ramon questioned him and said, "Well, come on up for a few drinks and we'll see what happens." The young man didn't have a car but told Ramon if he found a ride, he would call later for the address. As Paul was about to hang up, Ramon asked him, "By the way, how did you get my number?" He told Ramon that Larry had given it to him.

A few minutes later Ramon telephoned Larry Ortega, whom he had met through the escort service he used. Larry claimed that he had not given Ramon's number to anyone, nor did he know anyone named Paul. Ramon thanked Larry and returned to work in his garden. At 4:45 P.M., the phone rang again; it was Paul. "Oh, so you found a ride, good," Ramon said.[16] Paul told Ramon he was bringing Tommy, his 17-year-old brother, and would be there around 5:30 P.M.

Ramon had enough time to shower, trim his goatee, and splash on cologne. He put on his best robe, which was made of red and blue checkered silk, and a pair of blue canvas shoes. At 5:30 P.M. the doorbell rang and Ramon answered it, unaware of the events that were about to unfold.

Chapter Twenty-Seven

Murder (1968–1969)

Ramon aged gracefully. He never considered himself a "has-been" because he had enough money to choose his roles. He worked when he wanted and enjoyed his garden the rest of the time. He enjoyed a beautiful life."
—Leonard Shannon[1]

The following day was Halloween, and Edward Weber arrived at Ramon's at 8:30 A.M.[2] Finding the gates open, he parked his car and walked to the back door, which opened into the pantry. Entering the kitchen, he drew the curtains and discovered a sink full of dirty dishes.

As he entered the living room, it appeared to have been ransacked. Scanning the room, he saw Ramon's broken eye glasses on the parquet floor. Stepping over a chair, he walked to the bedroom door, which was slightly ajar, and peered into the darkened room. He whispered, "Ramon?" but there was no answer.

As Weber's eyes adjusted to the darkness, he noticed that the side of the bed that Ramon usually slept on was empty. Weber turned from the door and gazed around the living room, hoping to see some sign of the actor. He slowly entered the bedroom and walked into the master bathroom, whispering, "Ramon." His call was met with a numbing silence. Weber finally accepted the fact that something was seriously wrong. Where was Ramon? He wouldn't have been able to leave the house alone, and it was unlikely that someone had come by to pick him up.

Weber searched the house room by room, calling out Novarro's name.

179

As he once again stood in the doorway of the bedroom and peered into the darkness, he saw something on the far side of the bed and wondered why he had failed to notice it before.

As Weber pulled the drape cord, it jammed, allowing only a sliver of light to break through the darkness. What he discovered was the nude and lifeless body of Ramon Novarro. Weber desperately checked Novarro's breathing, but his chest was still. He gently searched for a pulse but felt only the cold dampness of Ramon's skin. Weber rushed to the living room and called Eduardo; then he notified the police and Novarro's priest at St. Charles.

Within five minutes, two black and whites pulled into the driveway, followed by an ambulance. Sergeants Norm Allen and Robert Smith of the North Hollywood Division arrived and were soon joined by Lt. Gerald Lauritzen, who would be in charge of the investigation.

Eduardo and Angel arrived at 9:15 A.M. and officially identified the body of their brother as sergeants Smith and Allen, along with a civilian criminalist, looked over the crime scene. They observed Novarro lying on his back, on the right side of the bed, with his head near the headboard. He was completely nude except for a sheet which partially covered his legs from the knees down. There was evidence of a struggle, and blood was smeared on the floor and ceiling of the bedroom. A tooth was lying on the floor at the foot of the bed.

Ramon's hands had been tied behind his back with brown electrical cord.[3] It was about 10 feet in length and had been doubled and made into a half loop and secured around his ankles. It had then been drawn up to the right wrist, where it had been wrapped three times. The other end had been used to draw the left hand to the right behind his back, causing the left arm to be bent horizontally across the small of his back.

On the right side of Ramon's neck, the initial "N" or "Z" had been carved. Lacerations were noted on his face and head. A broken, silver-tipped, black walking cane had been placed across his thighs, resting between the knee and hip of the right leg. As the body was turned over, the name "Larry" was found written on the sheet underneath him in letters approximately 12 inches high.[4] In Ramon's left hand was a ball point pen, and between his thumb and index finger of his right hand was an unused white condom. On the bedroom mirror was written in brown stick makeup, "Us girls are better than fagits." A check made out to "Cash" in the amount of $20 was found on the dresser.

In the kitchen sink were the remains of a dinner, which was later determined to have been prepared for three people. Behind the house, an officer found a garbage can filled with empty liquor bottles. "Looks like there may have been a party here last night," he told Lauritzen.

Outside, the gathering press corps was told by a detective: "The house is torn up and there's a lot of blood. We haven't determined what the method was, or the instrument used."[5]

Meanwhile, a photographer for a local newspaper strolled up the hill to get a different angle of the house. As he reached the top, he looked over a fence and saw something that stopped him dead in his tracks. There, just on the other side of the fence, was a pile of bloody clothing. All together, police catalogued and bagged six pieces of bloodstained clothing, including a small blue jacket, a small blue shirt, two large T-shirts, and two pairs of jockey shorts. "He [the killer] was probably afraid to go out with all that blood on his clothes," Smith told Lauritzen.

At 3:08 P.M., the Los Angeles Coroners Office removed the body of Ramon Novarro.

The following day the front pages of newspapers across the country reported the murder of Ramon Novarro. The entertainment industry reacted with shock and surprise. Novarro's one-time costar Anita Page was married and living in Coronado when she heard the news of Novarro's death. "I just couldn't believe it," she later recalled.[6]

Pancho Barnes was living in a trailer in the desert when she reminisced to a friend about her days in Hollywood, saying: "These were truly magnificent people.... There has to be a reason and we'll probably know why someday but right now all that we can do is bitch and wonder."[7]

"Forget how it happened," actress Mae Clarke said. "It's a fact that he was a great star, but he was also a great person."[8] Heartbroken, Dolores Del Rio said, "To meet such a death is so sad."[9] Alice Terry gave no statement but remained secluded in her house on Kelsey Avenue.[10] Actress Lupita Tovar, who was in Mexico at the time, said: "I feel just terrible, because he was such a nice person. Why? You say why?"[11]

Former costar Evelyn Laye told a friend: "I loved Ramon; he was one of my dearest friends. Whenever he came to London, we would walk arm in arm in Regents Park, perhaps have a cup of coffee together. I am very proud to think that I made a film with him. Both Frank [her husband] and I loved Ramon. What more can I say?"[12]

The only information released by police was that Novarro had been found nude and savagely beaten in his bedroom. Novarro's publicist and friend of 23 years, Leonard Shannon, theorized that someone walked in from Laurel Canyon wanting to borrow the phone. "When motorists ran out of gasoline or had engine problems," Shannon said, "they would often come here to telephone a mechanic."[13]

On Saturday, lieutenant Lauritzen and sergeant Smith released the findings of their investigation. "All the doors to the house were locked when Mr. Novarro's secretary first arrived," Smith said. "There are no signs of forced entry. This would indicate that Mr. Novarro was acquainted with his killer and let him in voluntarily."

"We have no evidence at this time of anything missing," Lauritzen added. "Of course, this is a large house and contains many valuable items. There are many things that we have to pursue."

Police believed Novarro had been killed with a single weapon that was recovered in the bedroom. They declined to identify it but called it "a striking instrument."[14] A search of Novarro's bank account revealed that he had written almost 140 checks to male prostitutes in the preceding six months.

At a press conference, Thomas T. Noguchi, the famed Los Angeles city coroner, reported that Novarro's autopsy revealed that the actor had died of "suffocation due to massive bleeding due to fracture of the nose and laceration of the lips and mouth."[15] Noguchi stated that Novarro lay dying on his bed for some time, apparently suffocating slowly on his own blood after being knocked out. He had multiple lacerations of the nose, lips, and mouth. His scalp was split, and there were contusions on his chest, neck, left arm, knees, and penis.

Because of the sexual overtones of the murder, oral and anal smears were taken to check for semen and sperm. The anal smear proved negative, but the oral smear mysteriously disappeared. There was 0.23 percent alcohol in Ramon's blood, and the time of death was set between 9 and 9:30 P.M.[16] Even though the injuries were serious, alone they would not have been enough to cause death. Had help arrived, Ramon Novarro probably would have survived.

The following day sergeant Smith was told that a county jail prisoner knew a Larry who was friends with Novarro. The prisoner admitted that he turned tricks for Larry Ortega, whose brother-in-law, Paul Ferguson, also hustled, and sometimes attacked his clients. Because Ortega's name kept coming up, the police posted a stakeout in front of his parents' house.

On Sunday, mourners arrived at the Cunningham and O'Connor Mortuary to pay their respects to Ramon Novarro. More than 1,000 people filed past the open casket during the six hours the actor's body lay in state. Among them was a former MGM employee who had once worked in the art department. He remembered Novarro as "a wonderful man who gave a lot of glamour to Hollywood." Even though producer William Self never met Novarro, he came to pay his respects. "I felt I had to come," Self said. "He was very important to our industry."[17]

That evening a rosary was recited at 8 P.M. for Novarro at St. Anne's Roman Catholic Church in North Hollywood. While Novarro's friends and family were mourning and preparing for the funeral, the Los Angeles Police Department was working full time to solve this high profile murder. Hoping that the murderers had made at least one mistake, the police continued to look for the one clue which would lead them to their suspects. They would get their wish within a matter of days.

The following morning the funeral and solemn requiem mass was held at St. Anne's Catholic Church. Sergeants Smith and Allen attended, as did Larry Ortega, who signed the guest register in the chapel but was not noticed by the officers. Five hundred people crowded into the small church to pay their final respects to Ramon Novarro. Angel and Eduardo knelt silently in front, surrounded by more than 40 members of Novarro's family. Hollywood was represented by Ida Lupino, Gilbert Roland, MGM publicist Howard Strickling, and actors Neil Hamilton, Les Tremayne, and Eddie Foy, Jr.

The Very Rev. Archimandrite Michel Bardaquil, pastor of St. Anne's, presided over the service, and in his eulogy he praised Novarro as a "good man and fine actor" and cited the evil in the world which had claimed his life.[18] After receiving permission from Eduardo, Sgt. Smith picked up the guest register. Following the church service, there was an hour-long motorcade to Calvary Cemetery, where Novarro was laid to rest in the family plot next to his mother.

Early the next morning, an envelope from the telephone company arrived containing Novarro's telephone records. As Allen glanced at the sheet, a smile crossed his face as he handed the papers to Lauritzen. "Take a look," he said calmly. A 48-minute telephone call to Chicago was made at about the time the coroner said Novarro had been murdered. This appeared to be the first big break in the case.

When Smith checked the funeral guest register, he was shocked that Ortega had signed it and escaped their notice. Shortly thereafter, however, officers from the stakeout had picked up Ortega and his sister Mary Ferguson and had brought them to the North Hollywood police station. "There's nothing to be frightened about," Smith assured them. "We'd just like to ask you a few questions."

Smith questioned Mary Ferguson about her relationship with her husband Paul. She explained that they had been separated for about a week. The couple had been having money problems and had argued over a can of evaporated milk. Paul had roughed her up, and she had gone to stay with her parents. She claimed she did not know Ramon Novarro and was uncertain whether Paul knew him.

The prison informant had told police that Paul was a "mean one," claiming that he might be a sadist. "I once saw him beat someone for no reason once," he told police. "If anyone knows about Paul, it would be Larry." Larry was, of course, hesitant to admit that he was friends with Ramon until he realized the police probably already knew. He reluctantly explained that Novarro had called him on Wednesday afternoon to ask if he had given his number to a hustler named Paul.[19] Larry had denied knowing anyone by that name, never dreaming it might have been Paul Ferguson, his brother-in-law. He also had assumed that Paul had given up hustling. Smith thanked them both and asked that they not discuss this matter with anyone.

The next day Chicago police spoke with Brenda Lee Metcalf, who had received the Wednesday night telephone call from Novarro's house. She claimed that she had spoken with her boyfriend, Tom Ferguson, who had said he was in a movie star's home. At first she hadn't believed him because he had a reputation for stretching the truth. In line with his character, he had

Paul Ferguson shortly after his arrest for the murder of Ramon Novarro.

told her that the house had 32 rooms and more than 700 pictures on the walls. Tom had then told her that he and his brother Paul were going to force the actor to reveal where he had hidden $5,000 in the house. After several minutes, she claimed she heard someone screaming in the background. Tom told her that Paul was with Novarro, trying to force him to tell where the money was. "I have to go now," Tom reportedly told Brenda. "I want to see what's going on."

That same day, in North Hollywood, a messenger delivered the Ferguson brothers' fingerprint records and rap sheet from the Chicago police department. Shortly after 2 P.M., they were positively matched to the set of prints taken from Novarro's house. The Fergusons were now the main suspects. Through a tip, the officers were told that the brothers were staying at the home of Paul's former employer in Bell Gardens. Along with four officers, they arrived at the house several hours later. A young man who identified himself as Thomas Ferguson opened the door. Sergeant Allen told him they were looking for Paul Ferguson on a burglary charge. He did not mention Ramon Novarro, nor did he mention murder.

Tom arrogantly told the officers that he did not know where Paul was but assumed he was at a bar playing pool or maybe at Taco Bell. Smith sent two policemen to search the area. Instead of questioning Tom, they sat in the small house and waited.

Shortly, the officers returned with Paul Ferguson, and both brothers were handcuffed, read their rights, and told they were being arrested for the murder of Ramon Novarro. An hour later they arrived at Parker Center, where they were fingerprinted and photographed.

Paul and Tom Ferguson went through hours of grueling interrogation by the North Hollywood police. Both were questioned separately, and both gave similar stories until asked about the actual murder. At that point, both brothers blamed each other. At a press conference, lieutenant Lauritzen told reporters, "We have substantial physical evidence to connect them with the crime scene."[20]

The next day Paul Ferguson was arraigned in Van Nuys Municipal Court, where robbery and murder complaints were issued against him. He was ordered held without bail pending a preliminary hearing. Tom was held in juvenile hall and was later ordered to stand trial as an adult.

On November 13, Ramon Novarro's will was filed for probate in superior court. He left an estate estimated at half a million dollars, the bulk of which included real estate holdings in the San Fernando Valley and his extensive stock portfolio. A trust fund was established for his family, except for Antonio, for whom the only provision was, "If my brother, Antonio Samaniego, is indebted to me at the date of my death, I hereby cancel and forgive all such indebtedness."[21]

Novarro left $15,000 to St. Anne's Catholic Church, where the funeral services were held, and provided for 20 friends, including Alice Terry, who was willed his paintings. His secretary, Edward Weber, received the framed sheet music, all "remaining tangible personal property," and the rosary from his Aunt Nachita, which Weber placed in the casket with Ramon.

Novarro also decreed that the rights to his autobiography and the proceeds thereof would be divided equally between his friends.[22] However, when a probate judge later asked Edward Weber what value he placed on the autobiography, Weber replied that it was too preliminary and in his opinion was worthless. The judge agreed.[23]

On December 17 the Ferguson brothers were brought before the Los Angeles County Grand Jury, which was told the motive for the murder was the attempted theft of $5,000 reportedly hidden in Novarro's home. Paul Robert and Thomas Scott Ferguson were later indicted and ordered to stand trial for the murder of Ramon Novarro.

Two months later, after entering innocent pleas for their clients, the brothers' attorneys made a motion to dismiss the murder charges, claiming the testimony brought before the grand jury was insufficient to sustain murder indictments. The motion was denied. The case was then turned over to the prosecution, whose duty it was to gather enough evidence to convict the brothers and put them away forever.

Chapter Twenty-Eight

The Trial (1969)

> *We will show that the Ferguson brothers were living in*
> *Gardena. They were in need of money. Paul Ferguson was*
> *what is known as a hustler—a male prostitute. He would*
> *earn money by having sex with older men. Now they were*
> *in need of a great deal more money than would be obtained*
> *by any one sexual act. So Paul Ferguson obtained the name*
> *of Ramon Novarro and called him.*
>
> —Deputy District Attorney
> James Ideman[1]

The murder trial against Paul Robert and Thomas Scott Ferguson began on July 28, 1969, in the Los Angeles Superior Court of Judge Mark Brandler. The court appointed attorney Richard A. Walton to defend Tom. Cletus J. Hanifin was retained by a cousin to represent Paul. Both lawyers entered a plea of "not guilty" of first degree murder for each of their clients. Had the charge been manslaughter, they would have pleaded guilty.

To Deputy District Attorney James Ideman, there was no doubt that the death of Ramon Novarro was first degree murder. Under California law, any death that occurs during a robbery is automatically first degree, even if it is accidental. Ideman was prepared to prove to the jury of seven men and five women that Paul and Thomas Ferguson went to the home of Ramon Novarro on the night of October 30, 1968, to rob him of the $5,000 they thought he kept hidden in the house. In his opening statements, Ideman

186

described to the jury what the prosecution was prepared to prove about the death of Ramon Novarro.

"The victim in this case, Mr. Ramon Novarro, lived by himself in a large Spanish-type house and it seemed obvious that he was a man of some wealth. Now Mr. Novarro was a homosexual and probably had been one for many years. But he was a discreet homosexual. He did not go out into the streets and try to pick up people. The young male prostitutes would come to his home and he was usually careful about who came to his home."

Ideman described to the jury the prosecution's version of what happened on the night of October 30, 1968. He told how Paul called Novarro and asked for an appointment to see him. Because they did not own a car, they asked an acquaintance to drive them to Novarro's residence. After arriving, they talked with Novarro and had a few drinks. Novarro then served dinner and more drinks. "Later on, apparently Paul Ferguson and Mr. Novarro went into the bedroom," he said.

Ideman claimed that somehow Paul thought there was a large amount of money concealed in the house. So when Novarro attempted to pay Paul with a check, the young hustler demanded money. But there wasn't any money to give, Ideman said, and Paul began to beat Novarro and was later joined by Tom.

Then Ideman began to recount for the jury the 22 different injuries to Novarro's body that he could only describe as torture. He told how Novarro was flailed with a silver-handled cane which had been a memento from one of his films. When he began to lose consciousness, they took him to a cold shower and revived him. Then they tied his hands behind his back and continued the beating. Novarro was unable to ward off the blows that were struck against the most sensitive parts of his body. They placed him on his back on the bed, and he ultimately lost consciousness. Blood dripped into his throat from his broken nose and drained into his lungs. "He drowned in his own blood," Ideman told the jury.

Ideman closed his statement by saying, "When I get through presenting the evidence, it will show Mr. Novarro was murdered. It will show who did it. It will show that the Fergusons did it and it will show why it was done. It was done for robbery."

The prosecution's star witness was Brenda Lee Metcalf, who was flown in from Chicago for the trial. Metcalf, who was near tears during her testimony, told the court about her 48-minute telephone conversation with Tom Ferguson on the night of the murder. Tom allegedly told her it would take too long to find the $5,000 so they would have to tie Novarro up and force him to tell where it was. She was warning Tom not to do anything foolish when she suddenly heard screaming. During her testimony, not once did she look in Tom's direction. He, however, sat transfixed, never taking his eyes off his former girlfriend, even as she was leaving the witness stand.

When the defense finally presented its side, the attorneys indicated each brother would claim the other one had murdered Ramon Novarro. Cletus Hanifin called Dr. Vernon J. Miller, a psychiatrist who had examined Paul. Dr. Miller claimed on the witness stand that Paul was legally sane but mentally ill. Dr. Miller testified that Paul's mental capacity was impaired or diminished under the influence of alcohol, which caused him to suffer blackouts. He said that because of a traumatic childhood, Paul had a long-standing personality disturbance and was a social misfit. "The abnormalities indicated brain damage—encephalitis," Miller said.

Paul Ferguson took the stand in his own defense on August 25, 1969. Cletus Hanifin asked his client several routine questions before asking about the night of the murder. Paul told how Novarro made them dinner and served drinks, how they played the piano, talked about Mexico, and discussed Novarro's music room which he had built for $5,000. Paul explained that Novarro and Tom went to the garden while he passed out on the couch. He said he heard Tom on the phone but didn't remember what was said. At this point in Paul's testimony, Tom became angry and told Walton, "Why don't you ask him what Novarro did during those 48 minutes that I was on the phone and he slept. The lying bastard."

Paul claimed that Tom later woke him and said that Novarro was dead. According to Paul's account, he followed his brother into the bedroom and hunched down to take a closer look at Novarro, touching him on the shoulder. His skin felt starchy and tight like paper. When they lifted the body on to the bed, Paul noticed that Novarro's hands were tied behind his back. He listened to his heart and determined that he was dead.

According to Paul's testimony, he said that they should call the police, but Tom insisted that they make it look like a robbery. Paul agreed and went into the dining room and overturned several chairs. Returning to the bedroom, he saw Tom writing "us girls are better than fagits" on the mirror. They replaced their bloody clothes with some from Novarro's closet. Tom then sat on Novarro's chest and cut marks on his neck with a knife. Bewildered, Paul asked him what he was doing. "I'm making it look like scratches, like a girl," was his reply. Paul followed Tom out the window, and both thumbed a ride to Sunset Boulevard.

"Did you at any time ever strike Mr. Novarro with that cane?" Hanifin asked him. Paul replied that he had never seen the cane until the prosecution entered it as an exhibit in court.

"Did you at any time ever strike Mr. Novarro with your fists, the palm of your hand, with a cane, with any other instrument or anything whatsoever?"

"No," he replied, looking at the jury. At one point during Paul's testimony, Tom sat at the table groaning and shaking his head violently. "No ... no ... it's not true," he said. "Not one word is true." The jury noticed the commotion, and the courtroom began to whisper.

Paul testified that Novarro wanted to make him a big star. Hanifin argued that Paul would have no reason to kill Novarro when he was going to help him launch a career in show business. Paul denied telling anyone he went to Novarro's to rob him of $5,000.

It was now Tom's turn to take the witness stand. Unlike his brother Paul, Tom appeared intelligent and in control. His calm and unflappable manner was a definite match for his interrogators. Under Richard Walton's expert questioning, Tom claimed that it was Paul, and not he, who beat Ramon Novarro to death. He told the court that he was on the telephone to Chicago for almost an hour while Paul was alone with Novarro.

Again, Tom claimed that he and his brother went to Novarro's house to hustle him, not to rob, burglarize, or kill him. He said that after drinks and dinner, Novarro agreed that both could spend the night. Tom was shown to the guest room and asked Novarro's permission to use the telephone. Later, when he passed through Novarro's bedroom to use the bathroom, he saw Paul and Ramon lying nude on the bed. "Get the hell out of here!" Paul screamed.

Tom testified that when he finished talking to Brenda, Paul called for him. As he entered the bedroom, he saw Paul, looking dazed and standing at the foot of the bed wearing blood-soaked shorts. Novarro was sitting, bent over on the bed, bleeding from his face, lips and forehead. Paul ordered Tom to take Novarro to the shower, where he washed the blood from his face. After helping him dry off, Tom returned to the bedroom with Ramon. Paul was not there.

"Hail Mary, full of Grace. The Lord is with Thee," Ramon mumbled. "Blessed art Thou amongst Women. And blessed is the Fruit of Thy womb, Jesus."

At this point in Tom's testimony, Paul flew into a rage and threw a pen at his brother, screaming, "Oh you punk liar ... you son of a bitch. Tell the truth." Judge Brandler sent the jury out of the courtroom and warned Paul that he would be bound and gagged if he disrupted the proceedings again. When the jury returned, Brandler instructed them to disregard the incident. Tom continued with his testimony.

As Tom helped Ramon back onto the bed, he looked up and saw Paul in the bathroom, dancing in front of a large mirror, with a soft gray fedora on his head. He was twirling an ivory crooked, black cane, and mumbling aimlessly to himself. "He said he looked crazy and should have been in vaudeville," Tom said.

Paul stormed from the bathroom, and Tom stepped in to urinate. As Ramon stood up Paul thought that he was going to attack him and began beating the actor with the cane. Ramon was knocked off balance and slipped on the blood, falling to the floor.

When Tom returned from the bathroom, he found Paul dressed, standing over Ramon, who was again covered with blood. Tom leaned down next

Tom Ferguson on trial for the murder of Ramon Novarro.

to the now still body and placed his ear on his chest, desperately listening for a heartbeat. "He looked dead," Tom told the hushed courtroom.

"Why didn't you ever stop Paul from beating Mr. Novarro?" Walton asked.

"I never saw him do anything," he answered.

As Tom knelt next to Ramon's body, Paul realized what he had done and began to sob. Tom admitted he was the one who suggested making it look like a robbery. After they tied his hands with the lamp cord, Paul turned Novarro's body on its side, wrote the name "Larry" on the bed sheet, and put the pen in Ramon's hand. He found a box of condoms and placed one in Novarro's right hand. Tom closed all the drapes in the house, locked the front door, turned out every light, and exited through the sliding glass doors, waiting outside for Paul.

Inside, Paul broke the cane he used to beat Novarro and placed each piece across his thighs. As they headed for Laurel Canyon, Paul ran to the fence and threw the bundle of bloody clothes into the next yard. "Paul Robert, you shouldn't have done that," Tom said shaking his head.

Tom told the court that he agreed to say he killed Novarro because he thought the courts would be lenient with him because he was underage. Besides, Paul told him he would go to a juvenile facility rather than prison. "But when it came out in court that Mr. Novarro had been beaten with a cane," Tom testified, "it turned my stomach against Paul."

Tom also claimed he was under pressure from many people, including his mother, to take the blame in order to save Paul from a possible death sentence. Unknown to Paul or Tom, their mother, Lorraine Smith, was called as a witness by the defense. Richard Walton quoted from a letter that she wrote to Tom shortly before the trial began. It read, "Tom, when you testify, *think* about what you're saying. You're holding Paul's life in your hands.... You can make him live or die."

Lorraine Smith testified that Tom wrote to her that both of them killed the actor. "Novarro deserved to be killed," she quoted Tom as saying. "He was nothing but an old faggot."

In an interview with the *Los Angeles Times*, Lorraine Smith said she thought both brothers were involved, "but there's something wrong some-place," she said. "I know Tom and his stories. I know he's told lies."[2]

In his closing remarks, James Ideman told the jury that Ramon Novarro was well liked and made great contributions to the entertainment industry. He explained that he was an alcoholic with homosexual tendencies. "I hope sincerely you will not put Mr. Novarro on trial," he cautioned the jury. "He has paid for whatever he did and now it is the Fergusons' turn to pay for whatever they have done.

"Three people know what happened in the house that night. Novarro is dead, so he can't tell us. Neither of the Ferguson brothers will admit striking Mr. Novarro even once. As a matter of fact, after listening to the Fergusons testify, I was beginning to wonder if what we were dealing with was a suicide. Perhaps Mr. Novarro wrapped himself in that electrical wire and beat himself to death."

Ideman emphasized the agony Novarro must have gone through as he lay tied up and was beaten about the most sensitive parts of his body. He showed the jury brutal photographs of the murder. "What kind of monster would do such a thing?" he asked them. "These two male whores are experienced. Why these injuries, if not to get him to tell where the money was?"

During the defense's closing statements, Hanifin, Paul's attorney, told the jury that Paul was either asleep when Novarro was killed or his excessive drinking that night caused him to black out and he was not responsible. Richard Walton, Tom's attorney, told the jury, "Novarro, the man who set female hearts a flutter, was nothing but a queer." He ended his summation by saying that Tom's family had conspired to have the youth take the sole blame for the murder because he was underage.

Judge Brandler then gave the jury members their instructions. After seven weeks of testimony, the jury deliberated for eight hours before reaching a verdict. The brothers were both convicted of first degree murder in the beating death of Ramon Novarro. This meant that Tom would automatically receive a life sentence because of his age. Paul would either be sentenced to life imprisonment or the gas chamber. That would be determined in the sentencing phase of the trial by the same jury that had convicted him.

At this part of the trial, held a week later, Paul's employer criticized Ideman for not allowing him to testify. "I'm sure he didn't do this murder," he said, before Judge Brandler rebuked him. Paul shouted at Ideman, calling him a pig for suppressing evidence. "You know and I know that I didn't do it!" he screamed.

The next day Tom took the stand and made a confession which sent reverberations across the entire courtroom. "I didn't kill him," he began. "It was my fault he died." Tom then explained to the court what he called the truth about that evening.

"Mr. Novarro came up to me when Paul was asleep on the couch," he explained. "We had a sex act—oral copulation. He kept trying to put his fingers up my rectum. I started hitting him."

He said that Novarro got up from the bed and went into the bathroom to remove the blood from his face. Tom forced him back into the bedroom and began hitting him. "I looked at him and it made me sick," he said. "I was just mad. I tied him up and I got the glove and cane out of the closet, twirling it like a baton. Then I hit him on the face and threw it on the floor. Just sickening he was. I went to wake up Paul. I told him he was trying to force me. He was like a sick punk!"

When Ideman asked him why he didn't come forward with this story before, Tom told him that he tried to confess three times but was not given the opportunity. "Are you saying these things now just to save your brother?" Ideman asked him.

"No," he replied. "I am saying these things because I want to tell the truth and I'd hate to send my brother to the gas chamber for something I did, while I sat in prison like Mr. Cool."

"Didn't it bother your conscience during the trial to blame the murder on Paul?"

"Not a bit," Tom shot back. "He was supposed to get manslaughter and I was supposed to get off. It's not our fault that we got a dumb jury."

Ideman asked Tom if he thought he would be a big man in jail. Tom sat straight up, looked Ideman in the eye and said: "I'm big already! I've been big all my life!"

"My brother's crazy, man," Paul said. "You care to solve your case? Look, I don't know what happened, man. Tommy is crazy! He didn't want to be screwed."

Ideman appeared to be truly disgusted with the entire proceedings. "I've about had it up to here with the Fergusons!" he exclaimed. He encouraged the jury to ignore Tom's confession. Later Judge Brandler asked Tom, "What did you mean, when you said that you didn't kill him but that you were responsible for his death?"

"He wasn't killed," Tom replied. "He died of a broken nose and I'm the one who busted his nose." He brazenly told Brandler that they were all responsible for Novarro's death—including Novarro.

Ideman insisted that Tom's confession was a last minute attempt to create doubt in the jury's mind and urged them to vote the death penalty for Paul. "He is the man who in my opinion deserves the ultimate penalty," he said.

The jury members seemed visibly shaken by the entire testimony. They deliberated for two and a half hours and returned with a verdict of life imprisonment. The jury members indicated they believed it would have been unfair to impose a greater penalty on Paul than on his brother. They were not convinced that the murder was intentional.

Judge Brandler called the jury "truly remarkable and extraordinary" and set October 27, 1969, as the date for sentencing. After Tom's testimony, Paul told a reporter, "I'm glad Tom finally told the truth. It sounds like Tom is really sorry for what he has done to me. And the very reason he was in Los Angeles was because I wanted to help him. I love my brother."[3]

At the sentencing, neither brother showed any sign of emotion as Judge Brandler called their crime a "horrendous murder" and ruled that they be confined to the state prison for life. Brandler recommended that they never be released on parole and said the evidence presented "established convincingly and conclusively the guilt of the Fergusons—Paul as well as Tom—to the brutal, vicious and torture killing. Both of them still are completely devoid of even a semblance of remorse or repentance." The brothers declared they were denied a fair trial.

"My father fought in World War II and Korea to guarantee us a fair trial," Paul told reporters. "The whole trial was unfair. The jury was not given all the evidence."[4]

As one obituary declared, "It was ex-star Ramon Novarro's tragedy not to recognize two bad actors when he saw them."[5]

During the murder trial of Ramon Novarro, Hollywood was once again shocked at the senseless murder of one of its own. Less than a year after Novarro's death, actress Sharon Tate and four others were murdered at Tate's mountain home by the Manson gang. Novarro contributed much to Hollywood's history and now his death brought about the beginning of a new era for Tinsel Town's elite, one that included tighter security, bodyguards, and a sense of paranoia.

Novarro, who had fought so hard to keep his private life private, would have been devastated at the pain his family and friends had to endure, not only because of the tragic way he died, but because of the way his life was now open to public scrutiny. Regardless of the way Ramon died, one must remember his life and how he used it to help others. His contributions to his church and to society far outweigh any vices that one may think he had. Novarro's friend and former agent Alan Brock summed up his life best when he said: "I never heard him say an unkind word about any of his contemporaries—nor of the stars of more recent years. And through the years, that sincere boyish enthusiasm the screen knew so well was ever present in his off screen life. The loss of Ramon Novarro leaves a tremendous gap in the ranks of the show business world that can never be filled."[6]

Epilogue

*He was himself, when not a prisoner of his own frailties,
a man of great charm, wit, and wisdom, and he had proved
himself a one time great star who could play a supporting
character role with authority and style. His death was both
barbaric and decidedly out of character. To the end, he could
not be typed.*[1]

—DeWitt Bodeen

If Tom Ferguson lied about killing Ramon Novarro in order to keep his brother from the gas chamber, it clearly worked. Jim Keppner, founder of the Gay and Lesbian Archives in West Hollywood, California, says that he attended the trial thinking the older brother had committed the murder, but as the trial continued, he began to have his doubts. Keppner, who was covering the trial for *The Advocate*, a national gay magazine, stated: "When attorneys Hanifin, Walton and Ideman had completed their summaries and replies, there was plenty of doubt. I could only say for myself that I had come to Judge Mark Brandler's court quite sure I knew who killed Ramon Novarro, and after sitting through more than 30 hours a week for seven weeks and filling 16 spiral notebooks with notes, I felt totally unsure."[2]

In any event, Ramon Novarro was on trial as much as the Ferguson brothers. The lifestyle he had kept so carefully hidden for more than 40 years was now out in the open for the entire world to dissect. As the deputy district attorney stated, Novarro should not be judged; he was the victim. While the reasons for Novarro's behavior do not excuse him, it seems clear that he had severe emotional problems.

As for the Fergusons, both were sent to San Quentin prison to serve life sentences. In 1978, author Joel Harrison published a book on the murder of Ramon Novarro titled *Bloody Wednesday*. Harrison argued that Tom was not the killer, but that his brother, Paul, in fact, had killed Ramon Novarro. He based his findings on extensive research of police files, court documents, and actual interviews with the two brothers while they were still at San Quentin.

Paul Ferguson allegedly confessed to the author that he was the one who killed Novarro. Paul's lawyer, Cletus Hanifin, reportedly showed Harrison a 19-page confession on lined yellow legal paper which was never entered as evidence during the trial.

In 1975, Tom Ferguson wrote a letter to the presiding judge of San Joaquin county asking him to appoint an attorney to file an appeal, or reopen his case. In the letter Tom told the judge, "On April 13, 1975, Mr. Harrison interviewed my brother in San Quentin. That interview was taped, and during the interview Paul reiterated his written confession. Mr. Harrison is now in possession of that tape."[3]

Because of Harrison's finding, Tom Ferguson was released from prison on probation sometime in 1976 and was placed on a work furlough program. He later violated the terms of his probation and was returned to prison, but he was released again several months later. In 1977 he was arrested and sent to prison for a sexual offense. After being released, he failed to report to the local police as a sex offender and was returned to jail. At the time of this writing, he is incarcerated in the Los Angeles jail system and is expected to be released in 2001.

As for Paul, he worked in the fire house at San Quentin and kept his record clean. "When I first came to San Quentin," he told a reporter, "I was extremely angry and bitter. I pretty much hated everyone." In 1970, Paul began taking several writing courses and graduated with an associate of arts degree in 1974. In 1975 he was the first prisoner to win first prize for fiction from the American Center of P.E.N., an international writers' association. He received $100 for a short story about a resentful young man arrested in Cook County, Illinois. "I've been in seven years," Paul said at that time, "and it's all been clean, so I could get out in November, and I can get a job in the coal industry in Pennsylvania and I'll continue writing."[4] In 1978, Paul Ferguson was paroled, after serving only nine years for murder.

Novarro's home at 3110 Laurel Canyon Boulevard, estimated at a value of $150,000, was sold on July 26, 1969, to screen writer Clifford Gould for $76,908.45.[5] The house then went through several owners until it was bought by a young actor named Ryan Kelly in the late 1970s. Kelly, a 35-year-old stunt man, thought he was the reincarnation of Ramon Novarro. After buying the house, Kelly dressed like Novarro and furnished the house as it was when the actor was murdered. He advertised for, and found, many of Novarro's belongings and was looking for the bed that the actor died on.

Around 1980, rumors began circulating that Novarro's former home was haunted. A local television show, *Two on the Town*, hosted by Connie Chung, contacted Kelly for a show they were doing on haunted houses. Although there had been no sightings or manifestations in the house, visitors reported that the house gave off eerie vibes. Ken Schessler, author of *This Is Hollywood*, worked on the show. "We went in there for *Two on the Town*," Schessler recalled, "and two of the crew wouldn't even go into the house. They had a strange feeling when they started to go in."

Schessler claims he didn't feel anything unusual while visiting the house but added, "The only thing that bothered me was Ryan Kelly. He was pretty strange."[6] Inside the house, they set up a camera in the bedroom where Novarro had been murdered. Suddenly, fear came over one of the crew members when he went near the bathroom, and he left the house. The segment was aired nationally before the Academy Awards.

Several years later a *Herald-Examiner* reporter was writing an article on Los Angeles haunted houses and visited 3110 Laurel Canyon Boulevard. Ryan Kelly no longer lived there, but the new owners told of the actor's bizarre fate. They said that one day Kelly was having an argument with his brother over some trivial matter. As Kelly was about to leave, his brother took out a gun and shot him in the head, killing him instantly. In the late 1980s, the old house was boarded up and a new one was built next to it.

As for Ramon Novarro's other Los Angeles residences, his early family home at 1340 Constance Street still stands, but the neighborhood has declined since he lived there. The longtime family estate at 2265 West 22d was torn down several years after Novarro sold it in 1949. Automobiles on the east-bound lanes of the Santa Monica Freeway now speed over the spot where Novarro once entertained movie stars and politicians in his Teatro Intimo.

The Lloyd Wright house that Novarro acquired in 1931 still stands in the Hollywood Hills at 2255 Verde Oak Drive. It was remodeled many times, and on July 17, 1974, the house was declared historic-cultural monument number 130 by the Los Angeles Cultural Heritage Board. Named the Samuel-Novarro House (after its first two owners), it was bought by actress Diane Keaton for $1.5 million in November 1988. She had it restored while in Rome filming *The Godfather, Part III*.[7] The outside was refurbished to its original beauty, and its glimmering copper trim was replaced.

Novarro's 1938 apartment building at 10938 Riverside Drive was sold by his family on August 30, 1971, to the North Hollywood Federal Savings and Loan for $111,405.05. It was later torn down and replaced with a service station. The J. C. Penney building at 6454 Van Nuys Boulevard was sold on February 17, 1977, for $275,000.[8]

In June 1980, James Cline, the executor of Novarro's estate, resigned and Angel Samaniego became sole executor. A few years later all of Novarro's stock holdings were sold. "The will as Ramon wrote it was very complicated," his brother explained. "It would have gone on forever."[9] The family retained a lawyer, and in January of 1984, the entire estate was discharged, with the proceeds divided among his surviving brothers and sisters and his secretary, Edward Weber.

As for the family of Ramon Novarro, many still survive as of this writing. Novarro's brothers Angel (now known to his friends as Jose) and Eduardo and his sister Carmen live near San Diego. Of his two sisters who were nuns, Guadalupe died in 1973 and Rosa in 1978. Novarro's brother Antonio died in 1988 of a heart attack he suffered in the parking lot of a Los Angeles restaurant. Luz died in 1991, and Mariano, who had arrived in the United States with Ramon in 1915, died in 1993. Novarro has many nephews and nieces, one of whom is a priest in Spain.

Ramon's lifelong friend, Alice Terry, lived in her home at 11554 North Kelsey Street in Studio City until she died of pneumonia on December 22, 1987. Anita Page, Novarro's only surviving costar from his glory days, is widowed and lives in Los Angeles. Edward Weber now resides in Massachusetts, and Novarro's friend and lover from the early 1940s, Don Atkins, is retired and lives in Florida.

The Ramon Novarro Film Club in England continued to meet and publish its newsletter through the '70s. Shortly after Novarro's death, the club leaders sadly wrote to their members, "No star has [been], nor will be as faithful to his fans as Ramon Novarro was."[10]

Filmography of
Ramon Novarro

It is reported that Ramon Novarro appeared as an extra in more than 100 films between 1916 and 1921. What follows is a listing of known extra roles and his complete feature roles, as well as his television and stage credits. Financial information is provided only for Metro-Goldwyn-Mayer films. Source: Eddie Mannix ledger, Howard Strickling Collection, AMPAS.

EXTRA ROLES

Joan the Woman—1916, Paramount. Directed by Cecil B. DeMille. Starring Geraldine Farrar and Wallace Reid.

The Little American—1917, Paramount. Directed by Cecil B. DeMille. Starring Mary Pickford and Jack Holt.

The Jaguar's Claw—1917, Triangle. Directed by Marshal Neilan. Starring Sessue Hayakawa.

The Hostage—1917, Famous Players–Lasky. Directed by Robert Thornby. Starring Wallace Reid and Dorthea Abril.

The Goat—1918, Paramount-Artcraft. Directed by Donald Crisp. Starring Fred Stone and Fanny Midgely.

Man, Woman, Marriage—1921, Universal. Directed by Allen Holubar. Starring Dorothy Phillips.

The Four Horsemen of the Apocalypse—1921, Metro. Directed by Rex Ingram. Starring Rudolph Valentino and Alice Terry.

A Small Town Idol—1921, Mack Sennett Productions. Directed by Erle C. Kenton. Starring Ben Turpin and Marie Prevost.

My American Wife—1922, Famous Players–Lasky. Directed by Sam Wood. Starring Gloria Swanson and Antonio Moreno.

FEATURED ROLES

1. *Mr. Barnes of New York*—1922, Goldwyn Pictures Corporation, drama. Released June 2, 1922. Produced by Samuel Goldwyn; directed by Victor Schertzinger; scenario by Gerald Duffy and J. E. Nash, based on the novel *Mr. Barnes of New York* by Archibald Clavering Gunter; photography by George Brewster.

Cast: Tom Moore (Mr. Barnes of New York), Anna Lehr (Marina Paoli), Naomi Childers (Enid Anstruther), Lewis Willoughby (Gerard Anstruther), Ramon Samaniego (Antonio), Otto Hoffman (Tomasso), Sidney Ainsworth (Danella).

Review: "It has plenty of romantic and adventurous interest, moves along at an even, well-tempered gait—and what is most important, is the sort of film from which exhibitors ought to reap satisfying rewards." *New York Morning Telegraph*, 6/25/22.

Silent. B & W. Running time, 5 reels, 4,804 ft.

2. *The Prisoner of Zenda*—1922, Metro, drama. Released at the Astor Theater, New York, July 31, 1922. Produced by Rex Ingram; directed by Rex Ingram; screenplay by Mary O'Hara based on the Edward Rose play (c. 1897) and Anthony Hope's novel *The Prisoner of Zenda*; art direction by Amos Myers; production manager, Starret Ford; edited by Grant Whytock; photographed by John F. Seitz.

Song: "Zenda"—words and music by Louis Breau and Ernst Luz.

Cast: Lewis Stone (Rudolf Rassendyll/King Rudolf), Alice Terry (Princess Flavia), Robert Edeson (Colonel Sapt), Stuart Holmes (Duke Michael), Ramon Samaniego (Rupert of Hentzau), Barbara La Marr (Antoinette de Mauban), Malcom McGregor (Count von Tarlenheim), Edward Connelly (Marshall Von Strakenez), Lois Lee (Countess Helga), John George (uncredited), Snitz Edwards (uncredited).

Review: "Ramon Samanyagos, who does a fine bit of acting as Rupert of Hentzau, seems a decided find and an entirely new type. With one flip of a monocle, he won the American public." *Photoplay*, 8/22.

Silent. B & W. Running time, 10 reels, 10,467 ft., 120 minutes.

3. *Trifling Women*—1922, Metro, romantic drama. Premiered at the Astor Theater, New York City, October 1, 1922 (released November 6, 1922). Produced by Rex Ingram; directed by Rex Ingram; screenplay by Rex Ingram from his own story, "Black Orchids"; art direction by Leo E. Kuter; edited by Grant Whytock; photographed by John F. Seitz.

Song: "Trifling Women"—words by George Kershaw, music by Ernst Luz and Louis Breau.

Cast: Barbara La Marr (Jacqueline de Severac/Zarenda), Ramon Novarro (Henri/Ivan de Maupin), Edward Connelly (Baron Francois de Maupin), Lewis Stone (Marquis Ferroni), Hughie Mack (Père Alphonse Bidondeau), Gene Pouyet (Colonel Roybet), John George (Achmet), Jess Weldon (Caesar), Hymen Binunsky (Hassan), Joe Martin (Hatim-Tai, a chimpanzee).

Review: "Other than the Rex Ingram name attached, it will be fortunate to command attention as a regular Metro release ... while Mr. Novarro's part could also have been assumed by almost any juvenile of pictures." *Variety*, 10/6/22.

Silent. B & W. Running time, 9 reels, 8,800 ft., 100 minutes.

4. *Where the Pavement Ends*—1923, Metro, melodrama. Released at the Capitol Theater, New York, March 19, 1923. Produced by Morton Spring and Rex Ingram; directed by Rex Ingram; screenplay adapted by Rex Ingram based on the short story "The Passion Vine" from John Russell's book *The Red Mark, and Other Stories*; technical direction by Gordon Mayer; edited by Grant Whytock; photographed by John F. Seitz.

Song: "Neath the Passion Vine"—words by Bert Herbert, music by Walter Havenschild.

Cast: Edward Connelly (Pastor Spener), Alice Terry (Miss Matilda), Ramon Novarro (Motauri), Harry T. Morey (Captain Hull Gregson), John George (Napuka Joe).

Review: "Ramon Novarro would be rather too conventionally and spiritually good looking for a regular hero, but in these surroundings he is a picturesque figure, and his slim, boyish type furnishes effective symbolic contrast to the burly figure of the drunken trader." *Variety*, 4/5/23.

Filmed on location near Miami, Florida, and in Cuba.

Silent. B & W. Running time, 8 reels, 7,706 ft., 70 minutes.

5. *Scaramouche*—1923, Metro, historical romance. Released at 44th Street Theater, New York, September 30, 1923. Produced by Rex Ingram; directed by Rex Ingram; screenplay adapted by Willis Goldbeck from the novel *Scaramouche: A Romance of the French Revolution* by Rafael Sabatini; wardrobe by

O'Kane Cornwell, Eve Roth, and Van Horn; edited by Grant Whytock; photographed by John F. Seitz.

Songs: "Scaramouche—Fox Trot March"—music by Joseph Jordan; "Scaramouche—Minuet"—words by P. S. Robinson, music by L. Beethoven.

Cast: Ramon Novarro (Andre-Louis Moreau), Alice Terry (Aline de Kercadiou), Lewis Stone (Marquis de la Tour d'Azyr), Lloyd Ingraham (Quinton de Kercadiou), Julia Swayne Gordon (Countess Therese de Plougastel), William Humphrey (Chevalier de Chabrillane), Otto Matiesen (Philippe de Vilmorin), George Siegmann (Georges Jacques Danton), Bowditch Turner (Le Chapelier), James A. Marcus (Challefau Binet), Edith Allen (Climene Binet), Lydia Yeamans Titus (Madame Binet), John George (Polinchinelle), Nelson McDowell (Rhodomont), De Garcia Fuerburg (Maximilien Robespierre), Roy Coulson (Jean Paul Marat), Edwin Argus (Louis XVI), Clotilde Delano (Marie Antoinette), Slavko Vorkapitch (Napoleon Bonaparte, a lieutenant of artillery), Edward Coxen (Jacques), Rose Dione (La Reuolte), Howard Gaye, (Viscount d'Albert), J. Edwin Brown (Monsieur Benoit), Carrie Clark Ward (Mme. Benoit), William Dyer (gamekeeper), Edward Connelly (minister to the King), Williard Lee Hall (king's lieutenent), Lorimer Johnston (Count Dupuye), Arthur Jasmine (a student of Rennes), Tom Kennedy (a dragoon), Kalla Pasha (keeper of the Paris gate), B. Hyman (extra), Louise Carver (extra), Mary Reynolds (extra).

Review: "Ingram has done himself proud in this picture. Ramon Novarro, as the young lawyer, actor-duelist hero of the story is made for the future." *Variety,* 9/20/23.

Silent. B & W. Running time, 10 reels, 9,850 ft., 120 minutes.

6. *Thy Name Is Woman*—1924, Metro-Goldwyn, romantic tragedy. Released at the Lyric Theater, New York, March 3, 1924. Produced by Louis B. Mayer; directed by Fred Niblo; screenplay adapted by Bess Meredyth from the play *The She-Devil* by Karl Schoenherr (translated by Benjamin Floyer Glazer, opened in New York City, November 15, 1920); art direction by Ben Carre; edited by Lloyd Nosler; photographed by Victor Milner.

Cast: William V. Mong (Pedro the Fox), Barbara La Marr (Guerita), Ramon Novarro (Juan Ricardo), Wallace MacDonald (Captain Roderigo de Castelar), Robert Edeson (Comandante), Claire MacDowell (Juan's mother), Edith Roberts (Delores).

Review: "There are portions of the second half where the sex stuff is permitted to run wild in the scenes between the trooper and the smuggler's wife. This may possibly prove the one box office asset, but that may not get by all censor boards." *Variety,* 3/5/24.

Silent. B & W. Running time, 9 reels, 9,087 ft., 102 minutes.

7. *The Arab*—1924, Metro-Goldwyn, melodrama. Released July 13, 1924. Produced by Rex Ingram; directed by Rex Ingram; screenplay adapted by Rex

Ingram from the play *The Arab, a Play* by Edgar Selwyn (opened in New York City, September 1911); edited by Grant Whytock; photographed by John F. Seitz.

Song: "The Arab"—words and music by Ted Barron.

Cast: Ramon Novarro (Jamil Abdullah Azam), Alice Terry Mary Hilbert), Gerald Robertshaw (Dr. Hilbert), Maxudian (Governor), Jean de Limur (Hossein, his aide), Adelqui Miller (Abdullah), Paul Vermoyal (Marmount), Alexandresco (Oulad Nile), Justa Uribe (Myrza), Paul Francesci (Marmount), Giuseppe De Compo (Selim).

Review: "This is the finest sheik film of them all. As a sheik, Novarro is the acme. Though this is in a measure a 'sex' picture, it may be recommended to high school classes." *Variety*, 7/16/24.

Filmed on location in Tunisia, North Africa.

Silent. B & W. Running time, 7 reels, 6,710 ft., 67 minutes.

8. *The Red Lily*—1924, Metro-Goldwyn, drama. Released at the Capitol Theater, New York, September 28, 1924. Produced by Louis B. Mayer; directed by Fred Niblo; assistant director, Doran Cox; screenplay adapted by Bess Meredyth from an original story by Fred Niblo; art direction by Ben Carre; edited by Lloyd Nosler; photographed by Victor Milner.

Cast: Enid Bennett (Marise La Noue), Ramon Novarro (Jean Leonnec), Wallace Beery (Bobo), Frank Currier (Hugo Leonnec), Rosemary Theby (Nana), Mitchell Lewis (D'Agut), Emily Fitzroy (Mama Bouchard), Georges Periolat (Papa Bouchard), Milla Davenport (Madame Poussot), Dick Sutherland (Toad), Gibson Gowland (Le Turc), George Nichols (concierge).

Review: "In addition to being unpleasant, condemnatory at the start, the plot is weak and hackneyed. Novarro's acting is almost negligible." *Variety*, 10/1/24.

Silent. B & W. Running time, 7 reels, 6,975 ft., 65 minutes.

9. *A Lover's Oath*—1925, Astor Distribution Corporation, fantasy. Released at Loew's New York, September 29, 1925 (filmed in 1921). Produced and directed by Ferdinand Pinney Earle; based on Edward Fitzgerald's *The Rubaiyat of Omar Khayyam, the Astronomer-Poet of Persia, Rendered into English Verse*; edited by Milton Sills; photographed by George Benoit.

Cast: Ramon Novarro (Ben Ali), Kathleen Key (Sherin), Edwin Stevens (Hassen Ben Sabbath), Frederick Warde (Omar Khayyam), Hedwig Reicher (Hassan's wife), Snitz Edwards (Omar's servant), Charles A. Post (Commander of the Faithful), Arthur Edmund Carew (Prince Yussuf), Paul Weigel (Sheik Rustum), Philippe de Lacy (his son), Warren Rodgers (Haja).

Review: "The Apolloesque Novarro has little to do but loll around.... On the other hand the sets are bizarre, imaginative and very often beautiful, rivalling any ever seen in such productions." *Variety*, 10/7/25.

Silent. B & W. Running time, 6 reels, 5,896 ft., 76 minutes.

10. *The Midshipman*—1925, Metro-Goldwyn-Mayer, romantic drama. Released at the Capitol Theater, New York, October 11, 1925. Produced by Bernard Hyman under the supervision of the U.S. Navy Department; technical supervision by Herbert A. Jones, USN; directed by Christy Cabanne; story by Carey Wilson; continuity by F. McGrew Willis and Christy Cabanne; edited by Harold Young; photographed by Oliver Marsh.

Song: "Midshipman"—words and music by Ted Barron.

Cast: Ramon Novarro (James Randall), Harriet Hammond (Patricia Lawrence), Wesley Barry (Ted Lawrence), Margaret Seddon (Mrs. Randall), Crauford Kent (Basil Courtney), Maurice Ryan ("Fat"), Harold Goodwin ("Tex"), William Boyd ("Spud"), Pauline Key (Rita).

Review: "It's a good picture and will be of general interest simply on the strength of the Naval Academy settings. Novarro makes a good looking undergraduate and plays both naturally and easily to convince." *Variety*, 10/14/25.

Filmed on location at the U.S. Naval Academy at Annapolis, Maryland.

Silent. B & W. Running time, 8 reels, 7,498 ft., 74 minutes. Cost: $175,000; domestic gross: $460,000; foreign gross: $490,000; profit: $450,000.

11. *Ben-Hur*—1925, Metro-Goldwyn-Mayer, religious spectacular. Premiered at the George M. Cohan Theater, New York, December 30, 1925. Produced by Irving Thalberg and Louis B. Mayer by special arrangement with A. L. Erlanger, Charles B. Delingham, and Florenz Ziegfeld, Jr.; directed by Fred Niblo; additional directors, Christy Cabanne, Alfred Raboch, B. Reaves Eason, and Ferdinand P. Earle; assistant director, Charles Stalling; assistants on chariot race, William Wyler and Henry Hathaway; production managers, Harry Edington and J. J. Cohn; screenplay by Carey Wilson and Bess Meredyth, based on June Mathis' adaptation of General Lew Wallace's novel; titles by Katherine Hilliker and H. H. Caldwell; musical score by David Mendoza and William Axt; art direction by Cedric Gibbons, Horace Jackson Grieve; assistant art director, A. Arnold Gillespie; special effects by Ferdinand P. Earle, Frank Williams (traveling mattes), Kenneth Gordon Maclean, Padre Berier; ships designed by Camillo Mastocinque; ship construction by Fratelli Neri; costumes by Henry J. Kaufmann; wardrobe and makeup by Mr. and Mrs. Adolph Seidel; edited by Lloyd Nosler (chief editor), Basil Wrangler, William Holmes, Harry Reynolds, and Ben Lewis; photographed by Karl Strauss, Percy Hilburn, Rene Guissart, and Clyde De Vinna; trick photography by Paul Eagler; additional photography by E. Burton Steene and George Meehan; technicolor staff, J. A. Ball, Rene Guissart, Ervin Roy Musgrave, and Wm. Howard Green.

Cast: Ramon Novarro (Ben-Hur), Francis X. Bushman (Messala), May McAvoy (Esther), Claire McDowell (Princess of Hur), Kathleen Key (Tirzah), Carmel Myers (Iras), Nigel de Bruiller (Simonides), Mitchell Lewis (Sheik Ilderim), Leo White (Sanballat), Frank Currier (Arrius), Charles

Belcher (Balthasar), Betty Bronson (Mary), Dale Fuller (Amrah), Winter Hall (Joseph), Rosita Garcia (bit), Myrna Loy (bit), Tom Tyler (bit).

Review: "As the industry today stands, so does Ben-Hur stand: the greatest achievement that has been accomplished on the screen for not only the screen itself, but for all motion picturedom. He [Novarro] may never have appealed before in former productions, but anyone who sees him in this picture will have to admit that he is without doubt a man's man and 100 percent of that. Novarro is made for all time by his performance here." *Variety,* 1/6/26.

Some scenes filmed on location near Rome, Italy.

Silent. B & W with Technicolor sequences. Running time, 12 reels, 11,693 ft., 128 minutes. Cost: $3,967,000; domestic gross: $4,359,000; foreign gross: $5,027,000; loss: $698,000. 1931 reissue: domestic gross: $199,000; foreign gross: $1,153,000.

12. *Lovers?* (working title: *The Great Goleoto*)—1927, Metro-Goldwyn-Mayer, romantic drama. Released at Capitol Theater, New York, April 15, 1927. Produced by Irving Thalberg and John Stahl; directed by John M. Stahl; assistant director, Sidney Algier; continuity by Douglas Furber and Sylvia Thalberg based on *El Gran Galeoto, drama en tres actos y en verso* by Jose Echegaray y Eizaguirre, adapted as *The World and His Wife* by Frederic Nordlinger; titles by Marion Ainslee and Ruth Cummings; settings by Cedric Gibbons and Merill Pye; wardrobe by Andre-Ani; edited by Margaret Booth; photographed by Max Fabian.

Cast: Ramon Novarro (Jose/Ernesto), Alice Terry (Felicia/Teodora), Edward Martindel (Don Julian), Edward Connelly (Don Severo), George K. Arthur (Pepito), Lillian Leighton (Donna Mercedes), Holmes Herbert (Milton), John Miljan (Alvarez), Roy D'Arcy (Senor Galdos).

Review: "A screenplay of stunning pictorial beauty, photographic excellence and fine acting, but lacking in the prime essential—sustained dramatic interest." *Variety,* 4/20/27.

Silent. B & W. Running time, 6 reels, 5,291 ft., 56 minutes. Cost: $347,000; domestic gross: $368,000; foreign gross: $268,000; profit: $104,000.

13. *The Student Prince in Old Heidelberg*—1927, Metro-Goldwyn-Mayer, romantic drama. Released at the Astor Theater, New York, September 21, 1927. Produced by Irving Thalberg; directed by Ernst Lubitsch; continuity by Hans Kraly, adapted from the operetta *The Student Prince* by Dorothy Donnelly and Sigmund Romberg (opened in New York City, December 2, 1924) and the play *Alt Heidelberg, Schauspiel in funf Aufzugen* by Wilhelm Meyer-Forster; titles by Marion Ainslee and Ruth Cummings; settings by Cedric Gibbons, Richard Day, Edgar G. Ulmer (asst.), and Eric Locke (asst.); original music by William Axt and David Mendoza; wardrobe by Ali Hubert; edited by Andrew Martin; photographed by John Mescall.

Cast: Ramon Novarro (Prince Karl Heindrich), Norma Shearer (Kathi), Jean Hersholt (Dr. Juttner), Gustav Von Seyffertitz (King Karl VII), Philippe de Lacy (Heir Apparent), Edgar Norton (Lutz), Bobby Mack (Kellerman), Edward Connelly (court marshal), Otils Harlan (Old Ruder), John S. Peters, George K. Arthur, Lionel Belmore, Edythe Chapman and Lincoln Stedman (students).

Review: "Lubitsch took his tongue out of his cheek when he directed this special. In toto, everything is okay except the story—and Novarro's make-up. Due to that make-up, Novarro is always the actor here despite a performance that is creditable." *Variety,* 9/28/27.

Silent. B & W. Running time, 10 reels, 9,435 ft., 105 minutes. Cost: $1,205,000; domestic gross: $894,000; foreign gross: $662,000; loss: $307,000.

14. *The Road to Romance* (working title: *Romance*)—1927, Metro-Goldwyn-Mayer, romantic melodrama. Released at the Capitol Theater, New York, October 8, 1927. Produced by Hunt Stromberg; directed by John S. Robertson; continuity by Josephine Lovett, based on the novel *Romance* (1903) by Joseph Conrad and Ford Maddox Ford; titles by Joe Farnum; settings by Cedric Gibbons and Richard Day; wardrobe by Gilbert Clark; edited by William Hamilton; photographed by Oliver Marsh.

Cast: Ramon Novarro (Jose Armando), Marceline Day (Serafina), Marc McDermott (Popolo), Roy D'Arcy (Don Balthasar); Cesare Gravina (Castro), Bobby Mack (drunkard), Otto Matiesen (Don Carlos), Jules Cowles (Smoky Beard).

Review: "A story of pirates, plenty of water on the side, and Ramon Novarro. Novarro did a neat bit as a nance aside in a court scene to fool the judge.... One must like Novarro a lot to like the picture, but those who do will." *Variety,* 10/12/27.

Silent. B & W. Running time, 7 reels, 6,544 ft., 60 minutes. Cost: $280,000; domestic gross: $425,000; foreign gross: $298,000; profit: $202,000.

15. *Across to Singapore* (working title: *China Bound*)—1928, Metro-Goldwyn-Mayer, drama. Released at the Capitol Theater, New York, April 29, 1928. Produced by Eddie Mannix; directed by William Nigh; screenplay adapted by Laurence Stallings and Ted Shane, based on the novel *All the Brothers Were Valiant* by Ben Ames Williams; continuity by Richard Schayer; titles by Joe Farnum; art direction by Cedric Gibbons; wardrobe by David Cox; edited by Ben Lewis; photographed by John F. Seitz.

Cast: Ramon Novarro (Joel Shore), Joan Crawford (Priscilla Crowninshield), Ernest Torrence (Captain Mark Shore), Frank Currier (Jeremiah Shore), Dan Wolheim (Noah Shore), Duke Martin (Matthew Shore), Edward Connelly (Joshua Crowninshield), James Mason (Finch), Anna May Wong (Bailarina).

Review: "On the technical side the film is a marvel of artistic excellence. Its settings are the finest kind of pictorial compositions, both ashore and on the majestic square-rigged ship.... There is a thrilling passage of the ship rounding Cape Horn in a 'snortin' nor'wester' that is a marvel for kick, indeed the first really convincing sea storm this reviewer has ever seen filmed." *Variety,* 5/2/28.

Silent. B & W. Running time, 7 reels, 6,805 ft., 78 minutes. Cost: $290,000; domestic gross: $548,000; foreign gross: $333,000; profit: $306,000.

16. *A Certain Young Man* (working titles: *Bellamy the Magnificent, The Heartbreaker*)—1928, Metro-Goldwyn-Mayer, romantic comedy. Released at the Capitol Theater, New York, June 9, 1928. Produced by Bernard Hyman, directed by Hobart Henly, screenplay by Doris Bureel, titles by Marion Ainslee, set design by Cedric Gibbons and Merrill Pye, wardrobe by Gilbert Clark, edited by Basil Wrangell, photographed by Merritt B. Gerstat.

Cast: Ramon Novarro (Lord Gerald Brinsley), Marceline Day (Phyllis), Renee Adoree (Henriette), Carmel Myers (Mrs. Crutchley), Bert Roach (Mr. Crutchley), Huntley Gordon (Mr. Hammond), Ernest Wood (Hubert), Willard Lewis.

Review: "Seemingly there have been numerous retakes and a new job of cutting and editing performed. The result is not bad, although plenty of details give a hint of what a palooka it probably was when first turned out." *Variety,* 6/13/28.

Note: Picture was filmed in 1926 with scenes added in 1928.

Silent. B & W. Running time, 6 reels, 5,679 ft., 58 minutes. Cost: $363,000; domestic gross: $263,000; foreign gross: $237,000; loss: $50,000.

17. *Forbidden Hours* (working title: *The Loves of Louis*)—1928, Metro-Goldwyn-Mayer, romantic melodrama. Released at the Capitol Theater, New York, July 22, 1928. Produced by Bernard Hyman; directed by Harry Beaumont; screenplay by A. P. Younger; titles by John Colton; art direction by Cedric Gibbons; sets by Richard Day; wardrobe by Gilbert Clark; edited by William Hamilton; photographed by Merritt B.Gerstad.

Cast: Ramon Novarro (His Majesty, Michael IV), Renee Adoree (Marie de Floriet), Dorothy Cumming (Queen Alexxia); Edward Connelly (Prime Minister); Alberta Vaughn (Nina), Roy D'Arcy (Duke Nicky), Mitzi Cummings (Princess Ena).

Review: "Light, frothy and inconsequential piece of work which Novarro's excellent light comedy playing will never be able to hold up for more than mediocre grosses. Tough break for the star that he had to waste such corking frivolous moments on such a yarn." *Variety,* 7/25/28.

Silent. B & W. Running time, 6 reels, 5,011 ft., 49 minutes. Cost: $293,000; domestic gross: $401,000; foreign gross: $198,000; profit: $109,000.

18. *The Flying Fleet* (working title: *Golden Braid*)—1929, Metro-Goldwyn-Mayer, drama. Released at the Capitol Theater, New York, February 9, 1929. Produced by Bernard Hyman with the sanction of the United States Navy; directed by George W. Hill; screenplay adapted by Richard Schayer, based on an original story by Lt. Commander Frank Wead, USN, and Byron Morgan; titles by Joe Farnham; art direction by Cedric Gibbons; wardrobe by David Cox; edited by Blanche Sewell; photographed by Ira Morgan with special air photography by Charles A. Marshall.

Song: "You're the Only One for Me"—words by Ray Klages, music by William Axt and David Mendoza.

Film is "Dedicated to the officers and men of Naval Aviation whose splendid co-operation made this production possible."

Cast: Ramon Novarro (Tommy), Ralph Graves (Steve), Anita Page (Anita), Edward Nugent (Dizzy), Carroll Nye (Tex), Sumner Getchell (Kewpie), Gardner James (Specs), Alfred Allen (Admiral), the Three Hawks.

Review: "In many ways, MGM's opus has serious claims to the distinction of being the most successful, technically and dramatically, of all the navy pictures. Ramon Novarro is a likeable, natural and clean-cut, but at the same time an unheroic hero." *Variety*, 2/13/29.

Filmed on location at the Hotel del Coronado and the naval base near San Diego, California.

Synchronized musical score and sound effects. Movietone (no dialogue). Also silent. B & W. Running time, 11 reels, 9,044 ft., 72 minutes. Cost: $385,000; domestic gross: $658,000; foreign gross: $628,000; profit: $443,000.

19. *The Pagan*—1929, Metro-Goldwyn-Mayer, melodrama. Released at the Capitol Theater, New York, May 11, 1929. Produced by Irving Thalberg; directed by W. S. Van Dyke; assistant director, Harry S. Bucquet; screenplay adapted by Dorothy Farnum from the short story by John Russell; titles by John Howard Lawson; art direction by Cedric Gibbons; edited by Ben Lewis; photographed by Clyde de Vinna.

Song: "The Pagan Love Song"—words by Arthur Freed, music by Nacio Herb Brown.

Cast: Ramon Novarro (Henry Shoesmith), Renee Adoree (Madge), Dorothy Janis (Tito), Donald Crisp (Henry Slater).

Review: "He [Novarro] gives profound understanding and pagan grace to his characterization of a half-caste youth whose 'only god is nature, and whose only law is love.' Under the delicate story surges the powerful undercurrent of Polynesian history, portrayed with heartfelt sympathy by the perfectly-chosen cast." *Photoplay*, 2/29.

Filmed on location in the Tuamotu Archipelago.

Synchronized musical score and sound effects. Movietone (no dialogue). Also silent. B & W. Running time, 9 reels, 7,459 ft., 80 minutes; silent version, 7,359 ft. Cost: $293,000; domestic gross: $639,000; foreign gross: $713,000; profit: $562,000.

20. *Devil-May-Care* (working title: *The Battle of the Ladies*)—1929, Metro-Goldwyn-Mayer, musical costume drama. Released at the Astor Theater, New York, December 22, 1929. Produced by Albert Lewin; directed by Sidney Franklin; based on the French play *La Bataille des dames ou un duel en amour* by Ernest Legouve and Eugene Scribe; adaptation by Richard Schrayer; scenario by Hans Kraly; dialogue by Zelda Sears; art direction by Cedric Gibbons; gowns by Adrian; ballet music by Dimitri Tiomkin; ballet directed by Albertina Rasch; sound by Douglas Shearer; edited by Conrad A. Nerug; photographed by Meritt B. Gerstad.

Songs: "Charming," "If He Cared," "March of the Old Guard," "The Old Guard Song," "Shepherd's Seranade," "The Gang Song," "Why Waste Your Charms," "Madame Pompadour"—words by Clifford Grey, music by Herbert Stothart.

Cast: Ramon Novarro (Armand), Dorothy Jordan (Leonie), Marion Harris (Louise), John Miljan (De Grignon), William Humphrey (Napoleon), George Davis (Groom), Clifford Bruce (Gaston).

Review: "An average good talker in the better class of near-specials now being turned out and a very good product for its star, Ramon Novarro.... Novarro sings well, with an accent, the only accent of this French character cast. He handles the well written dialog nicely." *Variety*, 12/25/29.

Sound (Movietone). B & W with a Technicolor sequence. Running time, 11 reels, 8,782 ft., 110 minutes. Cost: $487,000; domestic gross: $713,000; foreign gross: $703,000; profit: $357,000.

21. *In Gay Madrid* (working title: *The House of Troy*)—1930, Metro-Goldwyn-Mayer, musical comedy-drama. Released at the Capitol Theater, New York, June 7, 1930. Produced by Paul Bern; directed by Robert Z. Leonard; dialogue and continuity by Bess Meredyth, Salisbury Field, and Edwin Justus Mayer, based on the novel *La Casa de la Troya* by Alejandro Perez Lugin; art direction by Cedric Gibbons; gowns by Adrian; musical score by Fred E. Ahlert, Xavier Cugat and Herbert Stothart; sound by Douglas Shearer; edited by William S. Gray; photographed by Oliver Marsh.

Songs: "Dark Night," "Santiago," "Smile While We May"—words by Clifford Grey, music by Herbert Stothart and Xavier Cugat; "Into My Heart"—words by Roy Turk, music by Fred Ahlert.

Cast: Ramon Novarro (Ricardo), Dorothy Jordan (Carmina), Lottice Howell (La Goyita), Claude King (Marques de Castelar), Eugenia Besserer (Dona Generosa), William V. Mong (Rivas), Beryl Mercer (Dona Concha), Nanci Price (Jacinta), Herbert Clark (Octavio), David Scott (Ernesto), George Chandler (Enrique), Bruce Coleman (Corpulento), Nicholas Caruso (Carlos).

Review: "Unreal story, poor acting, ditto direction and general lack of popular appeal, are among the many negative marks of this one. Certainly looks like MGM was hard-up for a story for Novarro to go so far afield." *Variety,* 6/11/30.

Sound (Movietone). B & W. Running time, 9 reels, 7,654 ft., 78 minutes. Cost: $467,000; domestic gross: $551,000; foreign gross: $398,000; profit: $122,000.

22. *The March of Time* (working title: *Hollywood Revue of 1930/Show World*)—1930, Metro-Goldwyn-Mayer; musical revue. Unreleased. Produced by Harry Rapf; directed by Chuck Riesner.

Song: "Long Ago in Alcala"—words and music by Andre Messanzer.

Cast: Fay Templeton, Josephine Sable, Marie Dressler, Ramon Novarro, Buster Keaton, Bing Crosby, Joe Weber, Karl Dane, Cliff Edwards, Lon Chaney, Louis Mann, Barney Fagan, Lew Fields, William Collier, De Wolf Hopper.

Sound (Movietone). B & W and Technicolor sequence.

23. *Call of the Flesh* (working title: *The Singer of Seville*)—1930, Metro-Goldwyn-Mayer, musical romantic drama. Released at the Capitol Theater, New York, September 12, 1930. Produced by Hunt Stromberg; directed by Charles Brabin; story by Dorothy Farnum; dialogue by John Colton; art direction by Cedric Gibbons; wardrobe by David Cox; sound by Douglas Shearer and Ralph Shugart; edited by Conrad A. Nevig; photographed by Merritt B. Gerststad.

Songs: "Lonely"—words by Clifford Grey, music by Ramon Novarro and Herbert Stothart; "Just for Today," "Not Quite Good Enough for Me"—words by Clifford Grey, music by Herbert Stothart; "Cavatina" from *L'Elisir d'amore* by Donizetti; "Questa o quella" from *Rigoletto* by Verdi.

Cast: Ramon Novarro (Juan), Dorothy Jordan (Maria), Ernest Torrence (Esteban), Nance O'Neil (Mother Superior), Renee Adoree (Lola), Mathilde Comont (La Rumbarita), Russell Hopton (Enrique).

Review: "Some of the most delightful and artistic sequences ever photographed and recorded are in this. Acting of Ramon Novarro almost flawless." *Variety,* 9/17/31.

Sound (Movietone). B & W with Technicolor sequence. Running time, 11 reels, 9,178 ft., 100 minutes. Cost: $464,000; domestic gross: $619,000; foreign gross: $1,003,000; profit: $285,000.

24. *La Sevillana*—1931, Metro-Goldwyn-Mayer, musical romantic drama. Spanish-language version of *Call of the Flesh.* Produced by Hunt Stromberg; directed by Ramon Novarro; Spanish-language screenplay adapted by Ramon Guerrero; costumes by Lucia Coulter; music and lyrics by Ramon Novarro and Herbert Stothart; edited by Tom Held; photographed by Merritt B. Gerstad.

Cast: Ramon Novarro (Juan), Conchita Montenegro (Maria Consuelo), Sra. L.C. de Samaniego (Madre Superior), Jose Soriano Viosca (Tio Esteban), Rosita Ballestera (Lola), Martin Carralaja (Enrique Varga), Sra. Maria Caleo (Lulu Laponco), Michael Vavitch (Laponco Empresaria).

Review: "It is splendidly acted and compellingly sung by Mr. Novarro." *Los Angeles Times*, undated.

Sound (Western Electric Sound System). Foreign language. B & W. Running time, 102 minutes.

25. *La Chanteur de Seville*—1931, Metro-Goldwyn-Mayer, musical romantic drama. French-language version of *The Call of the Flesh*. Released at the Madeleine Theater, Paris, February 21, 1931. Produced by Hunt Stromberg; directed by Ramon Novarro; French language screenplay by Ivan Noe and Anne Mauclair; costumes by Lucia Coulter; music and lyrics by Ramon Novarro and Herbert Stothart; edited by Tom Held; photographed by Merrit B. Gerstad.

Cast: Ramon Novarro (Juan), Suzy Vernon (Maria Consuelo), Pierrette Gaillot (Lola), George Mauloy (Esteban), Mathilde Comont (La Ruinbarita), Marcel de la Brosse (Enrique).

Review: "Novarro, who directed the film, would have done better to leave direction to an expert. As an actor he is excellent. Though a French ear can detect a foreign ring in his accent, it is entirely satisfactory." *Variety*, 3/11/31.

Sound (Western Electric Sound System). Foreign language. B & W. Running time, 105 minutes.

26. *Daybreak*—1931, Metro-Goldwyn-Mayer, romantic drama. Released at the Capitol Theater, New York, May 29, 1931. Produced by Bernard Hyman; directed by Jacques Feyder; assistant director, Charles Dorian; adapted by Ruth Cummings from the novel *Daybreak* by Arthur Schnitzler (New York, 1927); dialogue by Cyril Hume; continuity by Zelda Sears; wardrobe by Rene Hubert; art direction by Cedric Gibbons; sound by Douglas Shearer; edited by Tom Held; photographed by Merritt B. Gerstad.

Cast: Ramon Novarro (Willi), Helen Chandler (Laura), Jean Hersholt (Herr Schnabel), C. Aubrey Smith (General von Hartz), William Bakewell (Otto), Karen Morley (Emily Kessner), Kent Douglass (Von Lear), Glenn Tryon (Franz), Clyde Cook (Josef), Sumner Getchall (Emil), Clara Bandick (Frau Hoffman), Edwin Maxwell (Herr Hoffman), Jackie Searle (August).

Review: "Daybreak can't draw beyond what its star, Ramon Novarro can draw by himself. Both of them, Novarro and Helen Chandler give a perfectly blah performance. Novarro tries the light juvenile style as the Lieut., but it flattens at every try." *Variety*, 6/20/31.

Sound (Western Electric Sound System). B & W. Running time, 9 reels, 73 minutes. Cost: $515,000; domestic gross: $418,000; foreign gross: $223,000; loss: $126,000.

27. *Son of India* (working title: *The Son of the Rajah*)—1931, Metro-Goldwyn-Mayer, romantic drama. Released at the Capitol Theater, New York, July 24, 1931. Produced by Hunt Stromberg; directed by Jacques Feyder; assistant director, Harry Bucquet; screenplay adapted by Ernest Vadja from the novel *Mr. Isaacs* by F. Marion Crawford; additional dialogue by John Meehan and Claudine West; art direction by Cedric Gibbons; wardrobe by Rene Hubert; sound by Douglas Shearer; recording engineer, Robert Shirley; technical director, Jerry Lynton; edited by Conrad A. Nervig; photographed by Harold Rossen.

    Cast: Ramon Novarro (Karim), Conrad Nagel (William Darsay), Marjorie Rambeau (Mrs. Darsay), Madge Evans (Janice Darsay), C. Aubrey Smith (Dr. Wallace), Mitchell Lewis (Hamid), John Miljan (Juggat), Nigel de Brulier (Rao Rama).

    Review: "Scenically and in general appearance the picture rates. Cast is all Novarro, with no chance for evens for anyone else, including the femme lead." *Variety*, 7/28/31.

    Sound (Western Electric Sound System). B & W. Running time, 8 reels, 75 minutes. Cost: $503,000; domestic gross: $491,000; foreign gross: $490,000; profit: $84,000.

28. *The Christmas Party*—1931, Metro-Goldwyn-Mayer, short. Released during Christmas season. Directed by Charles Reisner, screenplay by Robert E. Hopkins.

    Cast: Lionel Barrymore (himself), Wallace Beery (himself), Jackie Cooper (himself), Marion Davies (herself), Marie Dressler (herself), Jimmy Durante (Santa Claus), Cliff Edwards (himself), Clark Gable (himself), Charlotte Greenwood (herself), Jerry Madden (himself), Polly Moran (herself), Ramon Novarro (himself), Anita Page (herself), Norma Shearer (herself).

    Sound (Western Electric Sound System). B & W. Running time, 9 minutes.

29. *Mata Hari*—1931, Metro-Goldwyn-Mayer, spy drama. Released at the Capitol Theater, New York, December 31, 1931. Produced by Bernie Fineman; directed by George Fitzmaurice; assistant director, H. Cullen Tate; story by Benjamin Glazer and Leo Birinski; dialogue by Doris Anderson and Gilbert Emery; art direction by Cedric Gibbons; gowns by Adrian; sound by Douglas Shearer, Fred Morgan, Paul Neal, and James Brock; edited by Frank Sullivan; photographed by William Daniels; 2d cameraman, A. L. Lane; assistant cameramen, Charles W. Riley and Albert Scheving; still photography by Milton Brown.

    Cast: Greta Garbo (Mata Hari), Ramon Novarro (Lt. Alexis Rosanoff), Lionel Barrymore (General Shubin), Lews Stone (Andriani), C. Henry Gordon (Dubois), Karen Morley (Carlotta), Alex B. Francis (Caron), Blanche

Frederici (Sister Angelica), Edmund Breese (Warden), Helen Jerome Eddy (Sister Genevieve), Frank Reicher (cook/spy), Lennox Pawle (DiSignac), Mischa Auer (man executed), Cecil Cunningham (gambler), Michael Visaroff (Jacques), Sarah Padden (Sister Teresa), Harry Cording (Ivan), Roy Barcroft (bit), Reginald Barlow (bit), Frederick Burton (bit), Gordon de Main (bit).

Review: "Garbo, Novarro, Barrymore and Stone—the Metro Tragedy Four—are too strong a marquee combination of names to leave this film in box office doubt. Production is first rate in every department." *Variety*, 1/5/32.

Sound (Western Electric Sound System). B & W. Running time. 10 reels, 90 minutes. Cost: $558,000; domestic gross: $931,000; foreign gross: $1,296,000; profit: $879,000. 1940 reissue: domestic gross: $81,000; foreign gross: $81,000; profit: $27,000.

30. *Huddle*—1932, Metro-Goldwyn-Mayer, collegiate drama. Released at the Capitol Theater, New York, June 16, 1932. Produced by Bernard Hyman and Sam Wood; directed by Sam Wood; assistant director, John Waters; adapted by Robert Lee Johnson and Arthur S. Hyman, based on the novel *Huddle* by Francis Wallace (New York, 1931); dialogue continuity by Walton Hall Smith and C. Gardner Sullivan; art direction by Cedric Gibbons; gowns by Adrian; sound by Douglas Shearer and Charles Wallace; technical detail by Cully Butler and Elbridge Anderson; edited by Hugh Wynn; photographed by Harold Wenstrom.

Song: "The Wiffenpoof Song"—words by Meade Minnigeroode and George S. Pomeroy, music by Tod B. Galloway.

Cast: Ramon Novarro (Tony Amatto), Madge Evans (Rosalie Stone), Una Merkel (Thelma), Ralph Graves (Coach Malcom Gale), John Arledge (Jim "Pidge" Pidgeon), Frank Albertson (Larry Wilson), Kane Richmond (Tom Stone), Martha Sleeper (Barbara Winston), Henry Armetta (Mr. Amatto), Ferike Boros (Mrs. Amatto), Rockliffe Fellows (Mr. Stone), Joe Sauers (Slater), Charley Grapewin (doctor); Tom Kennedy (moving man).

Review: "Football film doing much to defeat its own purpose by extreme length. Novarro makes his Tony believable and they've opened up a sequence for him to strum a guitar and toss an Italian ballad to the girl in the case." *Variety*, 6/21/32.

Sound (Western Electric Sound System). B & W. Running time, 11 reels, 103 minutes. Cost: $514,000; domestic gross: $476,000, foreign gross: $333,000; loss: $28,000.

31. *The Son-Daughter*—1932, Metro-Goldwyn-Mayer, melodrama. Released at the Capitol Theater, New York, December 30, 1932. Produced by Hunt Stromberg; directed by Clarence Brown (some scenes directed by Robert Z. Leonard); assistant director, Harry Bucquet; screenplay adapted by John Goodrich and Claudine West, based on the play *The Son-Daughter* by David Belasco and George M. Scarborough (opened in New York City, November 19,

1919); additional dialogue by Leon Gorbert; musical score by Herbert Stothart; art direction by Cedric Gibbons; gowns by Adrian; sound by Douglas Shearer; edited by Margaret Booth; photographed by Oliver T. Marsh. Songs: by Anselm Goetzl and Herbert Stothart.

Cast: Ramon Novarro (Tom Lee/Prince Chun), Helen Hayes (Lien Wha), Lewis Stone (Dr. Dong Tong), Warner Oland (Fen Sha/the Sea Crab), Ralph Morgan (Fang Fou Hy), Louise Closser Hale (Toy Yah), H. B. Warner (Sin Kai).

Review: "It's old time stuff, moving slowly and laboriously toward a sad climax. Novarro, with his head shaved, is least fortunate of the lot, for his Latin dialect does not conform with the script's stilted and fancy English dialog." *Variety,* 1/3/33.

Sound (Western Electric Sound System). B & W. Running time, 9 reels, 86 minutes. Cost: $423,000; domestic gross: $379,000; foreign gross: $313,000; profit: $6,000.

32. *The Barbarian* (working title: *Man of the Nile*)—1933, Metro-Goldwyn-Mayer, romantic drama. Released at the Capitol Theater, New York, May 12, 1933. Produced by Bernard Hyman; directed by Sam Wood; screenplay and dialogue by Anita Loos and Elmer Harris from the play *The Arab* by Edgar Selwyn; musical score by Herbert Stothart; orchestra conducted by Oscar Radin; art direction by Cedric Gibbons; gowns by Adrian; sound by Douglas Shearer; sound mixer, James Brock; edited by Tom Held; photographed by Harold Rosson; 2d cameraman, Lester White; assistant cameraman, Harry Parkins.

Song: "Love Song of the Nile"—words by Arthur Freed, music by Nacio Herb Brown.

Cast: Ramon Novarro (Jamil El Shehab), Myrna Loy (Diana Standing), Reginald Denny (Gerald Hume), Louise Closser Hale (Powers), C. Aubrey Smith (Cecil Harwood), Edward Arnold (Pasha Achmed), Blanche Frederici (Mrs. Hume), Marcelle Corday (Marthe), Hedda Hopper (American tourist), Leni Stengel (German tourist), Akim Tamiroff (Colonel).

Review: "Ramon Novarro gains applause in *The Barbarian* because of his splendid characterization of an impertinent Egyptian guide who has no scruples in securing what he desires. The flaws of the picture are the artificiality of the story and the mediocre direction, but these are overcome by Novarro's fine acting, supported by Myrna Loy, and the fascinating scenes of the desert." *New York Daily News,* 5/13/33.

Sound (Western Electric Sound System). B & W. Running time, 9 reels, 82 minutes. Cost: $447,000; domestic gross: $337,000; foreign gross: $506,000; profit: $100,000.

33. *The Cat and the Fiddle*—1934, Metro-Goldwyn-Mayer, musical comedy-drama. Released at the Capitol Theater, New York, February 16, 1934.

Produced by Bernard Hyman; directed by William K. Howard; assistant director, Lesley Selander; retake director, Sam Wood; screenplay adapted by Bella and Samuel Spewack from the Max Gordon stage musical by Jerome Kern and Otto Harbach (opened in New York City, October 15, 1931); musical direction by Herbert Stothart; art direction by Alexander Toluboff; interior decoration by Edwin B. Willis; technicolor art direction by Natalie Kalmus; gowns by Adrian; sound by Douglas Shearer; sound mixer, Paul Neal; edited by Frank E. Hull; technicolor photography by Ray Rennahan; photographed by Harold Rossen and Charles Clarke.

Songs: "I Watched the Love Parade," "A New Love Is Old," "The Night Was Made for Love," "One Moment Alone," "She Didn't Say Yes," "Try to Forget," "Don't Ask Me Not to Sing," "Poor Pierrot," "The Breeze Kissed Your Hair," "Hh! Cha! Cha!"—words by Otto Harbach, music by Jerome Kern.

Cast: Ramon Novarro (Victor Florescu), Jeanette MacDonald (Shirley Sheridan), Frank Morgan (Jules Daudet), Charles Butterworth (Charles), Jean Hersholt (Professor Bertier), Vivienne Segal (Odette Brieux), Frank Conroy (theater owner), Henry Armetta (taxi driver), Adrienne D'Ambricourt (concierge), Joseph Cawthorn (Rudy Brieux); Sterling Holloway (flower messenger), Leonid Kinsky (conservatory violinist), Christian Rub (innkeeper), Otto Fries (piano mover), Yola D'Avril (housemaid), Sumner Getchel, Harry Swailes, George Davis, Andre Renaud (students), Herman Bing (eader firemen's band), Paul Porcasi (proprietor), Robert Graves (diner), Henry Kolker (theater manager), Alice Carlisle (vegetable seller), Grace Hayle (lettuce), Germaine De Neel (maid), Harry Depp (opera singer's husband), Bill Dooley (electrician), Leo White (prompter), Polly Bailey (ballet mistress), Frank Adams (musician), Irene Franklin (opera singer), E. Alyn Warren (orchestra leader), Phil Tead (reporter), Charles Crockett (Rudy's secretary), Harold Minjir (manager of travel bureau), Earl Oxford (leading man), Arthur Hoyt (meek and humble man), George Le Guere (elevator operator), Jacques Vanaire (singer), George Nardelli (singer's assistant), Dewey Robinson (Arabian singer), Armand Kaliz (king), J. H. Peters (stage manager), Reginald Barlow (king's aide), Max Davidson (dried-up old man), Rolfe Sedan, David Reese, Eugene Borden, Ludovico Tomarchio, Freddie Ford, Geneva Williams.

Enrico Ricardi (stand-in for Ramon Novarro), Dulcie Day (stand-in for Jeanette MacDonald).

Review: "Result isn't strong entertainment, but the music, production excellence and the combination of Ramon Novarro and Jeanette MacDonald as a singing team in the picture and a costarring pair for the billing should insure fair or better returns." *Variety*, 2/20/34.

Sound (Western Electric Sound System). B & W with a Technicolor sequence. Running time, 9 reels, 88 minutes. Cost: $843,000; domestic gross: $455,000; foreign gross: $644,000; loss: $142,000.

34. *Laughing Boy*—1934, Metro-Goldwyn-Mayer, romantic tragedy. Released at Met Theater, Brooklyn, New York, May 11, 1934. Produced by Hunt Stromberg; directed by W. S. Van Dyke; assistant director, Les Selander; screenplay adapted by John Colton and John Lee Mahin based on the Pulitzer Prize–winning novel *Laughing Boy* by Oliver LaFarge; musical score by Herbert Stothert; art direction by A. Arnold Gilespie; interior decoration by Edwin B. Willis; wardrobe by Dolly Tree; sound by Douglas Shearer; production manager, Bud Barsky; edited by Blanche Sewell; photographed by Lester White.

Song: "Call of Love"—words by Gus Kahn, music by Herbert Stothart.

Cast: Ramon Novarro (Laughing Boy); Lupe Velez (Slim Girl, also known as Lily); William Dickenson (George Hartshone); Chief Thunderbird (Laughing Boy's father); Catalina Rambula (Laughing Boy's mother); Tall Man's Boy (Wounded Face); F. A. Armeta (Yellow Singer); Deer Spring (Jesting Squaw's son); Pellicana (Red Man); Chief Meyers (Crooked Nose); Sidney Bracy (White Feather); Standing Bear (Quiet Hunter); Ki Yellowhorse, Night Hawk (Indian boys); Ferdinand Munier (Fred); Anita Sheldon (Yellow Singer's wife); Grace Hayle (Mabel); Dora Clement (mother); Joseph William Cody (leader of horsemen); Carol Flores (Rosie); Julius Bojua (Jesting Squaw's son); Dennett Dell (gossip); Romiere Darling (dancing girl); Anna Dupea (older wife); Aphed Elk (younger wife); Walks Alone, White Flower (Indian girls); White Dove, Agnes, Norcha, Clara Hunt (young married women); Winnona Nora, Glympia Houten (married gossips); William Steele (guide); Edward Hearn, Ruth Channing, Carl Stockdale (tourists); James Mason (cowboy); Tito H. Davison (Navajo); Katherine Sheldon, Nora Cecil (teachers); Frances Gillman (dancer); Bill McSwain (peanut vendor).

Review: "Laughing Boy is below average entertainment despite the handsome production and care it has received. For one thing, the simulation of Indian accents, notably by Ramon Novarro, leaves something to be desired. Most of the time the star sounds like Maurice Chevalier." *Variety*, 5/15/34.

Filmed on location at an Arizona Navajo reservation and near Cameron and Flagstaff, Arizona.

Sound (Western Electric Sound System). B & W. Running time, 8 reels, 75 minutes. Cost: $518,000; domestic gross: $180,000; foreign gross: $84,000; loss: $383,000.

35. *The Night Is Young* (working title: *Tiptoes*)—1935, Metro-Goldwyn-Mayer, musical romance. Released at the Capitol Theater, New York, January 11, 1935. Produced by Harry Rapf; directed by Dudley Murphy; story by Vicki Baum and adapted by Edgar Allan Woolf and Franz Schulz; libretto by Oscar Hammerstein II; music by Sigmund Romberg; musical conductor, Oscar Radin; orchestration and musical score directed by Herbert Stothart; dances choreographed by Chester Hale; art direction by Cedric Gibbons;

associate art directors, Frederic Hope and Edwin B. Willis; wardrobe by Dolly Tree; sound by Douglas Shearer; edited by Conrad A. Nervig; photographed by James Wong Howe.

Songs: "The Night Is Young," "When I Grow Too Old to Dream," "My Old Mare," "The Noble Duchess," "There's a Riot in Havana," "Lift Your Glass"—words by Oscar Hamerstein, music by Sigmund Romberg.

Cast: Ramon Novarro (Paul Gustave), Evelyn Laye (Lisl Gluck), Charles Butterworth (Willy Fitch), Una Merkel (Fanni), Edward Everett Horton (Szereny), Donald Cook (Toni), Henry Stephenson (Emperor), Rosalind Russell (Countess Rafay), Herman Bing (Nepomuk), Albert Conti (Moehler), Elspeth Dudgeon (Duchess), Charles Judels (Riccardi), Christian Rub (cafe proprietor), Gustav von Seyffertitz (Ambassador), Mitzi (the horse), Billy Dooley (coronetist), Edith Kingdon (dowager), Snub Pollard (drummer), Torben Meyer, Carlos de Valdez (adjutants), George Davis (milkman), Josef Swickard (coctor), Billy Gilbert, Kay English, Cecilia Parker.

Review: "The producers of *The Night Is Young* have gone to great effort to make this a big picture. The sets are handsome and the costumes costly. Good supporting players are cast and photographic expertness is present. But picture emerges a disappointment. Novarro gives a stilted performance." *Variety*, 1/15/35.

Sound (Western Electric Sound System). B & W. Running time, 9 reels, 80 minutes. Cost: $573,000; domestic gross: $268,000; foreign gross: $299,000; loss: $234,000.

36. *Contra la Corriente* (English trans.: *Against the Current*)—1936, RKO–Radio Pictures, comedy-drama. Released at the Teatro Campoamor, New York City, March 6, 1936. Produced and directed by Ramon Novarro; assistant director, Antonio Samaniego; screenplay by Ramon Novarro; musical score composed and directed by Professor Juan Aguilar; dances choreographed by Ernesto Piedra; art direction by Eduardo Samaniego; assistant art director, Stephen Stepanian; sound by Karl Zint; edited by Ethel Davey; photographed by Edward Snyder and Jerry Ash.

Cast: Jose Caraballo (Alberto Dortel), Luana Alcaniz (Rosalie Martin), Alma Real (Delores Palacios de Martin), Ramon Guerrero (Frank Martin), Marina Ortiz (Tia Pascuas), Luis Diaz Flores (Carlos Marco), Nena Sandoval (Juana), Carmen Samaniego (Maruca), Luz F. Moran (Sra. Torres), John Perez (Ricardo Gavilan), Corazon Montes, Jose Pena "Pepet."

Review: "When Ramon Novarro transferred his activities from acting to writing and directing, it did not signify any epoch-making changes or improvements in the world of motion pictures...." *New York Times*, 3/10/36.

Filmed on location around Los Angeles, California.

Sound (Balsey y Phillips). Spanish language. B & W. Running time, 11 reels, 89 minutes.

37. *The Sheik Steps Out* (working title: *She Didn't Want a Sheik*)—1937, Republic Pictures, romantic comedy. Released at Warner's Beverly Hills Theater, Beverly Hills, July 24, 1937. Produced by Herman Schlom; directed by Irving Pichel; assistant director, Phil Ford; story and screenplay by Adele Bullington; dialogue by Gordon Kahn; musical direction by Alberto Columbo; orchestration by Clarence Wheeler; costumes by Eloise; sound by Terry Kellum; edited by Ernest Nims and Murray Seldeen; photographed by Jack Marta.

Songs: "Song of the Sands"—words and music by Elsie Janis and Alberto Columbo; "Ride with the Wind"—words and music by Felix Bernard and Winston Tharp.

Cast: Ramon Novarro (Ahmed Ben Nesib), Lola Lane (Phyllis "Flip" Murdock), Gene Lockhart (Samuel P. Murdock), Kathleen Burke (Gloria Parker), Stanley Fields (Abu Saal), Billy Bevan (Munson), Charlotte Treadway (Polly Parker), Robert Coote (Lord Eustace Byington), Leonard Kinskey (Allusa Ali), Georges Benazent (Count Mario), Jamiel Hasson (Kisub), C. Montague Shaw (Dr. Peabody), George Sorel (Bordeaux), Martin Garralaga (hotel clerk), Josef Swickard (Mohammedan priest), Nick Shaid (Sandseer), Doria Caron (Marie), George David (telegraph clerk), Hercules Mendez (waiter), Jean De Briac (French lieutenant), Ronald Du Pont (French hotel clerk), Charles De Ravenne (bellboy), Tofik Mickey (Arab), Rudolf Myzet (aide), Andrew McKenna (Oadi).

Review: "Only interest for the trade in this one is the reappearance of Ramon Novarro, one time popular star in silent pictures. Novarro speaks English distinctly, and there is no reason why he should not regain some standing in films, if given a part in a major production where he would be assisted by competent actors." *Variety,* 7/28/37.

Sound (Western Electric Mirrophonic Recording). B & W. Running time, 7 reels, 5,631 ft., 85 minutes.

38. *A Desperate Adventure* (working titles: *It Happened in Paris, As You Are, A Romantic Age*)—1938, Republic Pictures, comedy-drama. Released August 15, 1938. Produced by John H. Auer; directed by John H. Auer; screenplay by Barry Travers; original story by Hans Kraly and M. Coates Webster; art direction by John Victor Mackay; costumes by Irene Saltern; production manager, Al Wilson; sound by Terry Kellum; edited by Murray Seldeen; photographed by Jack Marta.

Cast: Ramon Novarro (Andre Friezan), Marian Marsh (Ann Carrington), Eric Blore (Trump), Andrew Tombes (Cosmo Carrington), and introducing Margaret Tallichet (Betty Carrington), Tom Rutherford (Gerald Richards), Maurice Cass (Dornay), Erno Verebes (Marcel), Michael Kent (Maurice), Cliff Nazarro (Tipo), Rolfe Sedan (prefect of police), Gloria Rich (Mimi), Lois Collier (Angela).

Review: "A picture that does not live up to its promises. Ramon Novarro is a graceful, charming, romantic actor with qualities that are rare to the screen. Please Mr. Republic, give Novarro a real role." *Liberty,* undated, circa 1938.

Sound (RCA Victor "High Fidelity" Sound System). B & W. Running time, 7 reels, 5,659 ft., 65 minutes.

39. *La Comédie du Bonheur* (English trans.: *The Comedy of Happiness*)—1940 (a.k.a. *Ecco la felicita),* Paulve/Scaleta, comedy-drama. Directed by Marcel L'Herbier; screenplay by Marcel L'Herbier and Nicolas Evreinoff with additional dialogue by Jean Cocteau; music by Jacques Ibert; photographed by Massimo Terzano.

Cast: Michel Simon, Jacqueline Delubac, Sylvie, Ramon Novarro, Alerne Marcel Vallee, Louis Jourdan, Micheline Presle, Andre Alerme.

Review: "Subtle, whimsical and witty, this made-in-Rome picture was an excellent vehicle for the ebullient anarchic talents of Michel Simon. It also has an interestingly diverse cast, including former silent star Ramon 'Ben-Hur' Novarro...." Unidentified publication.

French-language film shot on location in Rome.

Sound. B & W. Running time, 108 minutes.

40. *La Virgen que Forjó una Patria* (English trans.: *The Saint That Forged a Country*)—1944, Clasa Studios, religious drama. Released in the U.S.A. at Belmont Theater, New York, May 19, 1944. Directed by Julio Bracho; story by Julio Bracho and Rene Garza.

Cast: Ramon Novarro (Juan Diego), Domingo Solar (Brother Martin), Gloria Marin (Aztec slave), Paco Fuentes (Pedro de Alonso), Felipe Montoya (Zinel), Julie Villareal (Don Miquel Hidalgo), Ernesto Alonso (Captiain Allende), Victor Urruchua (Captain Juan Aldama), Fanny Schiller (Josefa).

Review: "This story, however, has the advantage of Ramon Novarro playing the lead. Ramon Novarro is forthright as the peon who sees the saint, displaying some of his old screen skill. It's a difficult role, but he does it well." *Variety,* 6/7/44.

Filmed on location in Mexico. In Spanish with English subtitles.

Sound. B & W. Running time, 106 minutes.

41. *We Were Strangers*—1949, Columbia, suspense drama. Released New York City, April 15, 1949. Produced by S. P. Eagle and John Huston; directed by John Huston; assistant director, Carl Hieke; screenplay by Peter Viertel and John Huston, based on an episode in Robert Sylvestor's novel *Rough Sketch*; original music by George Antheil; musical direction by Morris Stoloff; costume design by Jean Louis; special effects by Lawrence W. Butler; sound by Lambert E. Day; art direction by Cary Odell; set decoration by Louis Diage; hair styles by Larry Germain; makeup by Robert J. Schiffer; edited by Al Clark; photographed by Russell Metty.

Cast: Jennifer Jones (China Valdes), John Garfied (Tony Fenner), Pedro Armendariz (Armando Arieta), Gilbert Roland (Gullermo), Ramon Novarro (chief), Wally Cassell (Miguel), David Bond (Ramon), Jose Perez (Toto), Morris Ankrum (bank manager), Tito Rinaldo (Manolo), Paul Monte (Roberto), Leonard Strong (bombmaker), Robert Tafur (Rubio).

Review: "In *We Were Strangers,* John Huston has come up with a finished job of directing that edges close to his best films. In his first film part in many years, Ramon Novarro is totally unrecognizable from his youthful, romantic stints. Novarro works in an effective metallic, fast-talking quality in the part of a rebel chief." *Variety,* 4/27/49.

Sound. B & W. Running time, 106 minutes.

42. *The Big Steal*—1949, RKO, chase thriller. Released at the Mayfair, New York, July 10, 1949. Produced by Jack J. Gross; directed by Don Siegel; screenplay by Geoffrey Homes and Gerald Drayson Adams, based on the magazine story "The Road to Carmichael's" by Richard Wormser; music by Leigh Harline; edited by Samuel E. Beetley; photographed by Harry J. Wild.

Cast: Robert Mitchum (Lieut. Duke Halliday), Jane Greer (Joan Graham), William Bendix (Capt. Vincent Blake), Patrick Knowles (Jim Fiske), Ramon Novarro (Colonel Ortega), Don Alvarado (Lieut. Ruiz), John Qualen (Julius Seton), Pascual Garcia Pena (Manuel), Dorothy Mitchum (tourist).

Review: "A breathtaking scenic excursion across the landscape of Mexico, following pursued and pursuer through villages, on lovely open roads and over towering mountains on switchback highway at a fast and sizzling pace, is the most genuine fascination of the RKO thriller The Big Steal." *New York Times,* 7/11/49.

Filmed on location in Mexico.

Sound. B & W. Running time, 71 minutes.

43. *The Outriders*—1950, Metro-Goldwyn-Mayer, Western. Released New York City, March 1, 1950. Produced by Richard Goldstone; directed by Roy Rowland; story and screenplay by Irving Ravetch; music by Andre Previn; photographed by Charles Schoenbaum.

Cast: Joel McCrea (Will Owen), Arlene Dahl (Jen Gort), Barry Sullivan (Jesse Wallace), Claude Jarman, Jr. (Roy Gort), James Whitmore (Clint Priest), Ramon Novarro (Don Antonio Chaves), Jeff Corey (Keeley), Ted de Corsia (Bye), Martin Garralaga (Father Damasco).

Review: "*The Outriders* is sturdy meat for the action fan. Ramon Novarro is excellent as the elderly Mexican who is lending his gold to the union."— *Variety,* 3/8/50.

Sound. Color. Running time, 93 minutes.

44. *Crisis*—1950, Metro-Goldwyn-Mayer, suspense drama. Released at the Capitol Theater, New York, July 3, 1950. Produced by Arthur Freed; directed

by Richard Brooks; screenplay by Richard Brooks based on a story by George Tabori; original music by Miklos Rozsa; art direction by Cedric Gibbons and E. Preston Ames; set decoration by Hugh Hunt and Edwin B. Willis; special effects by A. Arnold Gillespie and Warren Newcombe; sound by Douglas Shearer; hair styles by Sydney Guilaroff; makeup by Jack Dawn; edited by Robert J. Kern; photographed by Ray June.

Cast: Cary Grant (Dr. Eugene Ferguson), Jose Ferrer (Raoul Farrago), Paula Raymond (Helen Ferguson), Signe Hasso (Isabel Farrago), Ramon Novarro (Col. Adragon), Antonio Moreno (Dr. Nierra), Tersa Celli (Rosa), Leon Ames (Sam Proctor), Gilbert Roland (Gonzales), Pedro de Cordoba (Father Del Puento), Robert Cabal (Vyman).

Review: "Produced with less generous indulgence of acting and technical skill, this obviously fantastic fiction would probably be laughed off the screen, assuming it got any further than an action-house double-bill." *New York Times*, 7/4/50.

Sound. B & W. Running time, 95 minutes.

45. *Heller in Pink Tights* (working title: *Heller Without a Gun*)—1960, Paramount, Western. Released February 29, 1960. Produced by Carlo Ponti and Marcello Girosi; assistant producer, Lewis E. Ciannelli; directed by George Cukor; assistant director, Charles C. Coleman, Jr.; second unit director, Arthur Rosson; screenplay by Dudley Nichols and Walter Bernstein, based on the novel *Heller Without a Gun* by Louis L'Amour; art direction by Hal Pereira and Eugene Allen; set decoration by Sam Comer and Grace Gregory; sound by Winston H. Leverett and John Wilkinson; music by Daniele Amfitheatrof; choreography by Val Raset; technical advisor on theatre scenes, Warren Wade; costumes by Edith Head; hair styles by Nellie Manley; makeup by Wally Westmore; edited by Howard Smith; photographed by Harold Lipstein; photographer second unit, Irmin Roberts; process photographer, Farciot Edouart; special photographic effects, John P. Fulton; color consultant, Richard Mueller; color coordinator and technical advisor, Hoyningen Huene

Cast: Sophia Loren (Angela Rossinni), Anthony Quinn (Tom Healy), Margaret O'Brien (Della), Steve Forrest (Maybrey), Eillen Heckart (Lorna Hathaway), Ramon Novarro (De Leon), Edmund Lowe (Manfred Montague).

Review: "With *Heller in Pink Tights*, director George Cukor put tongue in cheek to turn an ordinary story into a gaudy, old-fashioned western satire with gleeful touches of melodrama. Ramon Novarro is aptly sinister as a well-heeled banker." *Variety*, 3/9/60.

Sound. Color. Running time, 100 minutes.

Television

1. *Ed Sullivan's Toast of the Town*—variety (CBS), December 23, 1952. Host: Ed Sullivan. Guests: Julie Harris, Gloria Swanson, Ramon Novarro, Billy DeWolf, Roger Price, St. Vincent Ferrer Boys Choir.

2. *Ken Murray's Blackout*—variety (CBS), February 6, 1952. Host: Ken Murray. Guests: Adolph Zukor, Buster Keaton, Ramon Novarro, Ruby Keeler.

3. *Walt Disney Presents*—drama (ABC), November 28, 1958. "Elfego Baca: Elfego—Lawman or Gunman (Part III)." Guests: Robert Loggia, James Dunn, Ramon Novarro.

4. *Walt Disney Presents*—drama (ABC), December 12, 1958. "Elfego Baca: Law and Order, Inc." (Part IV). Guests: Robert Loggia, James Dunn, Ramon Novarro.

5. *Hedda Hopper's Hollywood*—variety (NBC), January 9, 1960. Host: Hedda Hopper. Guests: Lucille Ball, Bob Cummings, Tony Perkins, Gary Cooper, Jody McCrea, Stephen Boyd, Ramon Novarro, Francis X. Bushman, Don Murray, Marion Davies, Teddy Rooney, John Cassavetes, King Vidor, Gloria Swanson, Debbie Reynolds, Judy Garland, Janet Gaynor, Bob Hope, others.

6. *Thriller*—drama (NBC), January 15, 1962. "La Strega." Starring: Boris Karloff. Guests: Ursula Andress (Luana), Alejandro Rey (Tonio Bellini), Jeanette Nolan (La Strega), Ramon Novarro (Maestro Giuliano).

7. *Combat*—drama (ABC), October 13, 1964. "Silver Service." Guests: Claudine Longet, Mickey Rooney, Norm Alden, Ramon Novarro.

8. *Rawhide*—Western (CBS), October 30, 1964. "Canliss." Starring: Clint Eastwood. Guests: Dean Martin (Canliss), Lauro Devon (Augusta Canliss), Michael Ansara (Don Miguel), Theodore Bikel (journalist), Ramon Novarro.

9. *Dr. Kildare*—drama (NBC), November 12, 1964. "Rome Will Never Leave You (Part I)." Starring: Richard Chamberlain. Guests: Alida Valli (Contessa Brabante), Mercedes McCambridge (Sister Theresa), Ramon Novarro (Gaspero Paolini), Paul Stewart (Dr. Murtelli), Daniela Bianchi (Francesca Paolini).

10. *Dr. Kildare*—drama (NBC), November 19, 1964. "Rome Will Never Leave You (Part II)." Starring: Richard Chamberlain. Guests: Alida Valli (Contessa Brabante), Mercedes McCambridge (Sister Theresa), Ramon Novarro (Gaspero Paolini), Paul Stewart (Dr. Murtelli), Daniela Bianchi (Francesca Paolini).

11. *Dr. Kildare*—drama (NBC), November 26, 1964. "Rome Will Never Leave You (Part III)." Starring: Richard Chamberlain (Kildare), Raymond

Massey (Gillespie). Guests: Alida Valli (Contessa Brabante), Mercedes McCambridge (Sister Theresa), Ramon Novarro (Gaspero Paolini), Paul Stewart (Dr. Murtelli), Daniela Bianchi (Francesca Paolini).

12. *Bonanza*—Western (NBC), September 26, 1965. "The Brass Box." Starring: Lorne Greene (Ben), Michael Landon (Little Joe). Guests: Ramon Novarro (Jose Ortega), Michael Dante (Miguel).

13. *Combat*—drama (ABC), December 21, 1965. "The Finest Hour." Starring: Rick Jason (Hanley), Pierre Jalbert (Caje). Guests: Luise Rainer (Countess Loraine De Roy), Ramon Novarro (Count De Roy), Kurt Krueger (Major Werner), Maurice Marsac (Claude), James Dobson (Lieutenant Schaefer).

14. *The Wild Wild West*—Western (CBS), September 22, 1967. "The Night of the Assassin." Starring: Robert Conrad (West), Ross Martin (Artemis). Guests: Robert Loggia (Colonel Barbossa), Donald Woods (Griswold), Conlon Carter (Halvorson), Ramon Novarro (Don Thomas), Nina Roman (Lucita), Nate Esformes (Perrico), Carlos Romero (lieutenant).

15. *High Chaparral*—Western (NBC), March 24, 1968. "A Joyful Noise." Starring: Leif Ericson (John), Linda Crystal (Victoria), Cameron Mitchell (Buck), Henry Darrow (Manolito) Mark Slade (Blue). Guests: Ramon Novarro (Padre Guillermo), Laurie Mock (Maria), Robert Yuro (Ramon), Penny Stanton (Sister Angelica), Angela Klarke (Sister Luke).

THEATER

A Royal Exchange—by Frederick Herendeen from a play by Lawrence Clarke. Adapted by Archie Menzies. Music by Edward Horan. Opened December 6, 1935, at His Majesty's Theatre, London.

    Cast: Leslie Bannister (attendant), Doris Carson (Countess Eloise), Hugh Wakefield (Baron Martinez), Doris Kenyon (H.R.H. Princess Sylvia), Man Torganoff (Andre Kessel), Carmen Samaniego (dancer), Ramon Novarro (Carlos Gavalin), Eddie Foy (Con Conley), Charles Wallen (Josef).

Infidel Caesar—A drama in two acts and fourteen scenes with a prologue. General manager, Milton Baron; Pres., Dorothy Ross; stage managers: Dan Doherty, Charles Rappaport; presented by Ray Shaw in association with J. and M. Mitchell, Bernard A. Lang, and Peter Petrello; production conceived and directed by Gene Wesson; scenery, lighting, and costumes by Burr Smidt; music composed and arranged by Joe Reisman; production supervisor, Paul Davis; assistant to the Producers, Max Wolfe. Opened Friday, April 27, 1962, at the Music Box, New York City and closed Saturday, April 28, 1962, after two preview performances.

Cast: Michael Ansara (Cesar), Marta Perez (Calpurnia), Gene Wesson (Antonio), Albert Popwell (soothsayer), John Cullum (Cassios), Mark Margolis (Casca), Armand Alzamora (Metellos Cimber), James Earl Jones (Cinna), Shelby Taylor (Octavios), Frank Ferrer (Lepidos), Agustin Mayor (Antonio's servant), John Ireland (Brutos), Rafael Campos (Lucios), Maria Brenes (Ligarios), Ramon Novarro (Ligarios), Vic Campos, Dan Fern, Guy Grasso, Robert Earl Jones, Joseph Roman (soldiers), Ann Johnson (dancer), Charles Gerald (diplomat), Manuel Suarez (Cinna the Poet), Charles Rappaport.

SUMMERSTOCK:

(Production notes and cast information not available.)

Command to Love, In the Shadow of the Harem, and *Tovarich* toured in summer 1949.

The Desert Song—June 4, 1962, Casa Manana Theater, Fort Worth, Texas.

The Flower Drum Song—June 18, 1962, Casa Manana Theater, Fort Worth, Texas.

Notes

Abbreviations:

AMPAS	Margaret Herrick Library, Academy of Motion Picture Arts & Sciences
LAHR	Los Angeles Hall of Records, Los Angeles
LWA-UCLA	Lloyd Wright Archives, University of California at Los Angeles
MGMSC-USC	MGM Script Collection, University of Southern California, Los Angeles
RN	Ramon Novarro
R.N.F.C.	Ramon Novarro Film Club, London

PROLOGUE

1. *Los Angeles Times*, September 28, 1965.
2. Bob Thomas, *Thalberg: Life and Legend* (New York: Doubleday, 1969), pp. 71.
3. Kevin Brownlow, *The Parade's Gone By* (New York: Dutton, 1981), p. 452.

CHAPTER ONE:
Childhood and the Revolution, 1899–1915

1. Dewitt Bodeen, "Ramon Novarro," *More from Hollywood* (Cranbury, N.J.: A.S. Barnes and Co., 1977), p. 193.

2. Unless otherwise noted, the information for this chapter was culled from Part 1 of Herb Howe's series of RN's life, "On the Road with Ramon," *Motion Picture Magazine*, February 1927, and an interview with RN's brother, Jose "Angel" Samaniego, Vista, California on April 16, 1994, .

CHAPTER TWO:
Remember My Name, Mr. De Mille, 1915–1920

1. "Ramon Novarro," *Hollywood (Then and Now)*, March 1991.
2. There has always been a discrepancy as to the year that RN actually arrived in Los Angeles. References mention the years from 1914 to 1917, but the most probable year seems to be 1915. In several sources, RN says that he arrived on Thanksgiving Day, and film historians and RN himself agree that he was an extra in DeMille's *Joan the Woman* (1917), which was filmed in late summer and fall of 1916. So the latest he could have arrived and been in the film was in 1915. In another interview, Novarro recollects being in Rome during filming of *Ben-Hur* on Thanksgiving 1924, saying it had been "nine years since he arrived." Jose "Angel" Samaniego also recalls that his brother was 16 years of age when he left home, which he would have been on Thanksgiving 1915.
3. Dewitt Bodeen, "Ramon Novarro," *More from Hollywood* (Cranbury, N.J.: A.S. Barnes and Co., 1977), p. 194.
4. "Hollywood's Hall of Fame," *New Movie Magazine*, August 1931. A few years later while in New York, RN approached Edison Company executives and proposed that they loan him $10,000 to train his voice; in return he offered to give them the exclusive phonograph rights. He did not return to hear their answer because he thought he was selling himself too cheaply.
5. "From Screen to Concert Stage," *Theatre Magazine*, January 1928.
6. The scenes of the boat sinking were filmed at the Los Angeles Harbor in San Pedro. A life-size deck of an ocean liner was built that could be tipped back and forth so the passengers would slip off into the cold waters of the Pacific. Many extras, including RN, received countless splinters from sliding down the deck.
7. Dewitt Bodeen, "Ramon Novarro," *The Silent Picture, No. 3*, Summer 1969.
8. "On the Road with Ramon," *Motion Picture Magazine*, May 1927.
9. Jose "Angel" Samaniego, interview, Vista, California, April 16, 1994.
10. Theresa Samaniego, telephone interview, October 1993. The Roosevelt Hotel did not open until 1927, one year after Valentino's death, but the events described by the "beloved female relative" could have taken place at any hotel.
11. Jose "Angel" Samaniego, interview, Vista, California, April 16, 1994.
12. Betty Lasky, "Star of Yesterday," *Players Showcase*, Summer 1965.
13. Lina Basquette in letter to author, November 21, 1993.
14. "The Man from the Mob," *Photoplay*, undated article.
15. RN to Joe Franklin on the *Joe Franklin Show*, 1962.
16. Michael Morris, *Madame Valentino: The Many Lives of Natasha Rambova* (New York: Abbeville Press, 1991), p. 264.
17. "On the Road with Ramon (Pt. 1)," *Motion Picture Magazine*, February

1927.

18. Fox, *Famous Film Folk*, p. 20.

19. Lina Basquette (1907–1996) had appeared at the 1915 San Francisco World's Fair and was later signed by Universal to star in a series of shorts called *The Lena Baskette Featurettes*. She later changed the spelling of her name to Lina Basquette.

20. Lina Basquette, in letter to author, September 7, 1993.

21. Lina Basquette, in letter to author, September 20, 1993.

22. *Ibid.*

23. Lina Basquette, in letter to author, September 7, 1993.

CHAPTER THREE: Stardom, 1920–1922

1. "On the Road with Ramon (Pt. 4)," *Motion Picture Magazine*, May 1927.

2. "The Savage Beating of Ramon Novarro," *Inside Detective*, February 1969.

3. Dewitt Bodeen, "Ramon Novarro," *More from Hollywood* (Cranbury, N.J.: A.S. Barnes and Co., 1977), p. 194.

4. Lillian Gish, telephone interview, January 8, 1993.

5. Dewitt Bodeen, "Ramon Novarro," *The Silent Picture*, No. 3, Summer 1969.

6. Unidentified publication.

7. "On the Road with Ramon (Pt. 3)," *Motion Picture Magazine*, April 1927.

8. Robert Taafe, telephone interview, March 8, 1994.

9. Dewitt Bodeen, "Richard Dix," *More from Hollywood* (Cranbury, N.J.: A.S. Barnes and Co., 1977), p. 303.

10. Ferdinand Pinney Earle (1878–1951) was a talented art director who had a reputation with the ladies that gained him the nickname "Affinity Earle."

11. The Hollywood Community Theater, located at 1742 Ivar, was a vine-covered extended bungalow which seated 100 people. On summer evenings, the doors stood open on both sides, giving the theater an open-air effect. This did not, however, prevent the fire department from condemning the theater because of a lack of exits. A few years later the Knickerbocker Hotel was built on the site.

12. The play is also referred to in some references as *The Royal Fandango*.

13. Dewitt Bodeen, "Rex Ingram and Alice Terry: Part One," *Films in Review*, February 1975.

14. "Join Novarro and See the World!" *Picture-Play*, November 1925.

15. Bodeen, "Ramon Novarro," *The Silent Picture*, No. 3, Summer 1969.

16. Novarro kept that letter with Ingram's illustration in a safe in his home for the remainder of his life.

17. "Whatever Happened to Ramon Novarro?" *Movie Illustrated*, June 1965.

18. "A Prediction," *Photoplay*, May 1924.

19. *Photoplay*, June 1922.

20. *Photoplay*, undated article, circa 1922, AMPAS.

21. "Ramon Novarro," *Hollywood Studio Magazine*, March 1991.

22. *Trifling Women* was written and directed by Rex Ingram and was based

on a picture he did for Universal called *Black Orchids* (1917).

23. Liam O'Leary, *Rex Ingram: Master of the Silent Cinema* (Dublin: Academy Press, 1980), p. 115.

24. *Variety*, October 6, 1922.

25. Michael Powell, *A Life in the Movies: An Autobiography* (New York: Alfred A. Knopf, 1987), p. 142.

26. Charles Donald Fox, *Famous Film Folk* (New York: George H. Doran Co., 1925), p. 21.

27. Jose "Angel" Samaniego, interview, Vista, California, April 16, 1994.

28. Dewitt Bodeen, "Ramon Novarro," *More from Hollywood*, p. 198.

CHAPTER FOUR: Rex Ingram, 1922–1923

1. Dewitt Bodeen, "Ramon Novarro," *More from Hollywood* (Cranbury, N.J.: A.S. Barnes and Co., 1977), p. 198.

2. Bodeen, "Ramon Novarro," *More from Hollywood*, p. 198.

3. Jose "Angel" Samaniego, interview, April 16, 1994, Vista, California.

4. *Ben-Hur* had been a successful stage play starring William S. Hart as Messala and William Farnum in the title role. In 1907, two years after General Wallace's death, Kalem Studios released a film version of *Ben-Hur* that consisted of a chariot race filmed at a fireworks rally, with some added interiors. The novel's publishers, Harper and Brothers, along with A. R. Erlanger, the play's producer, sued Kalem for breach of copyright. Kalem tried to protect its interest by claiming the film was good publicity for the book. Motion picture rights had never before been contested, and the case lingered in the courts until 1911 when Kalem admitted defeat and settled for $25,000.

5. Grant Whytock to Kevin Brownlow and David Gill in their documentary, *Hollywood*. Note: In the scene, the only chance Motauri and Matilda have of escaping their pursuers is to descend a dangerous path along the waterfall. Matilda is terrified, so Motauri picks her up and begins the treacherous descent down the path. As he begins, the scene fades and the title card reads, "Down the Virgin Falls!" At many theaters, patrons gasped, not realizing that "Falls" was meant as a noun.

6. "Novarro Sees What's Wrong," *Los Angeles Times*, April 1, 1923.

7. While Ingram was getting over his disappointment, his wife, Alice Terry, took over the directing reins of *Where the Pavement Ends*.

8. Kevin Brownlow, *The Parade's Gone By...* (New York: Dutton, 1981), p. 449.

9. "Novarro Sees What's Wrong," *Los Angeles Times*, April 1, 1923.

10. *Variety*, April 5, 1923.

11. *Morning Telegraph* (New York), April 8, 1923, AMPAS.

12. Unidentified publication, circa 1922.

13. Bodeen, "Ramon Novarro," *More from Hollywood*, p. 199.

14. "Novarro Bans Films for 'Sis,'" *San Francisco Chronicle*, May 18, 1931.

15. *Photoplay*, November 1923.

16. Production file, MGMSC-USC.

17. *Variety*, September 20, 1923.

18. "A Prediction," *Photoplay*, May 1924.

19. Marcus Loew (1870–1927) began in films with a penny arcade in Cincinnati. After seeing a picture show in nearby Covington, he rented the floor above his arcade. He ordered projection machines from the Vitagraph company and began showing movies the following Saturday. By 1907 he owned more than 40 Nickelodeons all over the country. By 1912 he had a chain of 400 theaters under the name of Loew's Theatrical Enterprises. He bought Metro Pictures to provide a supply of films to show in his theaters.

20. Brownlow, *The Parade's Gone By...*, p. 447.

21. *Photoplay*, May 1923.

22. "George Walsh Is Named Ben-Hur," *Morning Telegraph* (New York), September 1923, AMPAS.

23. J. J. Cohn, interview, April 12, 1993, Beverly Hills, California.

24. Samuel Goldwyn (1882–1974) had founded the studio in 1918 but was ousted in 1922 because of financial problems. He continued to produce pictures, releasing them through First National and later United Artists.

25. Louis B. Mayer (1885–1957) was a one-time junk dealer who owned the largest chain of movie theaters in New England. He eventually went into distribution and production, and he formed his own company in 1917. The next year he moved to Los Angeles and set up operations in space rented at the Selig Polyscope Studios at 3800 Mission Road.

26. Irving J. Thalberg (1899–1936) gained a reputation as a taskmaster running Universal at the age of twenty-three. Hollywood soon called him the "Boy Wonder," borrowing the moniker from a *Saturday Evening Post* article by a former Universal writer.

CHAPTER FIVE: Mayer and Thalberg, 1923–1924

1. Dewitt Bodeen, "Ramon Novarro," *More from Hollywood* (Cranbury, N.J.: A.S. Barnes and Co., 1977), p. 203.

2. Samuel Marx, *Mayer and Thalberg: The Make-Believe Saints* (New York: Random House, 1975), p. 46.

3. Barbara La Marr (1896–1926) was arrested at age fourteen in a police raid of a burlesque club. Even though she had broken no laws, a judge ordered her to leave Los Angeles, stating she was "too beautiful to be allowed alone in a big city."

4. "Ramon May Sing in Films," *Los Angeles Times*, August 5, 1928.

5. *Photoplay*, undated advertisement, circa 1922, AMPAS.

6. Bodeen, "Ramon Novarro," *More from Hollywood*, p. 202.

7. Herbert Howe started in publicity through his uncle, who was a motion picture exhibitor. He later wrote one- and two-reel shorts and contributed articles to movie magazines that caught the attention of James Quirk, editor of *Photoplay*. Quirk hired Howe, who proved to be one of the magazine's top writers.

8. "Hollywood's Hall of Fame," *New Movie Magazine*, August 1931.

9. "The Kiss That Shocked the Sheiks," *Photoplay*, undated article, AMPAS.

10. "Hollywood's Hall of Fame," *New Movie Magazine*, August 1931.

11. "A Prediction." *Photoplay*, May 1924.

12. Kevin Brownlow, *The Parade's Gone By...* (New York: Dutton, 1981), p. 78.

13. *Variety*, July 16, 1924.

14. Laurie Jacobson, *Hollywood Heartbreak* (New York: Simon & Schuster, 1984), p. 20.

15. Telegram to Abraham Lehr from June Mathis, February 7, 1924, MGMSC-USC.

16. Ephraim Katz, *The Film Encyclopedia* (New York: Harper Perennial, 1994), p. 1340.

17. "Meet Mr. Novarro," *Los Angeles Times*, April 26, 1924.

18. *Photoplay*, September 1924.

CHAPTER SIX: Metro-Goldwyn-Mayer, 1924

1. "A Prediction," *Photoplay*, May 1924.

2. Unidentified publication, circa 1925, AMPAS.

3. Production notes, MGMSC-USC.

4. "$65,000,000 Movie Merger Completed," *New York Times*, April 18, 1924.

5. *Ibid.*

6. The land that Goldwyn Studio was built on was given to Thomas Ince in 1916 by real estate developer Harry H. Culver. Ince built stages and became partners in Triangle Pictures with D. W. Griffith and Mack Sennett. Three years later, after Triangle went bankrupt, Samuel Goldwyn leased the 16-acre lot, later buying it and adding 23 adjacent acres.

7. Charles Higham, *Merchant of Dreams: Louis B. Mayer, M.G.M. and the Secret Hollywood* (New York: Donald I. Fine, 1993), p. 70.

8. Samuel Marx, *Mayer and Thalberg: The Make-Believe Saints* (New York: Random House, 1975), p. 56.

9. Letter to Marcus Loew from Joseph Schenck, May 2, 1924, MGMSC-USC.

10. Letter to Louis B. Mayer from Fred Niblo, May 20, 1924, MGMSC-USC.

11. Letter to Kevin Brownlow from George Walsh, March 1966, in Kevin Brownlow, *The Parade's Gone By...* (New York: Dutton, 1981), p. 452.

12. "On the Road with Ramon (Pt. 3)," *Motion Picture Magazine*, April 1927.

13. "Ramon Novarro in Europe," *Photoplay*, April 1925.

14. *Photoplay*, undated article, circa 1926, AMPAS.

15. "Ramon Novarro in Europe," *Photoplay*, April 1925.

16. Telegram to Louis B. Mayer from J. Robert Rubin, June 30, 1924, MGMSC-USC.

17. Letter to Kevin Brownlow from RN, March 1966, in Brownlow, *The Parade's Gone By...*, p. 453.

CHAPTER SEVEN: *Ben-Hur*, 1924

1. "On the Road with Ramon (Pt. 5)," *Motion Picture Magazine*, June 1927.

2. Letter to Louis B. Mayer from Bess Meredyth, July 14, 1924, MGMSC-USC.

3. J. J. Cohn, interview, April 12, 1993, Beverly Hills, California. RN was 5 ft. 8 in., George Walsh was 5 ft. 10½ in. and Francis X. Bushman was 5 ft. 11 in.

4. Telegram to Louis B. Mayer from Fred Niblo, July 24, 1924, MGMSC-USC.

5. Telegram to Louis B. Mayer from Fred Niblo, August 14, 1924, MGMSC-USC.

6. *Photoplay*, undated article, circa 1925, AMPAS.

7. "On the Road with Ramon (Pt. 3)," *Motion Picture Magazine*, April 1927.

8. "Ramon Novarro in Europe," *Photoplay*, April 1925.

9. Letter to Fred Niblo from Irving Thalberg, September 23, 1924, MGMSC-USC.

10. Irving Thalberg memo, August 16, 1924, MGMSC-USC.

11. "May McAvoy," *Films in Review*, undated article.

12. *Ibid.*

13. Kevin Brownlow, *The Parade's Gone By...* (New York: Dutton, 1981), p. 458.

14. "Brings First French Historical Film," *New York Times*, December 7, 1924. Bess Meredyth's father died during their voyage home. It was decided to have Mayer break the news to her.

15. Telegram to Carey Wilson from Irving Thalberg, October 21, 1924, MGMSC-USC.

16. Brownlow, *The Parade's Gone By...*, p. 461.

17. Niblo found four beautiful white steeds for replacements but was told that someone else was interested. Every bid Niblo made was immediately covered by the unknown buyer. Finally, Niblo discovered the unknown bidder was Pope Pius XI, with whom Novarro had just had a private reception. Needless to say, the pope got his horses.

18. Brownlow, *The Parade's Gone By...*, pp. 464–65.

19. "Novarro Used No Double in Raft Sequence," *Los Angeles Times*, September 8, 1926.

20. "On the Road with Ramon (Pt. 3)," *Motion Picture Magazine*, April 1927.

21. *Ibid.*

CHAPTER EIGHT: Rebellion in Italy, 1924–1925

1. Dewitt Bodeen, "Ramon Novarro," *The Silent Picture*, No. 3, Summer 1969.

2. Kevin Brownlow, *The Parade's Gone By...* (New York: Dutton, 1981), p. 460.

3. Letter to Irving Thalberg from Alexander Aronson, December 17, 1924, MGMSC-USC.

4. Telegram to Fred Niblo from Louis B. Mayer, December 1924, MGMSC-USC.

5. *Photoplay*, undated article.

6. Memo from Alexander Aronson, January 1925, MGMSC-USC.

7. "Ramon Novarro in Europe," *Photoplay*, April 1925.

8. Memo from Alexander Aronson, January 1925.

9. *Paris Tribune*, January 7, 1925.

10. Letter to J. Robert Rubin from Alexander Aronson, January 17, 1925, MGMSC-USC.

11. *Photoplay*, undated article, circa 1925, AMPAS.

12. "Ramon Novarro and Herb Howe, Back from Old World, Relate Their Adventures," *Los Angeles Times*, March 1, 1925.

13. Letter to J. Robert Rubin from Alexander Aronson, January 17, 1925, MGMSC-USC.

14. "Ramon Novarro and Herb Howe, Back from Old World, Relate Their Adventures," *Los Angeles Times*, March 1, 1925.

15. "On the Road with Ramon (Pt. 3)," *Motion Picture Magazine*, April 1927.

16. Letter column, *Photoplay*, January 1925.

17. Letter column, *Photoplay*, April 1925.

18. "Sheik of Films Is Auto Fan," *Los Angeles Times*, April 25, 1925.

19. Struggling actor Gilbert Roland doubled for Novarro during the filming of *The Midshipman*. He was paid $75 a week.

20. "Ramon Novarro Next Attraction at Loew's State," *Los Angeles Times*, October 1, 1925.

21. The Navy Department was so pleased with the film and Novarro's role that it used his likeness on navy posters with the invitation, "Join the Navy and See the World!" *Variety*, October 14, 1925.

CHAPTER NINE: The Chariot Race, 1925

1. Dewitt Bodeen, "Rex Ingram and Alice Terry: Part One," *Films in Review*, February 1975.

2. Lawrence J. Quirk, *Norma: The Story of Norma Shearer* (New York: St. Martin's Press, 1998), p. 70.

3. J. J. Cohn, interview, Beverly Hills, California, April 12, 1993.

4. William Haines (1900–1973) was finally "released" from his contract in 1931 after allegedly being arrested for picking up a sailor at the Pershing Square fountain (across from the Biltmore Hotel), infamous to the local homosexual community as a cruising area. Haines later found success as an interior decorator.

5. Quirk, *Norma*, p. 70.

6. J. J. Cohn, interview, Beverly Hills, California, April 12, 1993.

7. *Variety*, January 6, 1926. Greta Garbo and Myrna Loy were both considered for the part of the Virgin Mary. Loy was given an extra role as a hedonist.

8. That deal included the popular Wilhelm Meyer Forster play, *Old Heidelberg*, for which MGM owned the American rights. Unfortunately, UFA Studios owned the rights for all of central Europe, which MGM also wanted, so a trade was agreed upon. UFA would give up its European rights to *Old Heidelberg*

if Lillian Gish would appear in *Faust*.

    9. *Photoplay*, August 1925.

    10. "On the Road with Ramon (Pt. 4)," *Motion Picture Magazine*, May 1927.

    11. "Fulfillment of a Wink," *Photoplay*, April 1933.

    12. "On the Road with Ramon (Pt. 4)," *Motion Picture Magazine*, May 1927.

    13. Lon McAllister, telephone interview, July 4, 1993.

    14. *Variety*, October 7, 1925, p. 44.

    15. A. Arnold Gillespie to Kevin Brownlow and David Gill in their documentary, *Hollywood*. To match the action of real people, they mounted dolls on a dowel through a hole in the board. Activated by cams, they could be moved up or down to make it look as though there was a great throng of people.

    16. "Niblo Talks About Work in Filming Ben-Hur," *New York Times*, January 3, 1926. Cosmetics king Max Factor supervised the makeup, cooking up more than 300 gallons and literally spraying the extras as they stood in line. This was the largest amount of makeup ever used in one movie. (Max Factor Museum, Hollywood.)

    17. Niblo barked orders through a megaphone that Hilburn relayed over a loud speaker that was audible to each assistant in the various sections. Hilburn instructed the 42 cameras by using army and navy signal flags with the help of a United States Army sergeant. "Forty-Two Cameras Used on Scenes for Ben-Hur," *New York Times*, November 1, 1925.

    18. William Wyler to Kevin Brownlow and David Gill in their documentary, *Hollywood*. In 1959, Wyler directed the remake of *Ben-Hur*. The film won 11 Academy Awards, including Best Picture and the Best Director Award for Wyler.

    19. J. J. Cohn, interview, Beverly Hills, California, April 12, 1993.

    20. Forty-eight horses pulled the 12 chariots around the course, and another 150 were used in the scene. Each rider was part of Troop B of the U. S. Eleventh Cavalry. All men were of the same height and build, and the horses were all matched bays. Afterward, the men made a quick costume change and reappeared as buglers. "Forty-Two Cameras Used on Scenes for Ben-Hur," *New York Times*, November 1, 1925.

    21. Henry Hathaway to Kevin Brownlow and David Gill in their documentary, *Hollywood*.

    22. A. Arnold Gillespie to Kevin Brownlow and David Gill in their documentary, *Hollywood*.

    23. Henry Hathaway to Kevin Brownlow and David Gill in their documentary, *Hollywood*.

    24. Kevin Brownlow, *The Parade's Gone By...* (New York: Dutton, 1981), p. 468.

    25. J. J. Cohn, interview, Beverly Hills, California, April 12, 1993.

CHAPTER TEN: Novarro's Teatro Intimo, 1925

    1. "From Screen to Concert Stage," *Theatre Magazine*, January 1928.

2. "On the Road with Ramon (Pt. 4)," *Motion Picture Magazine*, May 1927.

3. "The Man No Woman Can Vamp," unidentified publication, February 1929.

4. "On the Road with Ramon (Pt. 5)," *Motion Picture Magazine*, June 1927.

5. "On the Road with Ramon (Pt. 4)," *Motion Picture Magazine*, May 1927.

6. Production notes, MGMSC-USC.

7. *New York Times*, December 31, 1925.

8. Telegram to Irving Thalberg from Nicolas Schenck, December 31, 1925, MGMSC-USC.

9. *Variety*, January 6, 1926.

10. Publicity photograph caption, circa 1926.

11. "Experiences with Ben-Hur," *New York Times*, January 31, 1926.

12. "On the Road with Ramon (Pt. 5)," *Motion Picture Magazine*, June 1927.

13. "Francis X. Bushman: Hollywood's First Star Talks About His Life & Times," Francis X. Bushman on a recorded interview released in 1975.

14. More than one million feet of film was shot during the previous three years, which was edited down to approximately 12,000 feet for the final cut. The picture played at the George M. Cohan Theater for more than a year. Grand premieres were held in the country's larger theaters until the fall of 1926, when the film received a wide release.

15. The film's financial backers, Erlanger and his Classical Cinema Corporation, which included C. B. Dillingham and Florenz Ziegfeld, Jr., insisted on half the profits.

16. "Barbara to Lie in State This Week," *Los Angeles Times*, February 1, 1926.

17. "Women Riot at Star's Funeral," *Los Angeles Times*, February 6, 1926.

18. "On the Road with Ramon (Pt. 5), *Motion Picture Magazine*, June 1927.

19. David Carol, *The Matinee Idols* (New York: Arbor House, 1972), p. 138.

20. "On the Road with Ramon (Pt. 1)," *Motion Picture Magazine*, February 1927.

21. *Photoplay*, June 1925.

22. "What Is the Mystery of Ramon Novarro?" *Motion Picture Classic*, October 1925.

23. George Hadley-Garcia, *Hispanic Hollywood: The Latins in Motion Pictures* (New York: Citadel Press, 1990), p. 34.

24. Dolores Del Rio (1905–1983) was the daughter of a Durango bank president and also escaped Mexico during the Huerta Revolution. Because Mexican families were sometimes so large and scattered over the city and country, it was not unusual that the two had never met. Lupita Tovar interview, June 2, 1994, Bel Air, California.

CHAPTER ELEVEN:
The Student Prince, 1926–1927

1. "Now It Can Be Told," *New Movie Magazine*, April 1932.

2. At the end of World War I, Elsie Janis (1889–1956) returned to New

York in triumph and was decorated by General John "Blackjack" Pershing.

3. "Now It Can Be Told," *New Movie Magazine*, April 1932.

4. Production notes, MGMSC-USC.

5. The Biltmore was a legitimate theater and did not have a projection booth, so the projector was hung in the second-floor balcony. The steep angle caused a distortion which made heads and necks slightly elongated.

6. "Famed Drama of Ben-Hur Wins Acclaim," *Los Angeles Times*, August 3, 1926.

7. "Novarro Is Praised by Warfield," *Los Angeles Times*, August 2, 1926.

8. Roger C. Peterson, *Valentino, The Unforgotten* (Los Angeles: Wetzel Publishing Co. Inc., 1937), pp. 140–141.

9. It was also rumored that Universal was going to film *Romeo and Juliet* and wanted Novarro to star opposite Mary Philbin. Carl Laemmle asked to borrow Novarro, but Mayer refused. *Photoplay*, September 1926.

10. "MGM to Film Romeo and Juliet," *Los Angeles Times*, September 16, 1926.

11. "On the Road with Ramon (Pt. 4)," *Motion Picture Magazine*, May 1927.

12. *Photoplay*, September 1926.

13. "Ramon Novarro Is Seriously Ill from Influenza," *Los Angeles Times*, October 6, 1926, AMPAS.

14. The film was based on two plays: Wilhelm Forster's popular play *Old Heidelberg* and a musical version called *The Student Prince*. MGM bought the rights to both plays. Even though the film was silent, the studio planned to use songs from the musical in the orchestral score. Thalberg later changed his mind and assigned David Mendez and William Axt to write a score that would capture the "flavor" of the original.

15. Lawrence J. Quirk. *Norma: The Story of Norma Shearer* (New York: St. Martin's Press, 1988), p. 94.

16. "Novarro at 50 'Steals' Picture in Comeback," *Los Angeles Times*, June 19, 1949.

17. "On the Road with Ramon (Pt. 5)," *Motion Picture Magazine*, May 1927.

18. Gavin Lambert, *Norma Shearer* (New York: Alfred A. Knopf, 1990), p. 90.

19. Quirk, *Norma*, p. 95.

20. *Ibid.*, p. 96.

21. Eddie Mannix ledger, Howard Strickling Collection, AMPAS.

CHAPTER TWELVE:
Talking Pictures, 1927–1928

1. "Ramon May Sing in Films," *Los Angeles Times*, August 5, 1928.

2. "Hollywood Structure Under Way," *Los Angeles Times*, August 5, 1928.

3. Jose "Angel" Samaniego, interview, Vista, California, April 16, 1994.

4. Ken Schessler, *This Is Hollywood* (11th ed.) (Redlands, Calif.: Ken Schessler Publishing Co., 1995), p. 8.

5. Sheilah Graham, *The Garden of Allah,* (New York: Crown Publishers, 1970), p. 31.

6. George Hadley Garcia, interview, West Hollywood, California, September 17, 1992.

7. *Photoplay*, undated article, AMPAS.

8. The studio had music and sound effects added at a New Jersey recording studio by its new recording director, Douglas Shearer, Norma's brother.

9. "What the Stars Think," *Photoplay*, undated, AMPAS.

10. Frances Marion, *Off with Their Heads* (New York: The Macmillan Co., 1972), p. 182.

11. "The Man No Woman Can Vamp," *Motion Picture*, February 1929.

12. "Novarro on Way to Spain," *Los Angeles Times*, April 8, 1928.

13. Jane Kesner Ardmore and Joan Crawford, *A Portrait of Joan: An Autobiography* (New York: Doubleday & Company Inc., 1962), p. 60–61.

14. Douglas Fairbanks, Jr., letter to author, November 18, 1992.

15. "Novarro on Way to Spain," *Los Angeles Times*, April 8, 1928.

16. Costars Carmel Myers and Bert Roach were no longer with MGM, and Willard Lewis died shortly after the original was shelved.

17. *Variety*, June 13, 1928.

CHAPTER THIRTEEN: Hurrell, 1928

1. Grover Ted Tate, *The Lady Who Tamed Pegasus: The Story of Pancho Barnes* (Bend, Ore.: Maverick, 1984), pp. 56–57.

2. Chuck Yeager and Leo Janos, *Yeager: An Autobiography* (New York: Bantam, 1985), p. 173.

3. Tate, *Lady Who Tamed Pegasus,* p. 57.

4. George Hurrell, *The Hurrell Style*, edited by Whitney Stine (New York: John Day Books, 1976), p. 4.

5. *Ibid.,* p. 5.

6. *Ibid.,* p. 6.

7. *Ibid.,* p. 7.

8. *Morning Telegraph* (New York), July 25, 1928, AMPAS.

9. Production file, AMPAS.

10. *Photoplay*, February 1929.

11. "Now It Can Be Told," *New Movie Magazine*, April 1932.

12. "Ramon May Sing in Films," *Los Angeles Times*, August 5, 1928.

13. *Ibid.*

14. George W. Hill (1895–1934) later directed several hits, including *The Big House* (1930) and *Min and Bill* (1930). Hill had a serious drinking problem which the crew and Frances Marion attempted to cover up. He would arrive drunk to meetings, and the studio threatened to fire him. While working on prepro-

duction for *The Good Earth*, Hill swerved his car to avoid hitting a group of children and slammed into a tree. He never fully recovered from the injuries, and two months later he killed himself with a gunshot to the head.

15. Letter from navy spokesman to J. Robert Rubin, May 23, 1928, MGMSC-USC.

16. Letter from Irving Thalberg to Adm. Pratt, USN, June 27, 1928, MGMSC-USC.

17. Anita Page quotes to end of chapter come from an interview with the author, August 20, 1993, Burbank, California.

CHAPTER FOURTEEN:
Pagan Love Song, 1928–1929

1. Anita Page, interview, Burbank, California, August 20, 1993.

2. In 1934, Anita Page married Nacio Herb Brown, the writer of such songs as "Singin' in the Rain" and "You Were Meant for Me," which he wrote for Anita. They divorced nine months later. In 1937 she married Adm. Herschel House, and she eventually settled in Coronado, where she had filmed *The Flying Fleet*.

3. Michael G. Ankerich, *Broken Silence: Conversations with 23 Silent Film Stars* (Jefferson, N.C.: McFarland, 1993), p. 166.

4. Harry Carr column, *Los Angeles Times*, August 5, 1928.

5. Death certificate, State of California, Vital Statistics.

6. Unidentified publication, circa 1935.

7. James Robert Parish and Gregory Mank, *The Best of MGM: The Golden Years: 1928–1959* (Westport, Conn.: Arlington House, 1981), p. xxii.

8. Dewitt Bodeen, "Ramon Novarro," *More from Hollywood* (Cranbury, N.J.: A.S. Barnes and Co., 1977), p. 204.

9. "From Screen to Concert Stage," *Theatre Magazine*, January 1928.

10. "Whatever Happened to Ramon Novarro?" *Movie Illustrated*, June 1965.

11. Unidentified publication, October 10, 1928, AMPAS.

12. Parish and Mank, *The Best of MGM*, p. xxii

13. "Ramon May Sing in Films," *Los Angeles Times*, August 5, 1928.

14. "From Screen to Concert Stage," *Theatre Magazine*, January 1928.

15. *Film Lovers Annual*, 1933.

16. Unidentified publication, June 22, 1929, AMPAS.

17. "From Screen to Concert Stage," *Theatre Magazine*, January 1928.

18. To publicize the opening of *Devil-May-Care*, MGM sent valentines to every female who ever wrote a fan letter to Novarro. When word spread about the promotion, the studio was deluged with requests for the valentine, a prime example of Novarro's popularity.

19. Sidney Franklin, "We Laughed and We Cried" (unpublished), p. 181.

20. *Variety*, December 25, 1929.

21. *Screen Play*, June 1931.

22. Jose "Angel" Samaniego, interview, Vista, California, April 16, 1994.

23. The house now known as the Samuel-Novarro House was completed in

1928 and was the first structure in which Lloyd Wright developed a concrete lightweight precast ring and plaster construction, where "U"-shaped sections were placed on top of one another to form a square, making the structure virtually earthquake proof.

24. *Variety*, June 11, 1930.

CHAPTER FIFTEEN: The Director's Chair, 1930

1. "A Screen Star Talks of the Films," *New York Times*, January 3, 1932.
2. Letter to Hunt Stromberg from Fred W. Beetson, February 23, 1929, MGMSC-USC.
3. The storyline went through more changes before it was finally agreed, at Novarro's urging, to make his character a fledgling opera singer. Eventually the title was changed to *Call of the Flesh*, much to Ramon's displeasure.
4. Roy Uselton, "Renee Adoree," *Films in Review*, undated article.
5. Through the years portions of *The March of Time* have been cannibalized and added to other MGM films. Three years later, when musicals started making a comeback, the studio revamped the story and used portions of the film in a new revue called *Broadway to Hollywood* (1933).
6. "Santa Monica House Leased by Film Actor," *Los Angeles Times*, April 17, 1930, AMPAS.
7. Jose "Angel" Samaniego interview, Vista, California, April 16, 1994.
8. *Picture Play Magazine*, May 1930.
9. *New York Times*, April 5, 1931.
10. *Screen Play*, June 1931.
11. "Hollywood's Hall of Fame," *New Movie Magazine*, August 1931.
12. "The Gay Cavalier," *Screen Play*, June 1931.
13. Jacques Samaniego (1910–?), who bore a striking resemblance to his famous cousin, was born in Juarez, Mexico, and was the son of Ramon's uncle Manual. He quit school because of a learning disability and was once arrested for possession of alcohol and various drugs, including veronal.
14. "Police Solve Two-Year Old Murder," *Los Angeles Examiner*, August 4, 1930.
15. *Variety*, February 21, 1931.
16. Bob Thomas, *Thalberg: Life and Legend* (New York: Doubleday, 1969), p. 129.
17. "'Play Dead' Outsmarts Actress," *Los Angeles Examiner*, October 20, 1930.

CHAPTER SIXTEEN: Secret Life, 1931

1. *Le Cinéma, Notre Métier Magazine*, undated article.
2. MGM bought the film rights for *Daybreak* in 1928 as a vehicle for John Gilbert, but by this time, Gilbert's career was beginning to slide so the part was

given to Novarro.

    3. William Bakewell, telephone interview, November 10, 1992.

    4. F. W. Murnau (1888–1931) was killed on March 11, 1931, under mysterious circumstances when his car careened off the road just outside Santa Barbara. Rumors alleged he was performing oral sex on his chauffeur, an attractive 14-year-old Filipino boy, but the story was never substantiated.

    5. Dewitt Bodeen, "Ramon Novarro," *More on Hollywood* (Cranbury, N.J.: A.S. Barnes and Co., 1977), p. 203.

    6. "A Screen Star Talks of the Films," *New York Times*, January 3, 1932.

    7. William Mossberg had been arrested on a gun concealment charge less than a month after the Trump murder. The gun, which had been confiscated, was found filed with the county clerk and was admitted as evidence.

    8. "Novarro Sought on Subpoena," *Los Angeles Herald-Examiner*, August 15, 1931.

    9. Court records, Los Angeles County. A motion for a new trial was denied, and on July 4, 1931, Mossberg and Jacques Samaniego entered San Quentin prison.

    10. LWA-UCLA. The ten-room, three-bathroom house had white exterior walls and copper moldings which made it resemble a Columbian temple. Wright estimated the remodeling would take seven months and cost a little over $43,000.

    11. "Extra! Novarro Quits!" Unidentified publication, circa 1935.

    12. *Movie Classic*, February 1932.

    13. Unidentified publication.

    14. Production notes, MGMSC-USC.

    15. *Variety*, January 5, 1932.

    16. "When Nordic Met Latin," *Photoplay*, February 1932.

CHAPTER SEVENTEEN: Garbo, 1931–1932

    1. Norman Zierold, *Garbo* (New York: Stein and Day, 1969), p. 89.

    2. *Ibid.*

    3. A scene depicting the execution of the spy Carlotta was cut by British censors and was deleted from American prints after the initial release. The British were also offended by the scene in which Mata Hari asks Alexis to extinguish the candle which he placed in reverence to the Virgin Mary, so MGM substituted for the Madonna a picture of Alexis' mother.

    4. "When Nordic Met Latin," *Photoplay*, February 1932.

    5. Zierold, *Garbo*, p. 77.

    6. Production file, MGMSC-USC.

    7. *American Film Institute Catalogue, Feature Films, 1931–1940*, pp. 1339–40.

    8. "The Boulevardier on Parade," *New Movie Magazine*, May 1932.

    9. "Estrellas De Ayer," unidentified publication, circa 1964.

    10. "One Drink O.K., Thinks Novarro," *Los Angeles Examiner*, Novem-

ber 14, 1931.

11. "Film Boon to Novarro in Motor Damage Suit," *Los Angeles Times*, November 18, 1931.

12. "Novarro Suit Verdict, $700," *Los Angeles Examiner*, November 18, 1931.

13. Arthur H. Lewis, *It Was Fun While It Lasted* (New York: Trident Press, 1973), p. 177.

14. *New York Times*, December 4. 1931.

15. *Variety*, June 21, 1932.

16. "The Hillside Home of Ramon Novarro," *California Arts & Architecture*, July 1933.

17. "'I'll Never Fall in Love,' Predicts Ramon Novarro," unidentified publication.

18. *Ibid.*

19. "The Gay Cavalier," *Screen Play*, June 1931.

20. Kenneth Barrow, *Helen Hayes: First Lady of the American Theater* (Garden City, N.Y.: Doubleday, 1985), p. 112.

21. "Helen Hayes and Novarro Linked by Strange Fate," *Los Angeles Examiner*, December 25, 1932.

22. "The Volunteer Grandma," *Photoplay*, April 1930.

CHAPTER EIGHTEEN:
European Concert Tour, 1932–1933

1. James Kotsilibas-Davis and Myrna Loy, *Myrna Loy: Being and Becoming* (New York: Alfred A. Knopf, 1987), p. 80.

2. "Novarro Writing Play," unidentified publication, January 1934, AMPAS.

3. William Bakewell, telephone interview, November 10, 1992.

4. Unidentified publication, March 18, 1933, AMPAS.

5. Unidentified publication, March 21, 1933, AMPAS.

6. David Bret, *The Mistinguett Legend* (London: Robson Books, 1990), pp. 167–68.

7. Lillian Gish in telephone interview with author, January 8, 1993; and *Los Angeles Examiner*, August 2, 1933.

8. Unidentified publication, August 11, 1933, AMPAS.

9. James Robert Parish, *The Jeanette MacDonald Story* (New York: Mason/ Charter, 1976), p. 71.

10. *Ibid.*

11. *Variety*, February 20, 1934.

12. *New York Times*, February 17, 1934.

13. *American Film Institute Catalogue, Feature Films, 1931–1940*, p. 303.

14. "Ramon Novarro Warmly Applauded at Concert Given for His Friends," *San Francisco Chronicle*, September 22, 1933.

15. *Ibid.*

16. Unidentified publication, October 26, 1933, AMPAS.

CHAPTER NINETEEN:
Nothing to Laugh At, 1933–1934

1. "'I'll Never Fall in Love' Predicts Ramon Novarro," unidentified publication.
2. Memo to John Lee Mahin from Hunt Stromberg, November 1933, MGMSC-USC.
3. "Movie Group Made Chiefs by Navajos," *Coconino Sun*, December 8, 1933, AMPAS.
4. Retakes were filmed at the Irvine Ranch at Chatsworth, California. Because of objections from the New York Censor Board, parts of the film, including a scene in which Ramon and Lupe's characters camp out together, were edited from screenings in New York.
5. *Variety*, May 15, 1934.
6. James Robert Parish and Gregory Mank, *The Best of MGM: The Golden years: 1928–1959* (Westport, Conn.: Arlington House, 1981), p. xxii.
7. "Novarro to Give Concerts," *Los Angeles Times*, February 7, 1934.
8. "'Fool To Wed' Says Novarro," *Los Angeles Examiner*, February 20, 1934.
9. "'I'll Never Fall in Love,' Predicts Ramon Novarro," unidentified publication.
10. "Novarro Quits!" unidentified publication, circa 1935.
11. Dewitt Bodeen, "Ramon Novarro," *More from Hollywood* (Cranbury, N.J.: A.S. Barnes and Co., 1977.), p. 206.
12. *Hollywood Citizen-News*, April 3, 1934.
13. "Admirers Mob Novarro," *Los Angeles Times*, April 24, 1934.
14. "Novarro Reaches Buenos Aires," *Los Angeles Times*, April 25, 1934.
15. "Four Film Stars' Names Drawn into Red Inquiry," *Los Angeles Times*, August 19, 1934.
16. "Velez and Del Rio Linked in Capital Communist Probe," *San Francisco Chronicle*, August 19, 1934.
17. "Four Film Stars' Names Drawn into Red Inquiry," *Los Angeles Times*, August 19, 1934.
18. "Action Nearing in Cagney Case," *Los Angeles Times*, August 20, 1934.
19. "Movie Actors Protected from Mexican Admirers," *New York Times*, September 30, 1934.
20. Jose "Angel" Samaniego, interview, Vista, California, April 16, 1994.
21. Dewitt Bodeen, "Ramon Novarro," *The Silent Picture*, No. 3, Summer 1969.

CHAPTER TWENTY:

Farewell, MGM, 1934–1936

1. "Extra! Novarro Quits!" unidentified publication, circa 1935.
2. J. J. Cohn, interview, Beverly Hills, California, April 12, 1993.
3. "Lonely Voyage of a Silent Star," *San Francisco Chronicle*, April 20, 1968.
4. Jose "Angel" Samaniego, interview, April 16, 1994, Vista, California.
5. "Novarro Leaves MGM to Make Own Pictures," *Illustrated Daily News*, February 8, 1935, AMPAS.
6. "Extra! Novarro Quits!" unidentified publication, circa 1935.
7. *Ibid.*
8. "Novarro Explains Dislike for Films," *New York Times*, July 7, 1935.
9. *American Film Institute Catalog, Feature Films, 1931–1940*, pp. 393–94.
10. *New York Times*, March 10, 1936.
11. "Mexican Star Makes Switch to Megaphone," *Los Angeles Times*, August 2, 1936.
12. *London Times*, December 7, 1935.
13. "Novarro in L. A.," *Los Angeles Examiner*, June 11, 1936.
14. "Extra! Novarro Quits!" unidentified publication, circa 1935.
15. "Novarro Back from Tour of Hectic Adventures," *Los Angeles Times*, June 10, 1936.
16. "Mexican Star Makes Switch to Megaphone," *Los Angeles Times*, August 2, 1936.
17. Dewitt Bodeen, "Ramon Novarro," *More from Hollywood* (Cranbury, N.J.: A.S. Barnes and Co., 1977), p. 204.

CHAPTER TWENTY-ONE:
The Republic Years, 1937–1941

1. "Novarro Returns," unidentified publication, circa 1937.
2. Republic Studios was located in the San Fernando Valley and was headed by Herbert Yates. It had a reputation as a "quickie joint" and specialized in serials and Westerns with Gene Autry, Roy Rogers, and John Wayne.
3. "Novarro Returns," unidentified publication, circa 1937.
4. *Variety*, July 28, 1937.
5. Letter to Eddie Zubbrick from RN, December 31, 1937.
6. Letter to Minnie Fisher from RN, December 29, 1937.
7. "Novarro Happy—His House Only Leaks!" unidentified publication, circa 1938.
8. Letter to Eddie Zubbrick from RN, April 22, 1938.
9. Unidentified publication, circa 1938.
10. "Novarro Loses Accident Case," *Los Angeles Times*, September 22, 1938.
11. The personal feats of Richard Halliburton (1900—1939) included climb-

ing Mount Olympus, being the first person to swim the Panama Canal ocean to ocean, and spending the summer as an observer on Devil's Island.

12. Samson DeBrier, interview, Hollywood, Calif., October 4, 1992.

13. Dewitt Bodeen, "Ramon Novarro," *More from Hollywood* (Cranbury, N.J.: A.S. Barnes and Co., 1977), p. 205.

14. "Actor Warns Nation to Keep Free Press," *Los Angeles Times*, June 8, 1940.

15. *Ibid.*

16. Edward Weber, telephone interview, July 14, 1994.

17. "Novarro's Glamour," unidentified publication.

18. Death certificate, State of California, Vital Statistics.

19. Letter to Minnie Fisher from RN, January 25, 1941.

CHAPTER TWENTY-TWO:
The Loss of Stardom, 1941–1944

1. All quotes from Don Atkins are taken from a telephone interview on February 24, 1993.

2. Norvel's real name was Anthony Truppo, and although he was known as an astrologer, he was more popular for his psychic readings. He had the uncanny ability to accurately predict things in the lives of his clients.

3. "Novarro Pays Liquor Fine," *Los Angeles Times*, October 30, 1941.

4. Boze Hadleigh, *Hollywood Babble On* (New York: Carol, 1994), p. 10.

5. "Novarro Put Under Strict Probation in Drunk Driving," *Los Angeles Times*, April 30, 1942.

6. "Is Novarro Tired—Or What?" *Picture Play*, December 1932.

7. Letter to Eddie Zubbrick from RN, December 31, 1937.

8. "Mexico Lets Novarro Enlist," *Los Angeles Times*, August 13, 1942.

9. Samson DeBrier was born in China, and at the age of 12, he claimed to have "certain powers." People said that he was a witch, which DeBrier denied, saying, "I always think of myself as just an All-American boy."

10. Letter to Samson DeBrier from RN, July 6, 1943.

CHAPTER TWENTY-THREE:
Comeback, 1944–1951

1. "Whatever Became of...," *Motion Picture*, January 1947.

2. The director of the film was Novarro's cousin, Julio Bracho (1909–1978), who was also born in Durango. Bracho started his career as a director in 1941 and was responsible for many of Mexico's box-office successes.

3. Lupita Tovar, interview, June 2, 1994, Bel Air, California.

4. *Variety*, June 7, 1944.

5. *Los Angeles Times*, September 28, 1965.

6. "Novarro at 50 'Steals' Picture in Comeback," *Los Angeles Times*, June 19,

1949.

    7. *Variety*, April 27, 1949.

    8. "Novarro at 50 'Steals' Picture in Comeback," *Los Angeles Times,* June 19, 1949.

    9. "Robert Mitchum," *Films in Review*, undated article.

    10. Jane Greer at Cinecon, Hollywood, California, September 1994.

    11. Ezra Goodman, *The Fifty Year Decline and Fall of Hollywood* (New York: McFadden Books, 1961), p. 353.

    12. *Time* magazine, undated article.

    13. "Novarro at 50 'Steals' Picture in Comeback," *Los Angeles Times*, June 19, 1949.

    14. *Ibid.*

    15. The building, at 10938 Riverside Drive in North Hollywood, had a collection of bungalows surrounding it and was shaded in tall magnolia and palm trees.

    16. "Novarro at 50 'Steals' Picture in Comeback," *Los Angeles Times*, June 19, 1949.

    17. *Hollywood Reporter*, undated article.

    18. Ezra Goodman, *Fifty Year Decline* (New York: McFadden Books, 1961), p. 353.

    19. J. J. Cohn interview, Beverly Hills, California, April 12, 1993.

    20. Freed Unit Records, MGMSC-USC.

CHAPTER TWENTY-FOUR:
Ramon Navarro Film Club, 1952–1959

    1. "My Friend Ramon," *Classic Film Collector*, Fall-Winter 1968.

    2. *Ibid.*

    3. *Irish Evening Herald*, January 21, 1954.

    4. *London Daily Mail*, January 19, 1954.

    5. *The R.N.F.C. News,* Summer 1954.

    6. *Irish Evening Herald,* January 21, 1954.

    7. Letter to R.N.F.C. from RN, February 3, 1954.

    8. The Pala Mission, where RN volunteered his time and money, is located midway between Los Angeles and San Diego. On the side of the mission is a plaque dedicated on April 26, 1959, to "the following individuals and groups of all faiths and to many more known to God, who gave generously of their material and spiritual help in the restoration of Mission San Antonio de Pala." RN's name is second on the list. Also listed here are director Frank Capra and his wife.

    9. "Ranch Idyllic Setting for Actor Novarro," *Los Angeles Times*, April 4, 1955.

    10. "Technical Know How of U. S. Film Makers Cited," *Los Angeles Times*, January 14, 1957.

    11. "My Friend Ramon," *Classic Film Collector*, Fall-Winter 1968.

12. Patrick Brock in letter to author, November 12, 1993.

13. Louis B. Mayer was ousted from his position at MGM in 1951, and over the next six years, he continued his struggle to regain control of the studio he had helped to create. That all ended in October of 1957 when the once mighty mogul died of severe anemia.

14. James Card, *Seductive Cinema* (New York: Alfred A. Knopf, 1994), p. 289.

15. Ramon Novarro Studio Biography, Walt Disney Productions, September 17, 1958, AMPAS.

16. "Ramon Novarro Held on Drunk Driving Charge," *Hollywood Citizen-News,* January 3, 1959, AMPAS.

17. Dewitt Bodeen, "Ramon Novarro," *More from Hollywood* (Cranbury, N.J.: A.S. Barnes and Co., 1977), p. 200.

CHAPTER TWENTY-FIVE: Broadway, 1960–1965

1. Dewitt Bodeen, "Ramon Novarro," *More from Hollywood* (Cranbury, N.J.: A.S. Barnes and Co., 1977), p. 205.

2. Margaret O'Brien interview, May 28, 1995, Hollywood, California.

3. Boze Hadleigh, *Conversations with My Elders* (New York: St. Martin's Press, 1986), p.170.

4. Lawrence J. Quirk, *Norma: The Story of Norma Shearer* (New York: St. Martin's Press, 1988), p. 95.

5. "Novarro Faces 2 Drunk Cases," *Los Angeles Times*, June 2, 1960.

6. *Ibid.*

7. "The Savage Beating of Ramon Novarro," *Inside Detective,* February 1969.

8. "Ramon Novarro," *Screen Stories*, November 1962.

9. *Ibid.*

10. *Hollywood Reporter*, August 5, 1962.

11. *Ibid.*

12. "Whatever Happened to Ramon Novarro?" *Movie Illustrated*, June 1965.

13. "The Savage Beating of Ramon Novarro," *Inside Detective*, February 1969.

14. *R.N.F.C. News,* Winter-Spring, 1963–1964.

15. David Carol, *The Matinee Idols* (New York: Arbor House, 1972), p. 138.

16. "Ramon Novarro," *Screen Stories*, November 1962.

17. Marvin Paige interview, September 28, 1993, North Hollywood, California.

18. "Novarro Rides Without Chariot," *New York Times*, November 15, 1964.

19. "Star of Yesterday," *Players Showcase,* Summer 1965.

20. Betty Lasky, interview (in person), Hollywood, California, April 10, 1993.

21. "Novarro Rides Without Chariot," *New York Times*, November 15, 1964.

CHAPTER TWENTY-SIX: Final Years, 1965–1968

1. "Novarro Rides Without Chariot," *New York Times*, November 15, 1964.
2. Kurt Kreuger, telephone interview, November 6, 1993.
3. Letter to Eddie Zubbrick from RN, December 31, 1965.
4. Kurt Kreuger, telephone interview, November 6, 1993.
5. "The Savage Beating of Ramon Novarro," *Inside Detective*, February 1969.
6. Dewitt Bodeen, *More from Hollywood* (Cranbury, N.J.: A.S. Barnes and Co., 1977), p. 206.
7. *The R.N.F.C. News*, Autumn, 1966.
8. Edward Weber, telephone interview, June 14, 1994
9. Dewitt, Bodeen, "Ramon Novarro," *Films in Review*,
10. Jose "Angel" Samaniego, interview, April 16, 1994, Vista, California.
11. Dewitt Bodeen, "Ramon Novarro," *The Silent Picture*, No. 3, Summer 1969.
12. Patrick Brock, letter to author, November 12, 1993.
13. Bodeen, "Ramon Novarro," *The Silent Picture*, No. 3, Summer 1969.
14. "Lonely Voyage of a Silent Star," *San Francisco Chronicle*, April 20, 1968.
15. Jose "Angel" Samaniego, interview, Vista, California, April 16, 1994.
16. Notes from police investigation.

CHAPTER TWENTY-SEVEN: Murder, 1968–1969

1. "Life Unrolled Like Film Legend," *Los Angeles Times*, November 1, 1968.
2. Unless otherwise noted, the quotes and information in this chapter are taken from two sources: notes from the police investigation and the book *Bloody Wednesday: The True Story of the Ramon Novarro Murder* by Joel L. Harrison.
3. The killers had taken the cord from the lamp next to RN's bed.
4. The name "Larry" was also written four times on a pad next to the living room phone.
5. "Did 'Friend' Kill Novarro?" *Los Angeles Herald-Examiner*, November 1, 1968.
6. Anita Page, interview, August 20, 1993, Burbank, California.
7. Grover Ted Tate, *The Lady Who Tamed Pegasus: The Story of Pancho Barnes* (Bend, Ore.: Maverick, 1984), p. 57.
8. Randal Malone interview, September 15, 1993, Pasadena, California.
9. Lupita Tovar, interview, June 2, 1994, Bel Air, California.
10. Robert Taafe, telephone interview, March 8, 1994.
11. Lupita Tovar, interview, June 2, 1994, Bel Air, California.
12. Dewitt Bodeen, "Ramon Novarro," *The Silent Picture*, No. 3, Summer 1969.

13. "Life Unrolled Like Film Legend," *Los Angeles Times*, November 1, 1968.

14. "Novarro Death Instrument Found," *Los Angeles Herald-Examiner*, November 2, 1968.

15. "Friend Slew Film Star, Police Say," *Houston Post*, November 3, 1968.

16. Chief medical examiner-coroner, Ramon Novarro, Case No. #68–11032, November 1, 1968.

17. "Nostalgia Unites Mourners at Novarro's Bier," *Los Angeles Times*, November 4, 1968.

18. "500 Attend Final Rites for Novarro," *Los Angeles Herald-Examiner*, November 4, 1968.

19. The person who gave Novarro's telephone number to Paul was Victor Nichols, a Hollywood realtor. Nichols often gave out telephone numbers of willing "johns" to his hustler friends and would cash the checks they received, keeping a percentage for himself. He called Novarro a "soft touch."

20. "Novarro Link! Two Men Face Murder Quiz," *Hollywood Citizen-News*, November 7, 1968.

21. Last will of Ramon Novarro Samaniego, third codicil, witnessed October 9, 1968.

22. Last will of Ramon Novarro Samaniego, first codicil, witnessed July 26, 1967.

23. Edward Weber, telephone interview, July 14, 1994.

CHAPTER TWENTY-EIGHT: The Trial, 1969

1. Unless otherwise noted, the quotes and information from this chapter are taken from court records of the People of the State of California versus Paul Robert Ferguson and Thomas Scott Ferguson for the murder of Ramon Novarro, July 28, 1969, to October 27, 1969; a series of articles on the murder from *The Advocate* by Jim Kepner; and the book *Bloody Wednesday: The True Story of the Ramon Novarro Murder* by Joel L. Harrison.

2. "A View of 2 Sons as Seen Through a Mother's Eyes," *Los Angeles Times*, September 7, 1969.

3. "Young Ferguson: 'I Killed Novarro,'" *Los Angeles Herald-Examiner*, September 25, 1969.

4. "Life in Prison for 2 Killers of Novarro," *Los Angeles Herald-Examiner*, October 28, 1969.

5. David Carol, *The Matinee Idols* (New York: Arbor House, 1972), p. 138.

6. "My Friend Ramon," *Classic Film Collector*, Fall-Winter 1968.

EPILOGUE

1. Dewitt Bodeen, "Ramon Novarro," *The Silent Picture*, No. 3, Summer 1969.

2. "Novarro Trial," *The Advocate*, 1969.

3. Joel Harrison, *Bloody Wednesday: The True Story of the Ramon Novarro Murder* (Canoga Park, Calif.: Major Books, 1978), p. 326.

4. "Jailed Killer Now Pens Prize Prose," *San Francisco Sunday Examiner & Chronicle*, June 29, 1975.

5. Probate records, Los Angeles County.

6. Ken Schessler, telephone interview, January 19, 1993.

7. *L.A. Style*, December 1991.

8. Probate records, Los Angeles County.

9. Jose "Angel" Samaniego, interview, Vista, California, April 16, 1994.

10. Jane Mercer, *Great Lovers of the Movies* (New York: Crescent Books, 1975).

Bibliography

Anderson, Gillian B., comp. *Music for Silent Films: 1894–1929*. Washington, D.C.: Library of Congress, 1988.

Anger, Kenneth. *Hollywood Babylon*. New York: Dell, 1975.

_____. *Hollywood Babylon II*. New York: E. P. Dutton, 1984.

Ankerich, Michael G. *Broken Silence: Conversations with 23 Silent Film Stars*. Jefferson, N.C.: McFarland, 1993.

Ardmore, Jane Kesner, and Joan Crawford. *A Portrait of Joan*. New York: Doubleday, 1962.

Bakewell, William. *Hollywood Be Thy Name: Random Recollections of a Movie Veteran from Silents to Talkies to TV*. Metuchen, N.J.: Scarecrow Press, 1991.

Barrow, Kenneth. *Helen Hayes: First Lady of the American Theatre*. Garden City, N.Y.: Doubleday, Inc., 1985.

Basquette, Lina. *Lina: DeMilles's Godless Girl*. Fairfax, Va.: Denlinger's, 1990.

Baxter, John. *The Hollywood Exiles*. New York: Taplinger, 1976.

Berg, A. Scott. *Goldwyn: A Biography*. New York: Alfred A. Knopf, 1989.

Bret, David. *The Mistinguett Legend*. London: Robson Books, 1990.

Brownlow, Kevin. *Hollywood: The Pioneers*. New York: Alfred A. Knopf, 1979.

_____. *The Parade's Gone By...* New York: Dutton, 1981.

Card, James. *Seductive Cinema*. New York: Alfred A. Knopf, 1994.

Carey, Gary. *All the Stars in Heaven: Louis B. Mayer's MGM*. New York: Dutton, 1981.

Carroll, David. *The Matinee Idols*. New York: Arbor House, 1972.

Crockett, Art, ed. *Celebrity Murders*. New York: Windsor, 1990.

Crowther, Bosley. *The Lion's Share: The Story of an Entertainment Empire.* New York: Dutton, 1957.

_____. *Hollywood Rajah: The Life and Times of Louis B. Mayer.* New York: Henry Holt, 1960.

Culbertson, Judi, and Tom Randall. *Permanent Californians: The Illustrated Guide to the Cemeteries of California.* Chelsea, Vt.: Chelsea Green, 1989.

DeMille, William. *Hollywood Saga.* New York: Dutton, 1939.

Edmonds, I. G. *Hollywood, R.I.P.* Evanston, Ill.: Regency Books, 1963.

Eells, George. *Hedda and Louella.* New York: Warner Paperback Library, 1973.

Endres, Stacey, and Robert Cushman. *Hollywood at Your Feet: The Story of the World-Famous Chinese Theater from the Silents to "Star Trek."* Los Angeles: Pomegranate Press, 1992.

Eyyman, Scott. *Mary Pickford: America's Sweetheart.* New York: Donald I. Fine, 1990.

Fernett, Gene. *American Film Studios: An Historical Encyclopedia.* Jefferson, North Carolina: McFarland, 1988.

Fox, Charles Donald. *Famous Film Folk.* New York: George H. Doran Company, 1925.

Franklin, Joe. *Classics of the Silent Screen.* Secaucus, N.J.: Citadel Press, 1959.

Franklin, Sidney. "We Laughed and We Cried." Unpublished.

Goodman, Ezra. *The Fifty Year Decline and Fall of Hollywood.* New York: McFadden Books, 1961.

Graham, Sheilah. *The Garden of Allah.* New York: Crown Publishers, 1970.

Hadleigh, Boze. *Conversations with My Elders.* New York: St. Martin's Press, 1986.

_____. *Hollywood Babble On.* New York: Carol, 1994.

_____. *The Lavender Screen: The Gay and Lesbian Films: Their Stars, Makers, Characters and Critics.* New York: Citadel Press, 1993.

Hadley-Garcia, George. *Hispanic Hollywood: The Latins in Motion Pictures.* New York: Citadel Press, 1990.

Hamilton, Ian. *Writers in Hollywood: 1915–1951.* New York: Harper and Row, 1990.

Harrision, Joel. *Bloody Wednesday: The True Story of the Ramon Novarro Murder.* Canoga Park, Calif.: Major Books, 1978.

Hayes, Susan Lloyd. *3-D Hollywood: Photographs by Harold Lloyd.* New York: Simon & Schuster, 1992.

Heisner, Beverly. *Hollywood Art: Art Direction in the Days of the Great Studios.* Jefferson, N.C.: McFarland, 1990.

Higham, Charles. *Cecil B. DeMille: A Biography of the Most Successful Film Maker of Them All.* New York: Charles Scribners' Sons, 1973.

_____. *Merchant of Dreams: Louis B. Mayer, M.G.M. and the Secret Hollywood.* New York: Donald I. Fine, Inc., 1993.

Hopper, Hedda. *From Under My Hat.* Garden City, N.Y.: Doubleday, 1952.

_____, and James Brough. *The Whole Truth and Nothing But.* Garden City, N.Y.: Doubleday, 1963.

Hurrell, George. *The Hurrell Style.* Edited by Whitney Stine. New York: John Day Books, 1976.

Katchmer, George A. *Eighty Silent Film Stars: Biographies and Filmographies of the Obscure to the Well Known.* Jefferson, N.C.: McFarland, 1991.

Katz, Ephraim. *The Film Encyclopedia.* New York: Harper Perennial, 1994.

Keller, Gary D. *A Biographical Handbook of Hispanics and United States Films.* Tempe, Ariz.: Bilingual Review/Press, 1997.

Keylin, Arleen, and Suri Fleischer, eds. *Hollywood Album: Lives and Deaths of Hollywood Stars from the Pages of the New York Times.* New York: Arno Press, 1977.

Kobal, John. *People Will Talk.* New York: Alfred A. Knopf, 1985.

Kotsilibas-Davis, James, and Myrna Loy. *Myrna Loy: Being and Becoming.* New York: Alfred A. Knopf, 1987.

Lambert, Gavin. *Norma Shearer.* New York: Alfred A. Knopf, 1990.

Lamparski, Richard. *Whatever Became of...? The New Fifth Series.* New York: Bantam Books, 1974.

Lasky, Betty. *RKO: The Biggest Little Major of Them All.* Santa Monica, Calif.: Roundtable, 1989.

Lewis, Arthur H. *It Was Fun While It Lasted: A Lament for the Hollywood That Was.* New York: Trident Press, 1973.

Maltin, Leonard. *TV Movies and Video Guide.* New York: New American Library, 1987.

Marion, Frances. *Off with Their Heads! A Serio-Comic Tale of Hollywood.* New York: Macmillan Company, 1972.

Marx, Samuel. *Mayer and Thalberg: The Make Believe Saints.* New York: Random House, 1975.

Mercer, Jane. *Great Lovers of the Movies.* New York: Crescent Books, 1975.

Mordden, Ethan. *The Hollywood Musical.* New York: St. Martin's Press, 1981.

Morris, Michael. *Madam Valentino: The Many Lives of Natacha Rambova.* New York: Abbeville Press, 1991.

O'Leary, Liam. *Rex Ingram: Master of the Silent Cinema.* Dublin: Academy Press, 1980.

Parish, James Robert. *The Jeanette MacDonald Story.* New York: Mason/Charter, 1976.

_____ and R. L. Bowers. *The M.G.M. Stock Company.* New York: Bonanza, 1972.

_____ and Gregory Mank. *The Best of MGM: The Golden Years: 1928–1959.* Westport, Conn.: Arlington House, 1981.

Peterson, Roger C., *Valentino, the Forgotten.* Los Angeles: Wetzel Publishing Co., Inc., 1937.

Powell, Michael. *A Life in the Movies: An Autobiography*. New York: Alfred A. Knopf, 1987.

Quirk, Lawrence J. *Norma: The Story of Norma Shearer*. New York: St. Martin's Press, 1988.

Ringgold, Gene, and DeWitt Bodeen. *The Films of Cecil B. DeMille*. Secaucus, N.J.: Citadel Press, 1960.

Rogers St. Johns, Adela. *Love, Laughter and Tears: My Hollywood Story*. Garden City, N.Y.: Doubleday, 1978.

Schessler, Ken. *This Is Hollywood: An Unusual Movieland Guide*. Redlands, Calif.: Ken Schessler Publishing, 1995.

Schulberg, Budd. *Moving Pictures*. New York: Scarborough House, 1981.

Schulman, Irving. *Valentino*. New York: Trident Press, 1967.

Scott, Evelyn F. *Hollywood: When Silents Were Golden*. New York: McGraw Hill, 1972.

Selznick, Irene. *A Private View*. New York: Alfred A. Knopf, 1982.

Slide, Anthony. *Silent Portraits: Stars of the Silent Screen in Historic Photographs*. New York: Vestal Press, 1989.

Stubblebine, Donald J. *Cinema Sheet Music: A Comprehensive Listing of Published Film Music from the Squaw Man (1914) to Batman (1989)*. Jefferson, N.C.: McFarland, 1991.

Tate, Grover Ted. *The Lady Who Tamed Pegasus: The Story of Pancho Barnes*. Bend, Ore.: Maverick, 1984.

Thomas, Bob. *Thalberg: Life and Legend*. New York: Doubleday, 1969.

Tryon, Thomas. *Crowned Heads*. New York: Dell, 1976.

Vermilye, Jerry. *The Films of the Twenties*. Secaucus, N.J.: Citadel Press, 1985.

Wiley, Mason, and Damien Bona. *Inside Oscar: The Unofficial History of the Academy Awards*. New York: Ballantine Books, 1986.

Yeagar, Chuck, and Leo Janos. *Yeagar: An Autobiography*. New York: Bantam, 1985.

Zierold, Norman. *Garbo*. New York: Stein and Day Publishers, 1969.

_____. *The Moguls*. New York: Cowan McCann, 1969.

Index